Illustrators:
Jose L. Tapia
Sue Fullam
Keith Vasconcelles

Editors:
Concetta Doti Ryan, M.A.
Karen J. Goldfluss, M.S. Ed.

Editor-in-Chief:
Sharon Coan, M.S. Ed.

Art Director:
Elayne Roberts

Cover Artist:
Sue Fullam

Imaging:
Alfred Lau
Rick Chacón

Production Manager:
Phil Garcia

Publishers:
Rachelle Cracchiolo, M.S. Ed.
Mary Dupuy Smith, M.S. Ed.

TEACHING BASIC SKILLS THROUGH LITERATURE
PHONICS
PRIMARY

Authors:
*Sylvia Ferrer-McGrade, M.Ed.
and Sandra Wuillmier, M.A.*

Teacher Created Materials, Inc.
P.O. Box 1040
Huntington Beach, CA 92647
©1995 Teacher Created Materials, Inc.
Made in U.S.A.

ISBN-1-55734-791-3

The classroom teacher may reproduce copies of materials in this book for classroom use only. The reproductions of any part for an entire school or school system is strictly prohibited. No part of this publication may be transmitted, stored, or recorded in any form without written permission from the publisher.

Table of Contents

Introduction 3
Taking a Closer Look 4
Cooperative Learning 14
Learning Centers 20
Assessment 28
Phonics Skills in Context 42

- Letter "B" 42
- Letter "C" 53
- Letter "D" 64
- Letter "F" 82
- Letter "G" 88
- Letter "H" 100
- Letter "J" 109
- Letter "K" 120
- Letter "L" 133
- Letter "M" 145
- Letter "N" 154
- Letter "P" 164
- Letter "Q" 176
- Letter "R" 188
- Letter "S" 197
- Letter "T" 206
- Letter "V" 217
- Letter "W" 227
- Letter "X" 236
- Letter "Y" 243
- Letter "Z" 252
- Short "A" 259
- Long "A" 272
- Short "E" 278
- Long "E" 293
- Short "I" 300
- Long "I" 314
- Short "O" 327
- Long "O" 337
- Short "U" 343
- Long "U" 354
- "ch" Blend 358
- "th" Blend 367
- "wh" Blend 375

Related Poetry 384
Children's Literature Bibliography 390
The 300 Most Frequently Used English Words 396
Caldecott Award Winners 398
Newbery Award Winners 399
Professional Book Bibliography 400

Introduction

What are basic skills?

Basic skills are those skills you feel are necessary for your students to learn for your particular grade level. Teachers often select the basic skills to teach their students from state frameworks, district mandates, and textbook scope and sequence charts. The teacher, as a professional, selects the skills his or her students have a need to learn and are ready to learn. For example, it is pointless to try to teach how to use quotation marks to students who have never used dialogue in their story writing. They do not have a need to learn about quotation marks at that particular point in time. By teaching skills as they are necessary, you allow students to immediately apply what they have learned in an authentic context, like practicing the use of quotation marks using their own writing.

The literature selections and activities in *Teaching Basic Skills Through Literature: Phonics* provide an authentic context for students by making the learning of the skills both timely and meaningful.

Basic Skills Lessons

Each of the lessons in *Teaching Basic Skills Through Literature: Phonics* focuses on a specific piece of literature and emphasizes a basic skill through activities which connect it to the literature. Each lesson in this book is organized as follows:

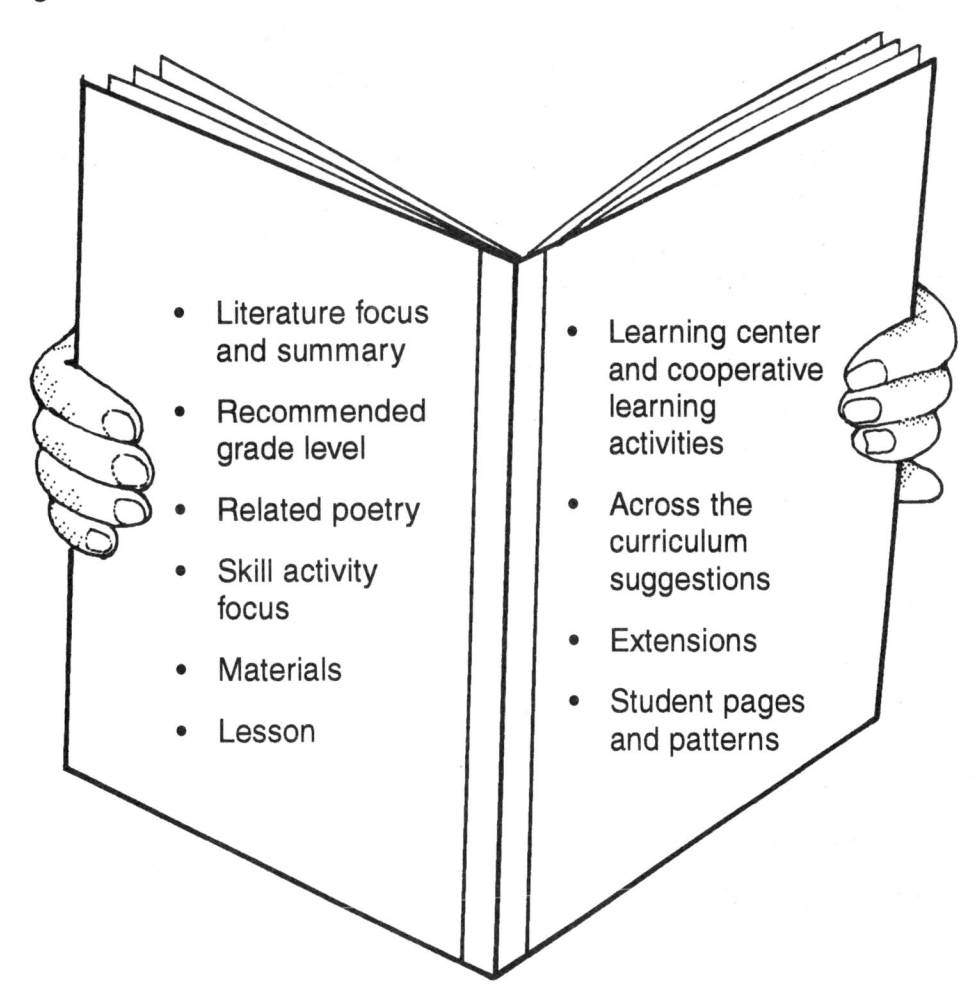

- Literature focus and summary
- Recommended grade level
- Related poetry
- Skill activity focus
- Materials
- Lesson

- Learning center and cooperative learning activities
- Across the curriculum suggestions
- Extensions
- Student pages and patterns

Before You Begin

Further information about basic skills and strategies, as well as guidelines for cooperative learning, learning centers, and assessment, is provided on pages 4 through 41.

Taking a Closer Look

How does a skill become a strategy?

By choosing to teach skills only when they are needed, you create an immediate opportunity for students to use and practice the skill. A skill becomes a strategy when the learner can use it purposefully and independently. Application of a skill to a broader context is far more likely if it has been taught in an authentic, meaningful context. The following example of a skill becoming a strategy is based on the previous lesson idea about quotation marks.

Example

In a whole-language classroom children do a great deal of writing. Let us imagine that in reviewing the students' writing the teacher notices that they are beginning to use dialogue. At this point the teacher would want to teach students how to use quotation marks because they have a real need to know. In preparation for the quotation mark lesson, the teacher would request that all students write a story that includes the characters talking.

Using a literature base, the teacher would begin the quotation mark skill lesson. First, the literature book is read. The book should contain a great deal of dialogue so students will be able to see the way quotation marks are used in context. After reading the book, point out the quotation marks to students and discuss why they are used (to make it clear to the reader that a character is speaking). Allow students to practice using quotation marks by putting several sentences from the story on the board. Volunteers can put quotation marks around the text on the board. The teacher returns the stories students wrote prior to the lesson using character dialogue. Students go through their own stories putting quotation marks wherever appropriate.

Results

This lesson creates a meaningful and authentic context to learn an important skill, the use of quotation marks. By immediately using the skill with their own writing, it becomes a strategy that students understand and will surely be able to apply to a broader context in the future.

Taking a Closer Look (cont.)

What is whole language?

Whole language was started by teachers, teachers who feel learners are ultimately in control of what they learn. The curriculum develops as the teacher learns about the interests and needs of the students. For this reason, whole language classrooms are like snowflakes, no two are alike. However, there are certain characteristics of the learning environment that are common to whole-language classrooms because they are the underpinning of the whole language philosophy. These commonalties are described below.

A whole-language program surrounds children with language. Children are taught the skills of reading, writing, speaking, and listening through experience with language. These skills are not taught in isolation, but are related to a particular story, book, or poem. Meaning is emphasized in whole language. Children are taught to focus on meaning construction while reading and to constantly ask themselves whether the story makes sense. Reading is, after all, constructing meaning from text.

Whole language classrooms are child centered because the curriculum develops from the interests and needs of the child. This child-centered view encourages the teacher to make a special effort to understand each child's unique experiences and ways of thinking and to then capitalize on this information when designing units of study. This idea is synonymous with developmental psychologist Piaget's theory that education must stem from a child-centered perspective.

Within this student-centered arrangement, students are allowed to make some of their own choices. This makes them feel as though they are taking a more active role in their own learning, and they are, therefore, more motivated to learn.

In whole-language classrooms children are encouraged to use all four reading cueing systems in order to construct meaning while reading text. The four cueing systems are described in detail on page 6.

In whole-language classrooms children are surrounded by print. Walls and bulletin boards are covered with labeled pictures and creative writing. All types of books, including quality children's literature, poetry, magazines, student-published books, and big books, are available for children to read in the classroom. Allowing children to experience written language in a variety of forms gives them a good foundation for learning.

Taking a Closer Look (cont.)

What is the role of phonics in the classroom?

Phonics is part of the whole language classroom, but only to the extent that it is one of four cueing systems that students use when reading. Traditionally phonics has been taught in isolation. This makes it difficult for students to make the connection between the letter-sound relationship and what that has to do with reading or the comprehension of text. Also, because English is such an irregular language, there are many exceptions to phonics rules. Therefore, more often than not students need to see the word in a broader context in order to determine its pronunciation.

When phonics is taught in isolation it is a skill, not a strategy. In order for phonics to be meaningful, connections of sounds and letters must be made to real contexts, such as literature, signs, labels, charts, etc. For example, after reading a story to students, particularly if there are a great many rhyming words, you can point out the similarities in sounds among the words. You may ask students to contribute other words that sound like those in the literature. By connecting the phonics skill to the literature, as well as having students contribute words they know on their own, you have turned a skill into a strategy. Students will understand phonic generalizations only when they are used along with the other three cueing systems of reading and presented in a meaningful, authentic context.

What are the cueing systems of reading?

There are four cueing systems a reader uses when constructing meaning from text: the semantic system, the syntactic system, the grapho-phonic system, and the pragmatic system. The semantic cueing system refers to the way language is used and the words chosen to convey meaning. The semantic system gives language its life. It has to do with the way in which we express meaning, sense, ideas, and thought. This system relies heavily on context clues for word identification. In the syntactic cueing system, the reader uses knowledge of language patterns and grammatical structure to identify unknown words. This system is the frame that supports the meaning. The grapho-phonic cueing system is based on letter-sound relationships. This system is visually expressed. In other words, it is the black marks on the page. When relying on this system, students sound out words they do not know. The pragmatic system refers to the practical use of language. Proficient readers use all four cueing systems simultaneously in order to construct meaning.

How do I find the time?

Finding the time for basic skills lessons can be challenging. This book provides you with three sample schedules that incorporate basic skills lessons. These schedules are on pages 8 through 10. In addition, there are three sample room arrangements to assist you in organizing your classroom. These are located on pages 11 through 13.

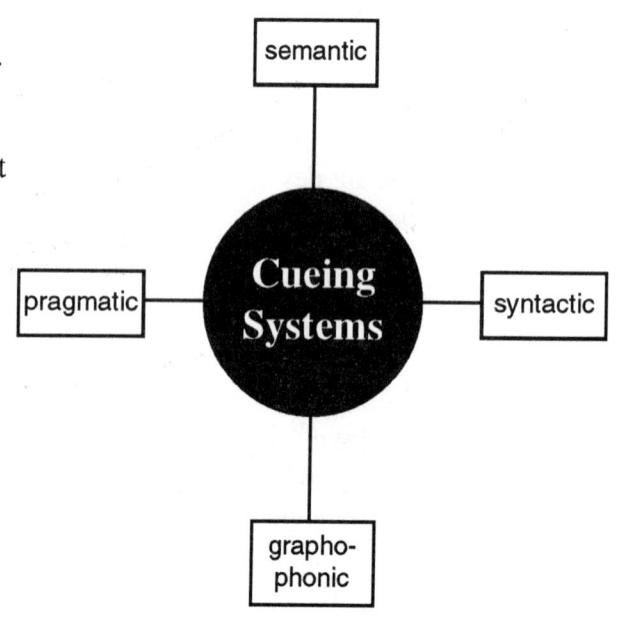

Language Arts Model

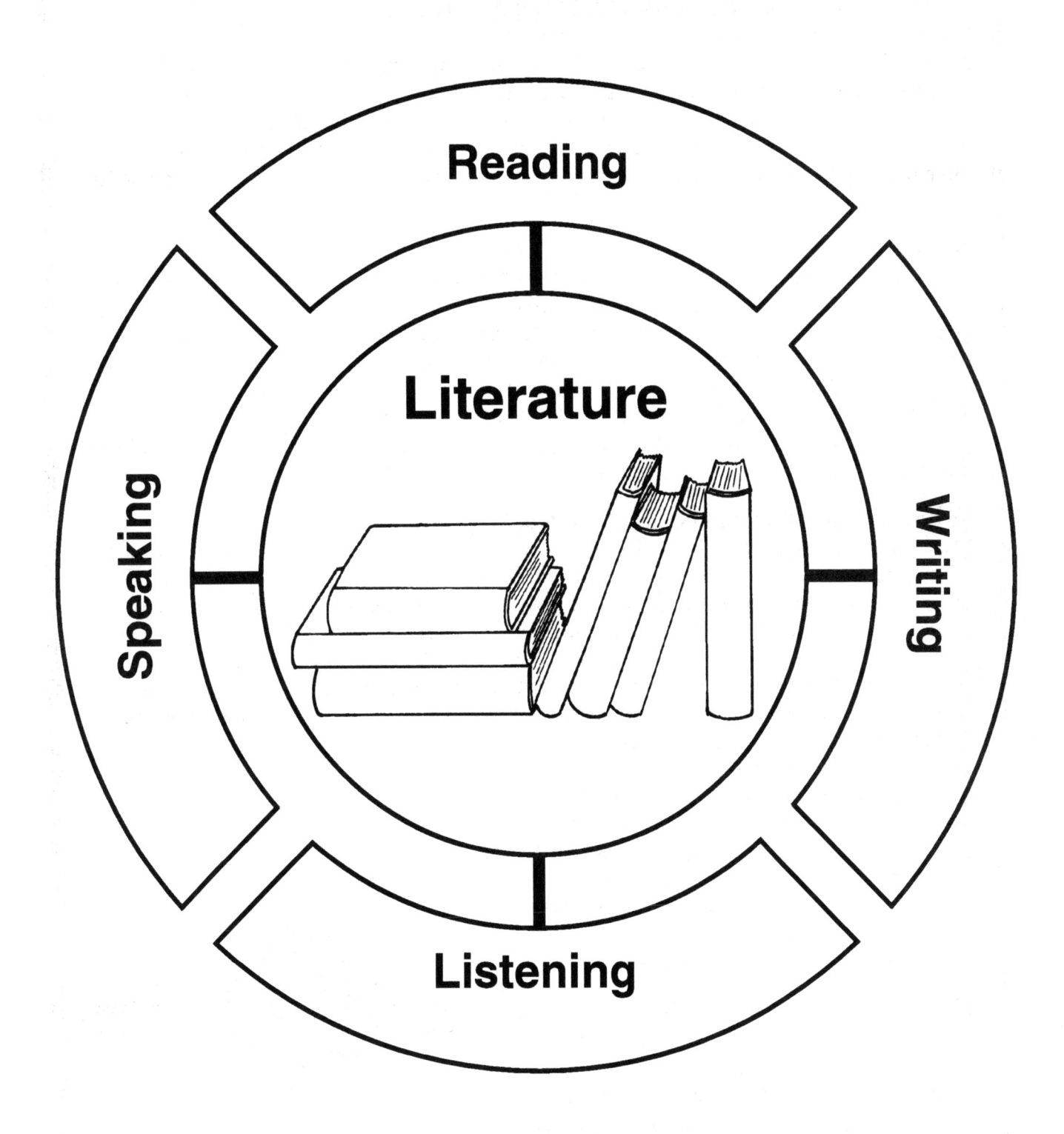

- Reading
- Writing
- Listening
- Speaking
- Literature

Sample Schedule #1

Full Day

Opening Exercises	8:30–9:00
Skill Mini-Lesson	9:00–10:00
Recess	10:00–10:15
Specialist Time (Art/Music/PE/Library)	10:15–10:45
SSR	10:45–11:00
Cooperative Work/Centers	11:00–11:45
Lunch	11:45–12:30
Thematic Teaching Lessons	12:30–2:30
Homework/Cleanup/Closing	2:30–2:45

Sample Schedule #2

Full Day

Opening Exercises	8:30–9:00
Cooperative Work/Centers	9:00–10:00
Recess	10:00–10:15
Thematic Teaching Lessons	10:15–12:00
Lunch	12:00–12:45
SSR	12:45–1:00
Specialist Time (Art/Music/PE/Library)	1:00–1:30
Skill Mini-Lesson	1:30–2:30
Homework/Cleanup/Closing	2:30–2:45

Sample Schedule #3

Half Day

Opening Exercises	8:30–8:45
Cooperative Work/Centers	8:45–9:30
Recess	9:30–9:45
Skill Mini-Lesson	9:45–10:30
Specialist Time (Art/Music/PE/Library)	10:30–11:00
Thematic Teaching Lessons	11:00–11:45
Cleanup/Closing	11:45–12:00

Room Arrangement Suggestion #1

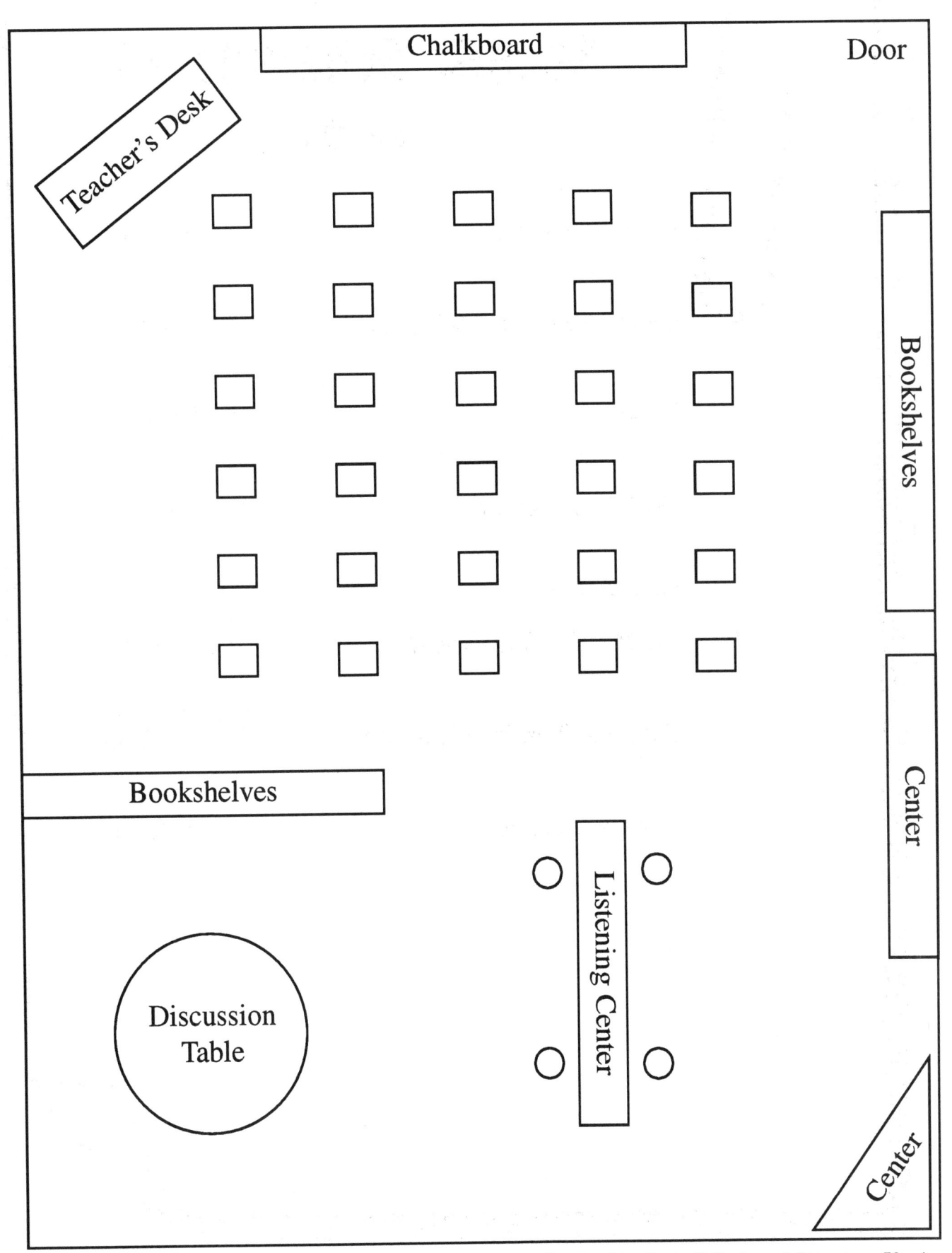

©1995 Teacher Created Materials, Inc.   11   #791 Teaching Basic Skills through Literature: Phonics

Room Arrangement Suggestion #2

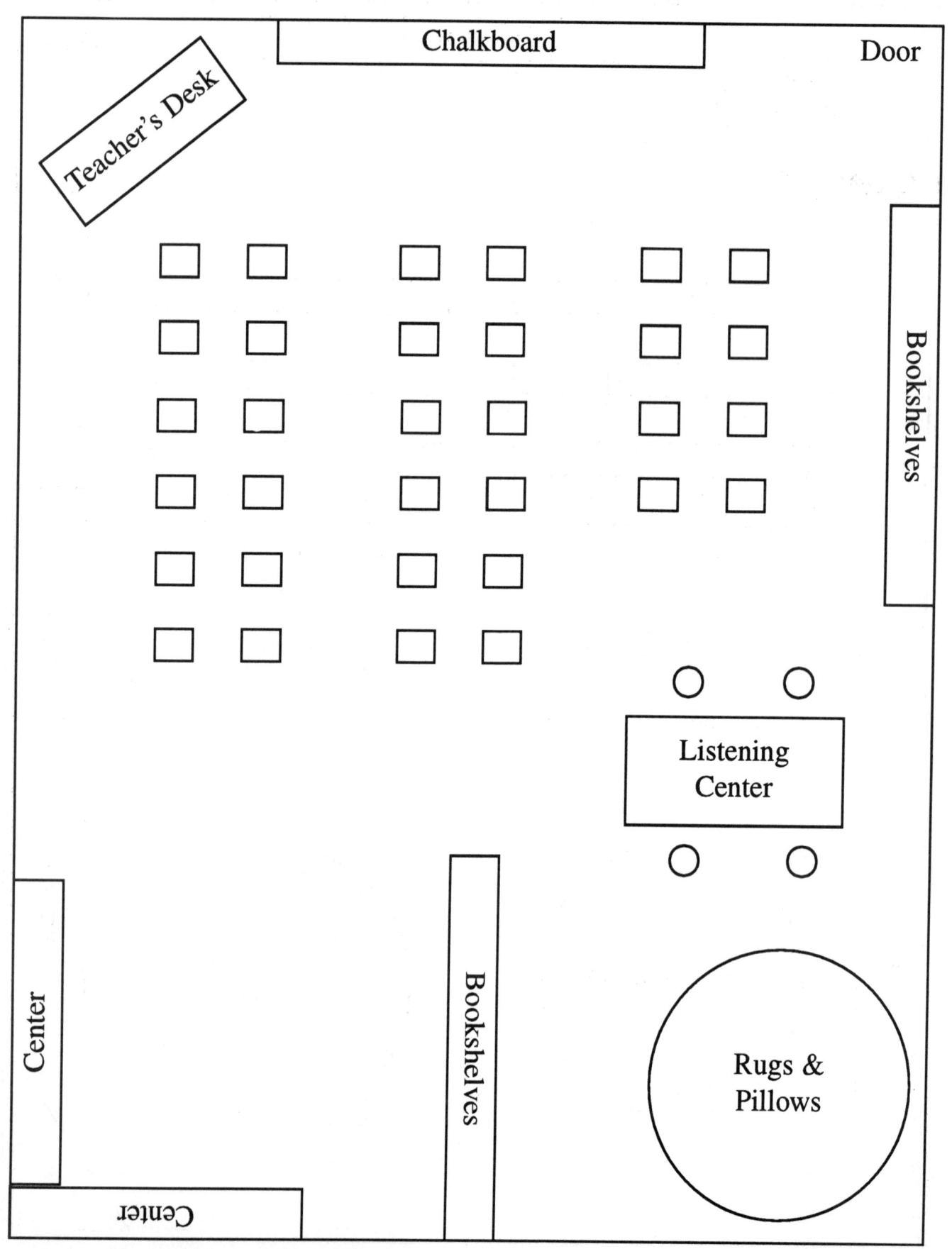

#791 Teaching Basic Skills through Literature: Phonics   12   ©1995 Teacher Created Materials, Inc.

Room Arrangement Suggestion #3

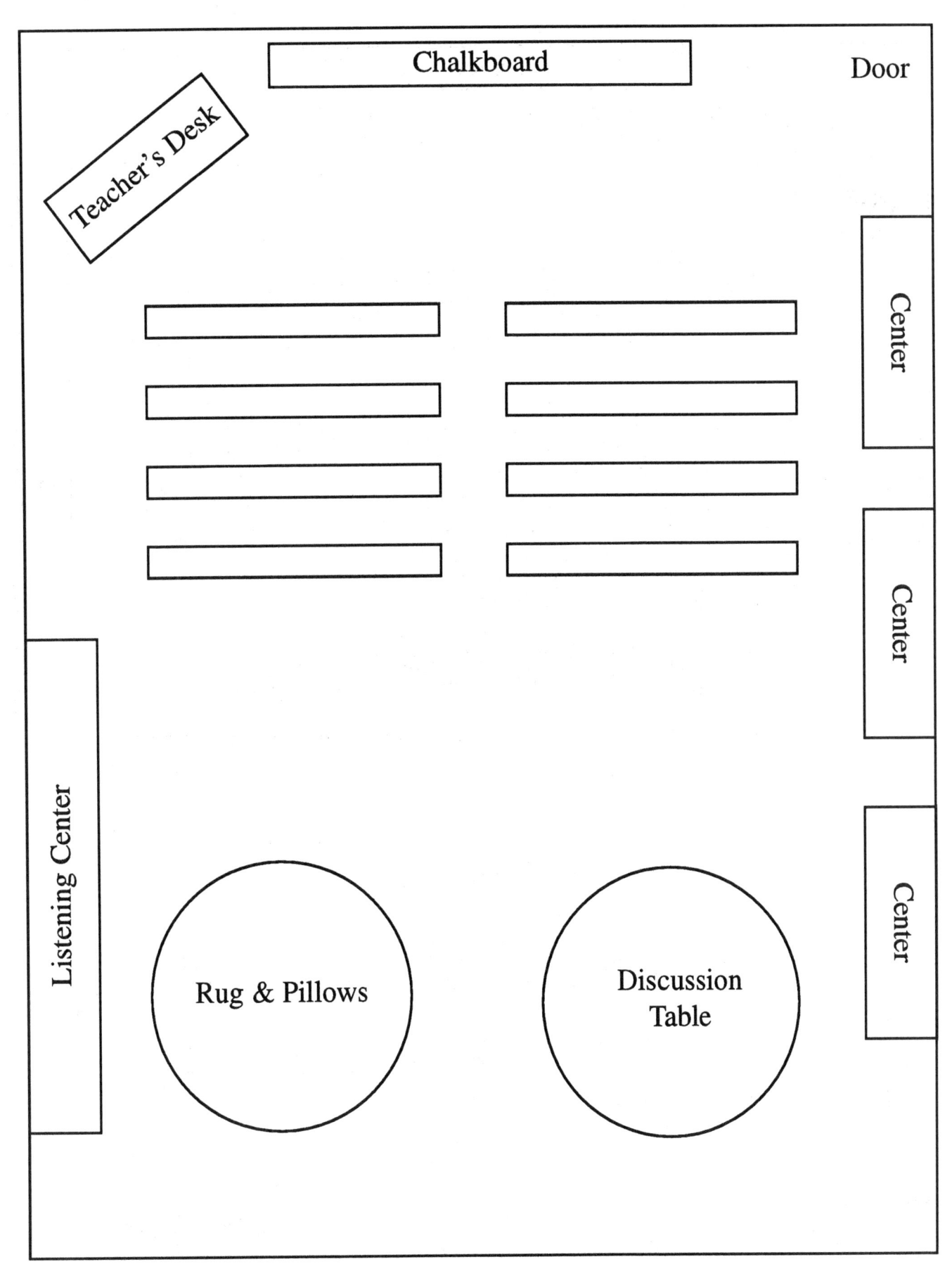

| | Chalkboard | Door |

Teacher's Desk

Center

Center

Center

Listening Center

Rug & Pillows

Discussion Table

©1995 Teacher Created Materials, Inc. 13 #791 Teaching Basic Skills through Literature: Phonics

Cooperative Learning

What is cooperative learning?

Cooperative learning is a group-oriented problem-solving process. It is a way of finding out answers while integrating social skills. Using this method, small groups of students work together to complete a task. The task might be a game, a problem requiring a correct answer, or an open-ended activity. It is accomplished by students collaborating and pooling their resources to come up with a solution. An important component in achieving a goal is cooperating while completing the task, with everyone in the group participating.

What are the components of cooperative learning?

In cooperative learning all group members need to work together to accomplish a task. No one is finished until the whole group is finished. The task or activity needs to be designed so that members are not each completing their own parts but are working to complete one product together.

Cooperative groups should be academically balanced. It is helpful to start by organizing groups so that there is a balance of abilities and cultures within and between groups. Heterogeneous groups foster success for all your students. The first step in planning your groups is to rank your students. You can base this on past grades or general class work. Choose group members who represent a variety of achievement levels. Also, keep gender in mind when organizing groups. Do not create groups that are all boys or all girls. Keep children apart who do not get along or who are best friends.

Cooperative learning activities need to be designed so that each student contributes to the group and individual group members can be assessed on their performances. This can be accomplished by assigning each group member a role that is essential to the completion of the task or activity. When input must be gathered from all members of the group, no one can go along for a free ride. Change the roles for each group with each new activity or task. Members of cooperative groups need to be changed occasionally to allow students to work with different classmates.

Cooperative learning groups need to know the social as well as the academic objectives of a lesson. Students need to know what they are expected to learn and how they are supposed to be working together to accomplish this learning. Students need to think and talk about how they worked on social skills as well as to evaluate how well their group worked on accomplishing the academic objective.

Cooperative Learning (cont.)

What is the teacher's role in cooperative learning?

The teacher's role is quite different from what it is during a teacher directed lesson. During the cooperative learning activity the teacher acts as facilitator. The teacher enables the children to create the parameters within which the activity operates. The teacher's involvement will vary based on the specific activity and the developmental level of the children and their previous experiences with cooperative learning.

What are the students' roles and responsibilities?

In cooperative learning students are able to interact effectively, assigning tasks and forming leadership patterns. Students involved in cooperative learning benefit by developing increased socialization and communication skills.

At the end of an activity, members of a group should be given the opportunity to discuss and compare the various ways in which they approached the problem and ultimately solved it. This time for reflection will help bring closure to the activity. It is important to encourage class discussion of each group's results. The sharing of information among groups can be a valuable learning experience too.

Teachers often find that using job assignments or roles helps students to know what part of the task or activity they are responsible for completing. It gives them specific information on what they need to do to help their group. The teacher can select specific roles for group work, depending on the task or activity. Roles need to be taught or modeled for the class. After a period of experience with cooperative learning, specific roles may not be necessary each time for groups that work well together. In this case, groups will naturally divide up the tasks, with group members doing what they like or are especially capable of doing. Some cooperative learning roles are described on page 16.

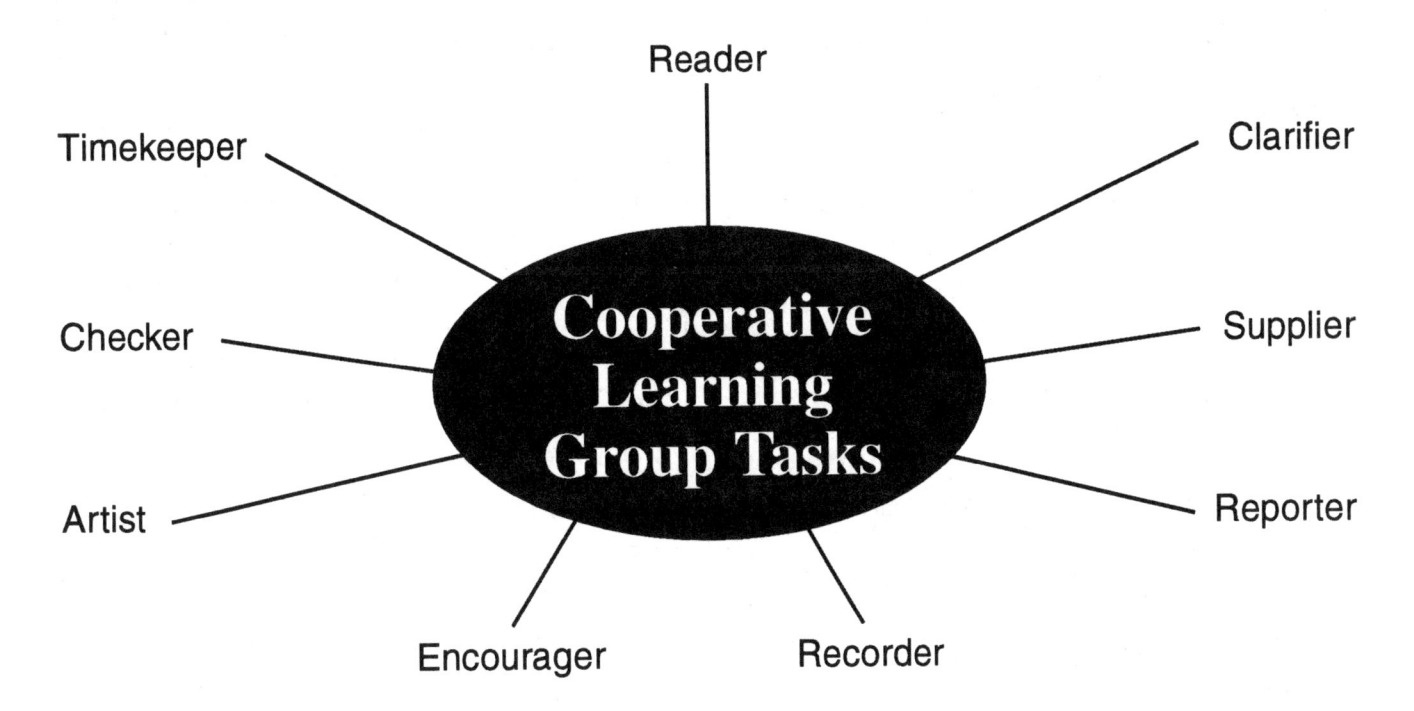

Cooperative Learning Group Tasks
- Reader
- Clarifier
- Supplier
- Reporter
- Recorder
- Encourager
- Artist
- Checker
- Timekeeper

Cooperative Learning (cont.)

The following is a list of possibilities of roles you may decide to use for a cooperative learning activity.

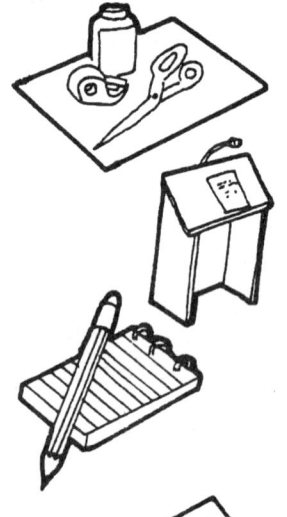

Supplier: Gets materials and supplies for the group.

Reporter: Reports to the class for the group.

Recorder: Writes down what the group does, completes the written part of the task or activity, and records the group's response during reflection time.

Encourager: Gives group members praise for the participation and collaboration on the group task or activity.

Artist: Produces all the artwork.

Checker: Checks completed work for completeness, neatness, and accuracy.

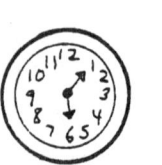

Reader: Reads directions, text, or looks up information during group work.

Timekeeper: Keeps the group on task and gives time prompts so the group will complete their task on time.

Cooperative Learning (cont.)

How do I prepare my students for cooperative learning?

Prepare your students for cooperative learning by conducting whole-class activities. Whole-class cooperative activities are especially conducive to creating a comfortable, safe environment in which students have some knowledge and understanding of one another. It is helpful to ease into the cooperative experience since many beginning students have never had the experience of cooperative interaction.

The younger the children are, the less comfortable they may feel in group situations. To begin the transition to cooperative learning, teachers can focus on teaching children how to get along within the classroom setting. Concepts such as sharing and taking turns are understood by precooperative learners. Emphasize these skills when introducing students to cooperative tasks. Remember, training students to be cooperative learners takes time. Try to be patient.

How do I assess students in cooperative groups?

After groups have worked on some task or activity, they need an opportunity to look more closely at their finished product and to process how well they worked together as a group to complete the task. This gives students an opportunity to look at their own learning and to see how well they met the objectives of the lesson. When students reflect on how well they worked together, it gives them a chance to consider not only how they did, but also what they should work on next.

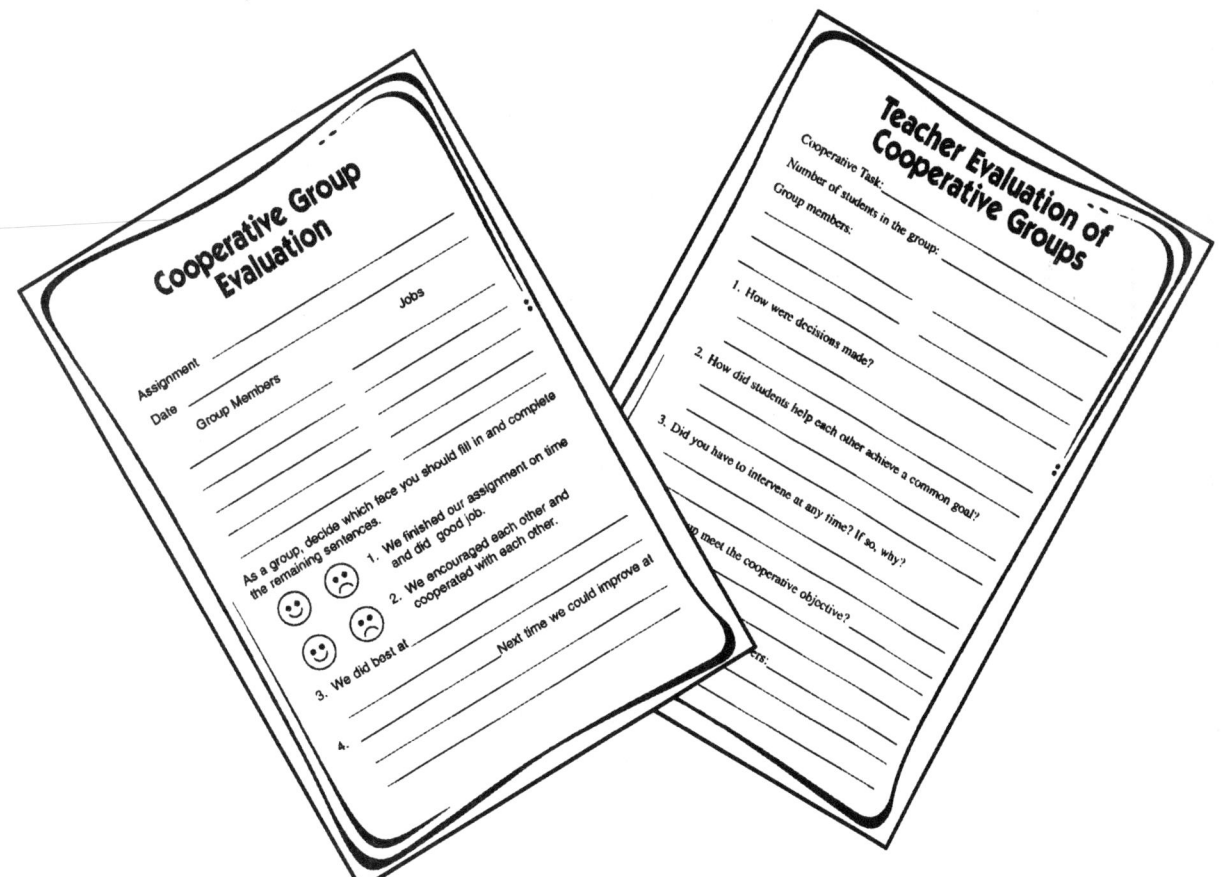

A cooperative group evaluation form can be found on page 18. Be sure to allow adequate time for group processing. It is a major component of successful cooperative group management.

A teacher cooperative evaluation form is provided on page 19. As the teacher, when evaluating the group you should consider both the academic and social objectives of the lesson.

©1995 Teacher Created Materials, Inc.

Cooperative Group Evaluation

Assignment _____

Date _____

    Group Members   Jobs

_____   _____

_____   _____

_____   _____

_____   _____

_____   _____

As a group, decide which face you should fill in and complete the remaining sentences.

☺ ☹   1. We finished our assignment on time and did a good job.

☺ ☹   2. We encouraged each other and cooperated with each other.

3. We did best at _____

4. Next time we could improve at _____

_____

_____

Teacher Evaluation of Cooperative Groups

Cooperative Task: _____

Number of students in the group: _____

Group members:

_____   _____

_____   _____

_____

1. How were decisions made?

   _____

   _____

2. How did students help each other achieve a common goal?

   _____

   _____

3. Did you have to intervene at any time? If so, why?

   _____

   _____

4. Did the group meet the cooperative objective? _____
   Evidence: _____

   _____

Comments on individual group members: _____

   _____

   _____

Learning Centers

What is a learning center?

A learning center is an area in a classroom where one or more children can participate in activities designed for enrichment, and review of current learning, and reinforcement of the skills being taught. A learning center coordinated with the curriculum enhances skills and learning.

A center can consist of games, activities, reading materials, or manipulatives. The games can be board games that have been purchased for use in your classroom or simple file folder games that you have created. Activities can consist of art projects, science experiments, or puzzles. For students who have difficulty reading the assigned literature book, a listening center equipped with a tape recorder and tape-recorded version of the book can be created. Students can use the manipulatives located in the math center to extend the learning concepts of cooperative problem solving.

As new topics are introduced or areas of special interest develop, new centers may be created. Rather than serve as primary instruction, a learning center supports what is taught in the classroom. A center provides an alternative to the traditional concept of seatwork. It allows students the opportunity to independently practice skills and assume responsibility for learning, while freeing the teacher to work with small groups or individual students.

A learning center should not serve as a place where students can merely spend their free time. A successful center has a clearly stated task or objective for each activity. Children should have the opportunity to use the centers daily.

#791 Teaching Basic Skills through Literature: Phonics   ©1995 Teacher Created Materials, Inc.

Learning Centers (cont.)

How do I create the learning center?

Choose a piece of literature that corresponds to the skill or activity that will be the focus of the learning center. The extensive bibliography located at the back of this book is an excellent resource for you. Then, design the learning center activity so students will have an opportunity to read the piece of literature, and then practice the skill. Leave specific instructions for students at the learning center so they can be self-directed and will not have to interrupt you. Also, make sure all necessary materials to complete the activity are at the center for students. Each lesson in this resource book has a learning center activity.

How do I set up the learning center?

Below are some general suggestions for things to keep in mind as you set up your learning centers.

1. **Have some form of symbolic directions for students** even if you have to orally explain a center. These symbols are for students who are not yet reading. Sample signs are provided on pages 24 through 26.

2. **Decorate centers so they are inviting to students.** Have a partially completed model for students to see so that they know what they are expected to do. Use the bottom part of a bulletin board, a chart taped to a wall, a wooden stand, or a cardboard carrel to post directions and display completed projects.

3. **Have all materials that students will need at the center** so that students will not have to interrupt to get glue, scissors, etc. Folders or boxes are useful so that students remember where to put the center supplies when they are finished or when time is up.

4. **Design a method for students to check the work** they do at the centers whenever possible. Perhaps a parent could help check for accuracy of work if you set the standards.

5. **Determine a recording system** to help you keep track of which students have visited which centers. The chart on page 27 will help you keep students organized.

How will my students benefit from learning centers?

The enthusiasm for and results of using learning centers is well worth the time and effort required to set them up. They offer an avenue for reaching each child. Learning centers can play an important part in the daily schedule for primary children. Your children will learn by doing and enjoy learning while it is taking place.

Using Centers

In a classroom rich with reinforcement and exploratory activity centers, students are able to expand their knowledge of basic skills, topical information, and critical thinking skills. Center areas can be created using desk or table tops countertops, floor space, a corner of the room, an easel, a window area, or even a bathtub! Eight to ten center areas work well.

The hardest time to develop center activities is during the first year of implementation. Coming up with the activities and ideas, gathering necessary materials, and making ample samples can be very time consuming. Send home a supply request letter at the beginning of the year, with an additional follow-up letter sent home with each report card. Along with the supply letter, send a center helper list to enlist parents to act as classroom helpers (or to help with behind-the-scenes preparations).

The most common center frustration is getting students to use all of the center areas. To solve this problem, you must first determine the purpose for using centers in your classroom. If they are to facilitate reinforcement experiences during free time (the period of time after a student has finished an assignment or project), then it should be acceptable for students to go back over and over again. The reason students go back to the same center consistently may be that they are achieving and experiencing success from that center activity. If your goal is for students to experience extra practice in specific skill areas, a structured center rotation design would be needed. Listed below are suggestions for both open and structured center rotation designs.

Open Center Rotation Design

1. If centers are being used for free-time exploration, either at the beginning of the day or after work has been completed, place a number (1, 2, 3, 4) above each center area to signal how many students are allowed in each area at any one time. Keep in mind that the number of students may be changed as activities are changed.

2. If centers are used for a designated daily free-choice "center time" (for example, 30 minutes per day), signal students to change center areas by ringing a bell after 10 to 15 minutes. Students then move to a different center area of their choice.

Structured Center Rotation Design

1. Create a pocket chart using colorful tagboard and library card pockets. Glue the pockets to the tagboard and laminate. Using a razor blade, cut a slit through the lamin at each pocket opening so center cards will slide in easily.

Using Centers (cont.)

Structured Center Rotation Design (cont.)

Write a student's name on each pocket with a permanent marker. On 3" x 5" (8 cm x 13 cm) index cards draw a picture or write the name of each center area. (**Note:** If four students are allowed at the counting center, make four counting center index cards; if two students are allowed at the tangram center, make two index cards, etc.) Place prepared index cards in the pockets. (**Note:** Do not place two like center cards directly to the right of each other. If you do this, when cards are rotated to the right, some students will go to the same center two days in a row). During structured center time, each student looks to see in which center he/she will work. After school, rotate cards one pocket to the right so students will go to a different center the following day.

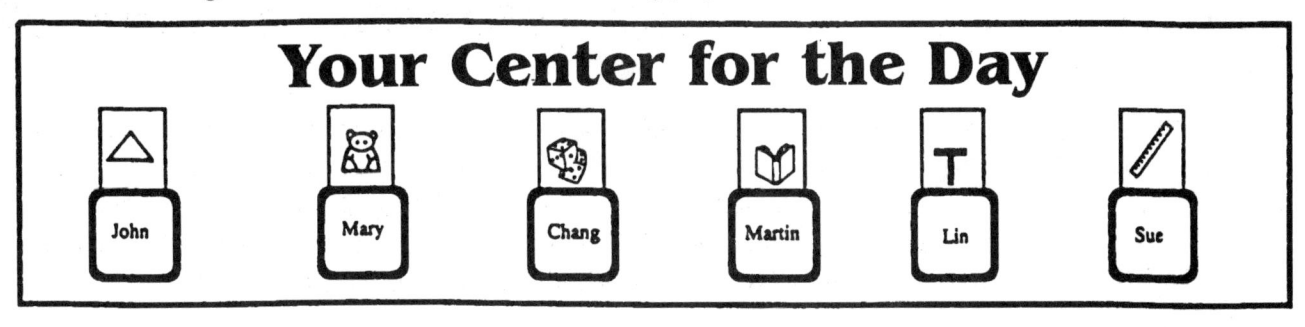

2. If utilizing a small group instruction time, you may wish to divide the class into four groups. During small group time, students participate in one of four learning activities: working with the teacher, completing seatwork, working in cooperative groups, or working in a center area. To manage this time effectively, create a chart using the center circle; colorful tagboard divided into four sections, a paper fastener, and markers.

Four group names (let students brainstorm and vote) are placed on the tag board. If you would like, draw or add a picture, too. Students will participate in two of the four learning experiences each day. For example:

Monday: First Rotation

Octopi—working with teacher

Sharks—cooperative groups

Whales—seatwork

Dolphins—centers

Approximately one half hour later, turn wheel on chart clockwise.

Monday: Second Rotation

Octopi—centers

Sharks—working with teacher

Whales—cooperative groups

Dolphins—seatwork

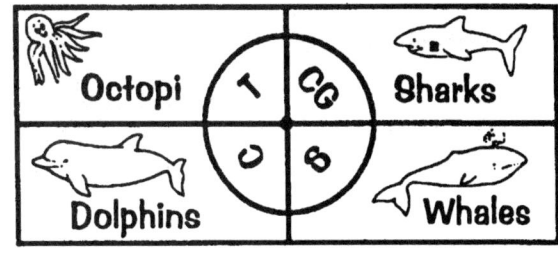

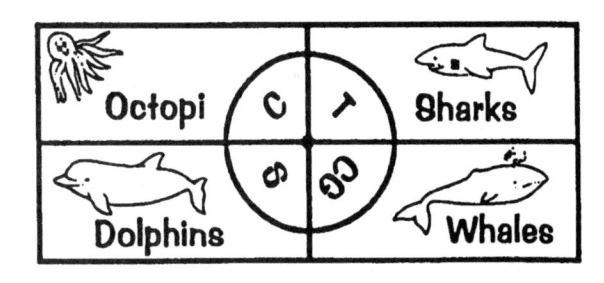

©1995 Teacher Created Materials, Inc.   23   #791 Teaching Basic Skills through Literature: Phonics

Learning Center Signs

Some form of symbolic directions for students will make the centers easier to use even if you explain what a center is. These symbols will be especially helpful for those who are not yet reading.

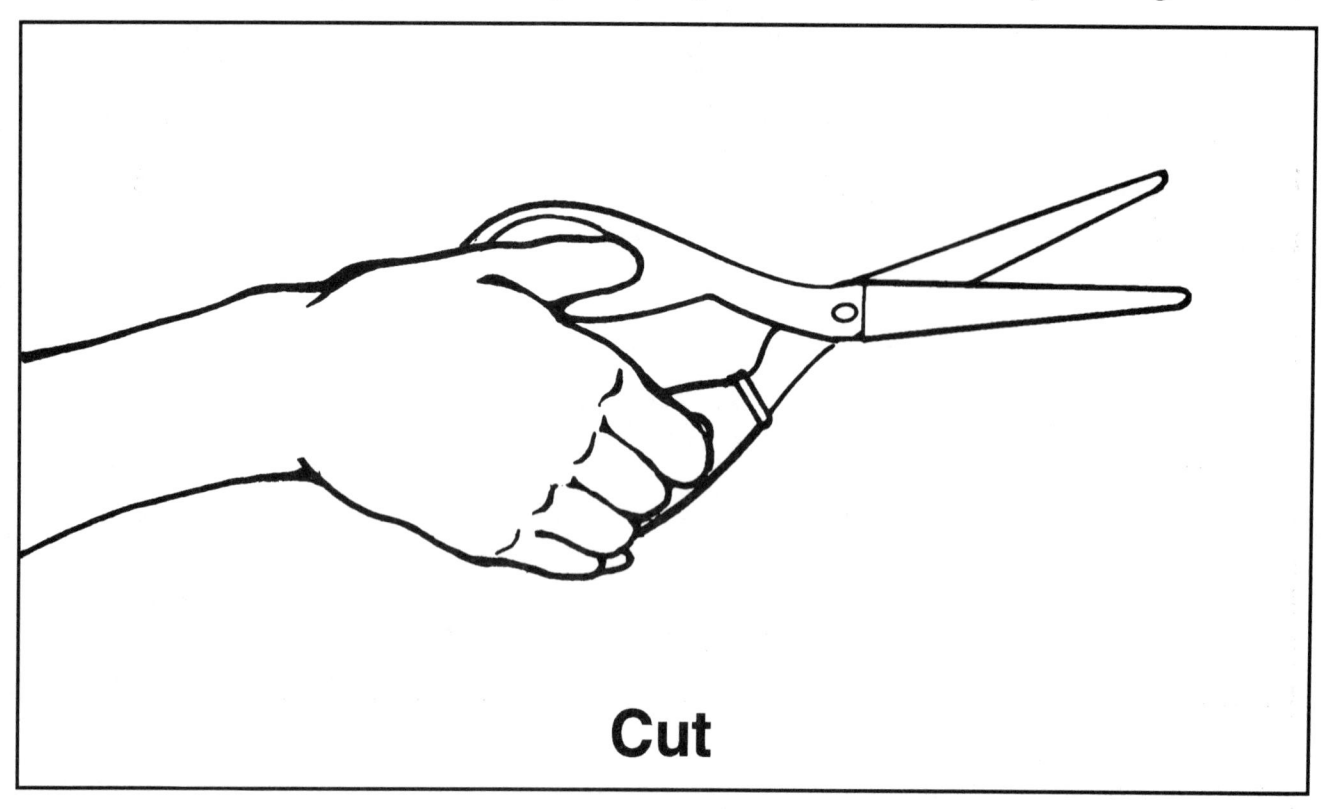

Cut

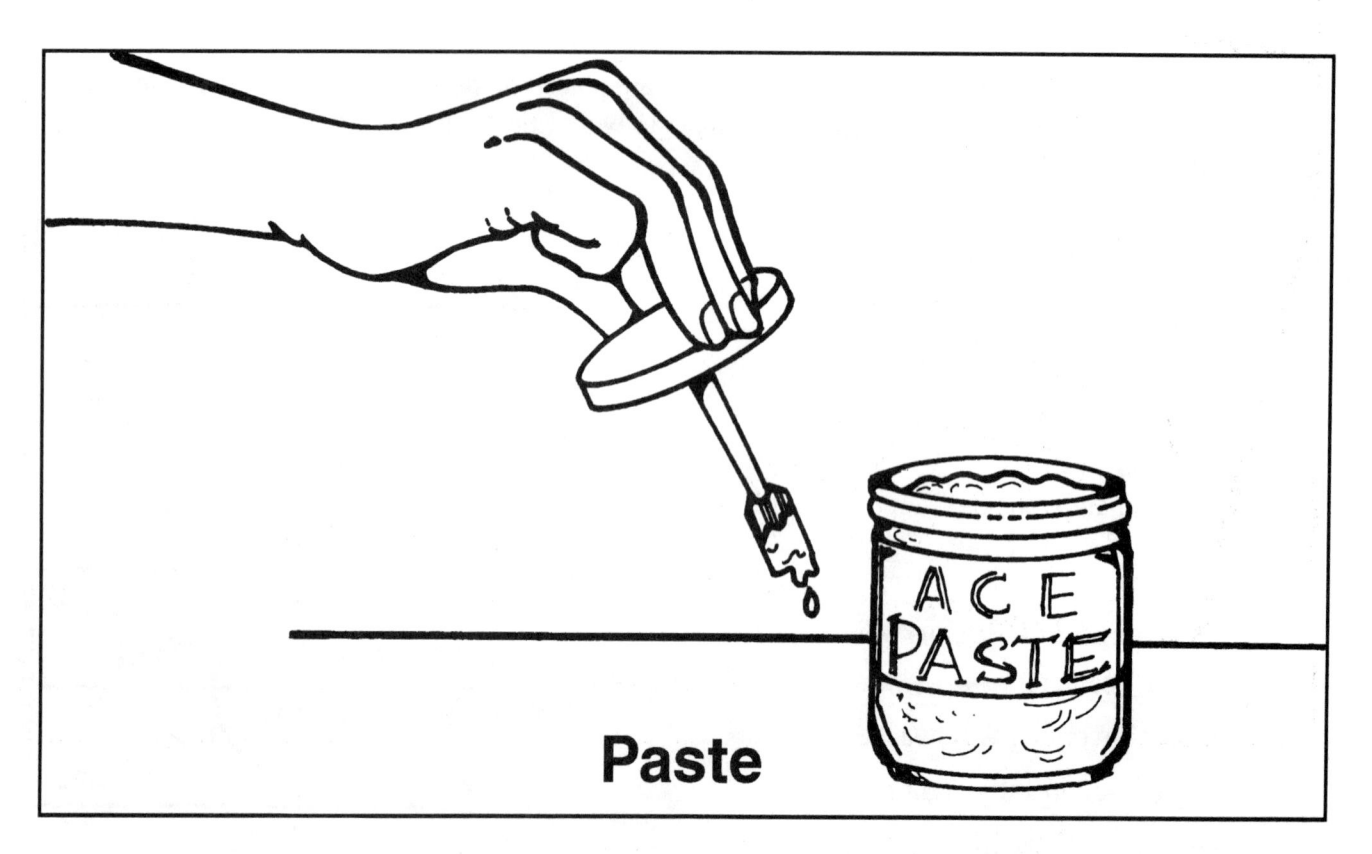

Paste

#791 Teaching Basic Skills through Literature: Phonics

Learning Center Signs *(cont.)*

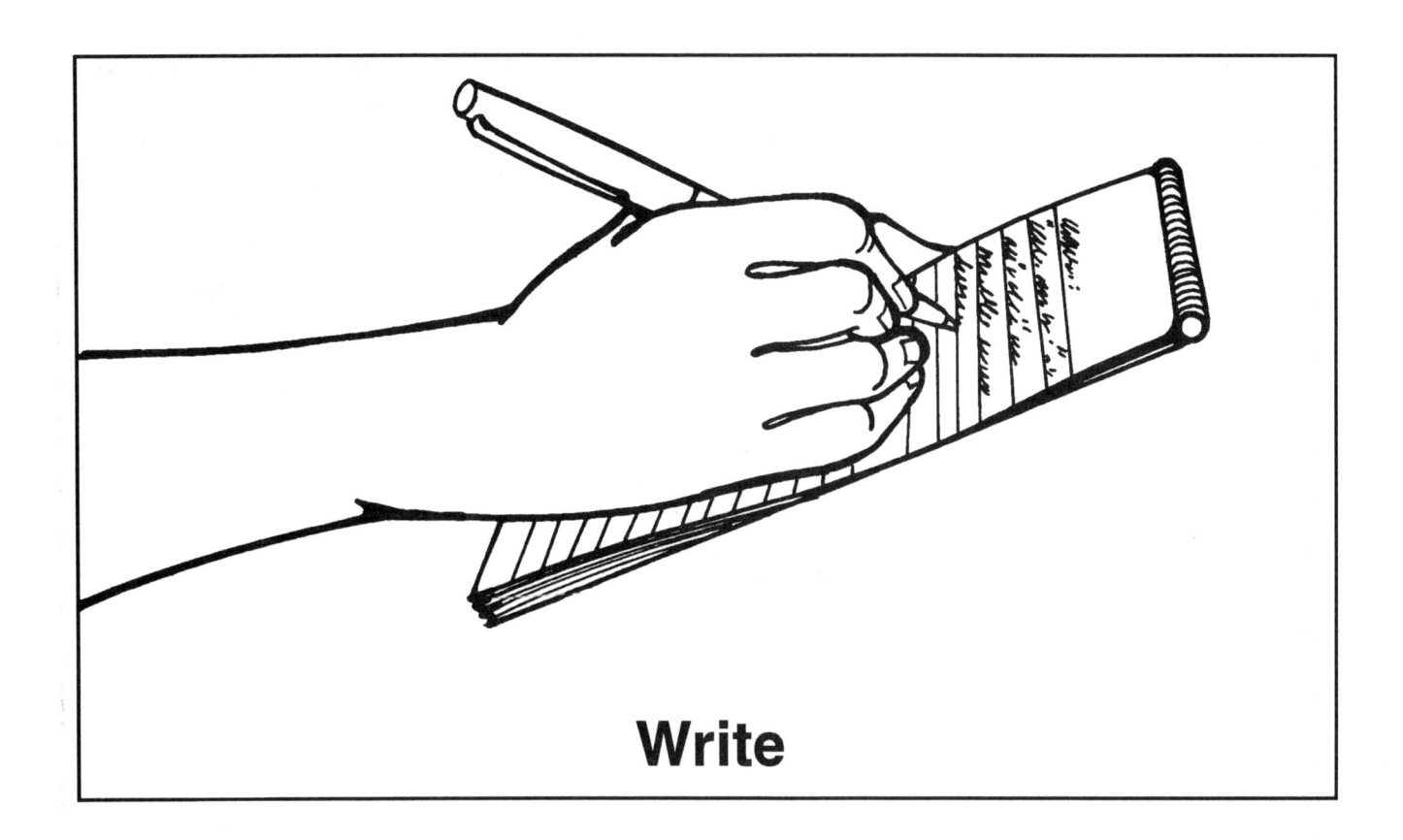

Write

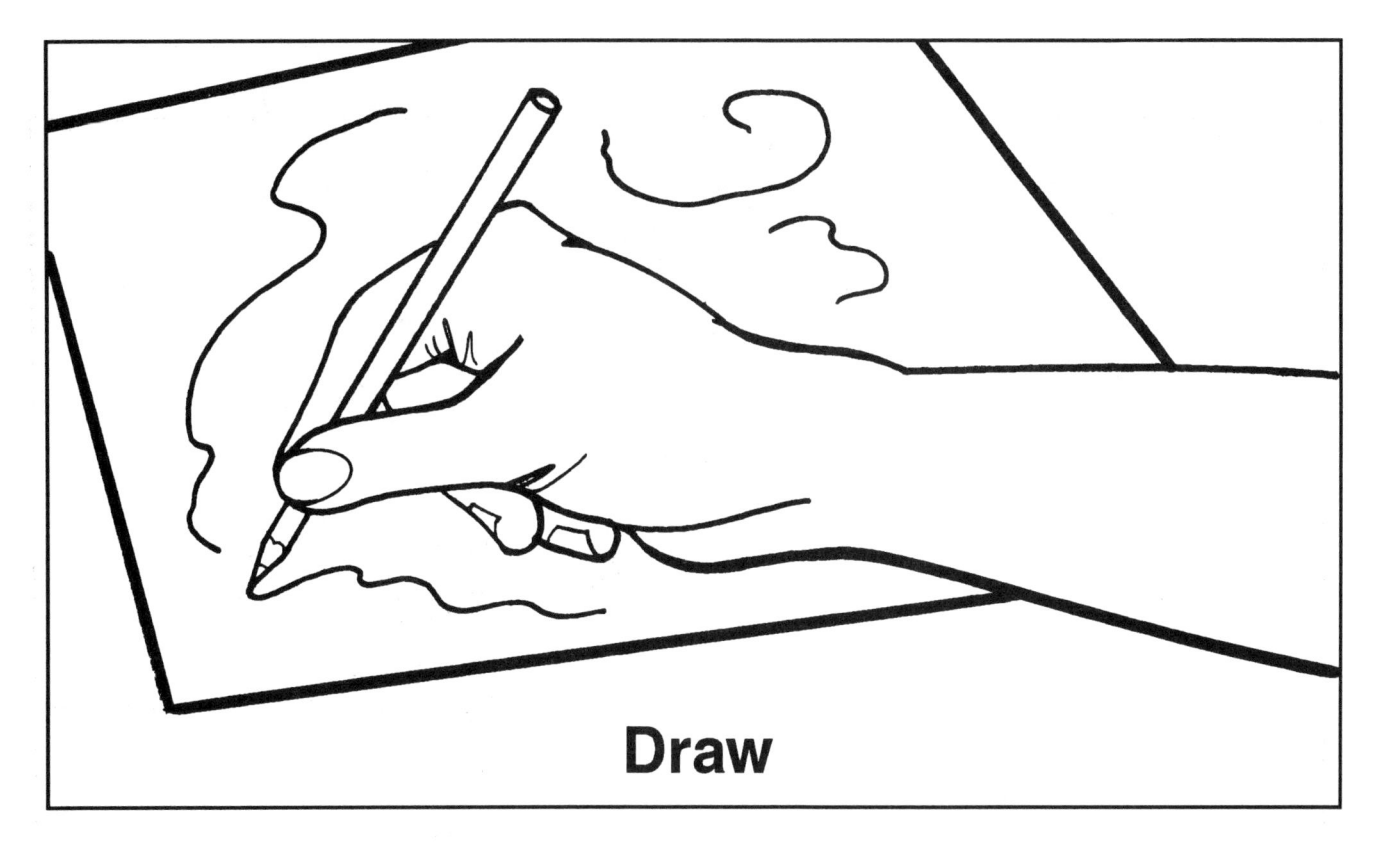

Draw

Learning Center Signs (cont.)

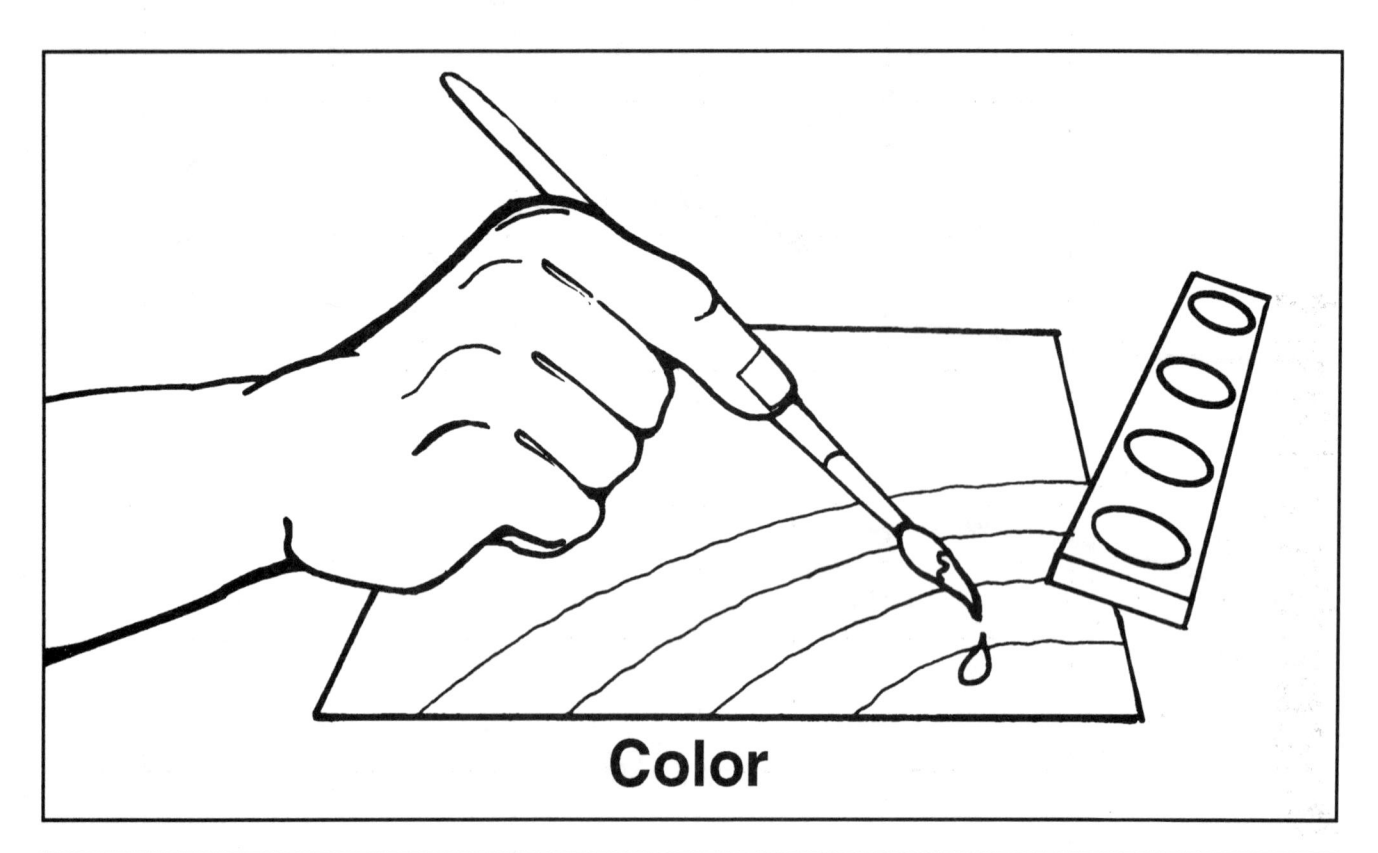

Color

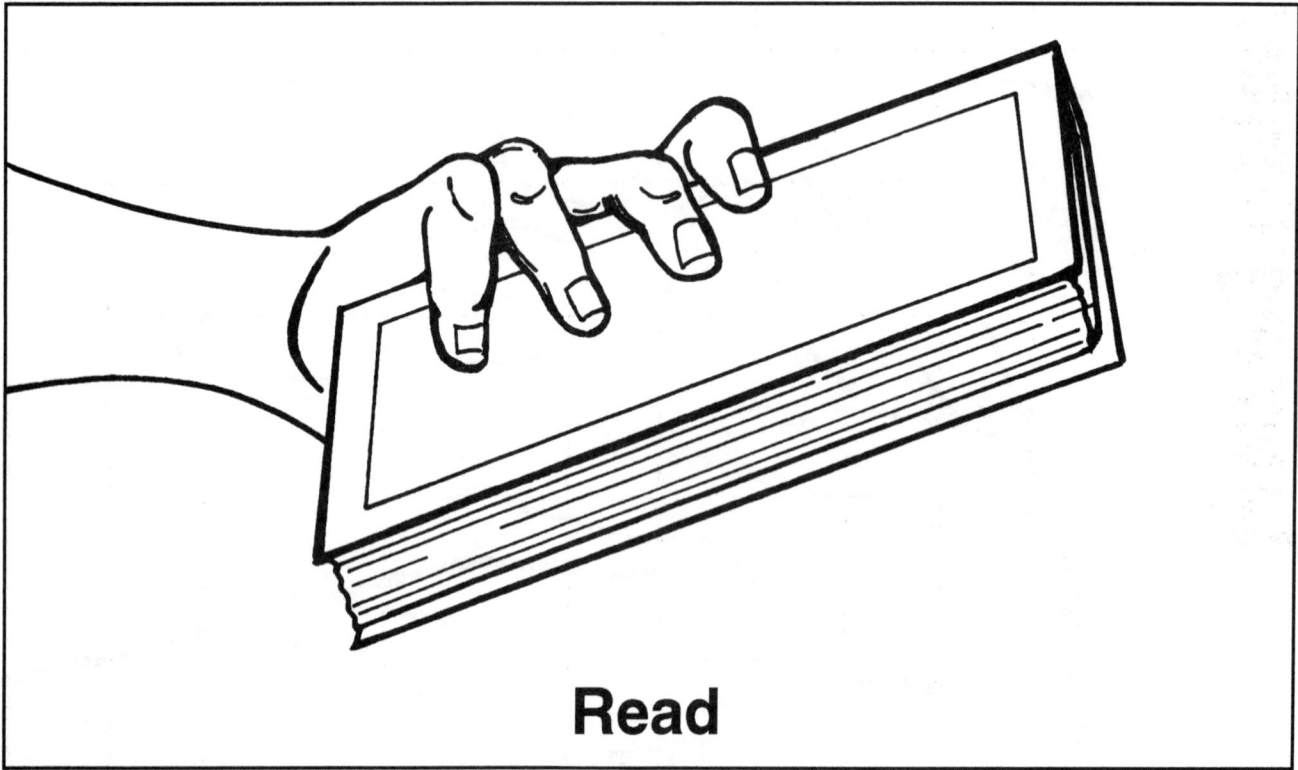

Read

Learning Center Recording Chart

Centers

Students' Names

©1995 Teacher Created Materials, Inc. 27 #791 Teaching Basic Skills through Literature: Phonics

Assessment

When should I assess?

Assessment should happen continuously in your classroom. New information pertaining to a particular child's strengths and weaknesses will be gained daily. Attention should be paid to areas that have been mastered and areas where reteaching and additional practice are needed. By making assessment an ongoing, continuous process, we are in a better position to make decisions regarding curriculum, skills, and lessons. Teachers can assess a student's progress at any moment by reviewing the portfolio contents and then determine if there needs to be a review of certain skills. The ongoing nature of authentic assessment means that we no longer have to wait until the end of an instructional unit before assessing a student's understanding of skills and concepts.

Whole-language teachers have specific skill objectives; however, they are not always sequential in nature. Furthermore, literacy is not easily broken down into measurable skills. Instead, it is a complex building of numerous concepts and abstract thinking processes and should be considered as such when evaluating student achievement.

Once a literature-based skill lesson has been taught and ample practice has been provided, students can be evaluated for mastery. There are many ways you can assess students. These options include portfolio assessment, observation-based assessment, and rubrics.

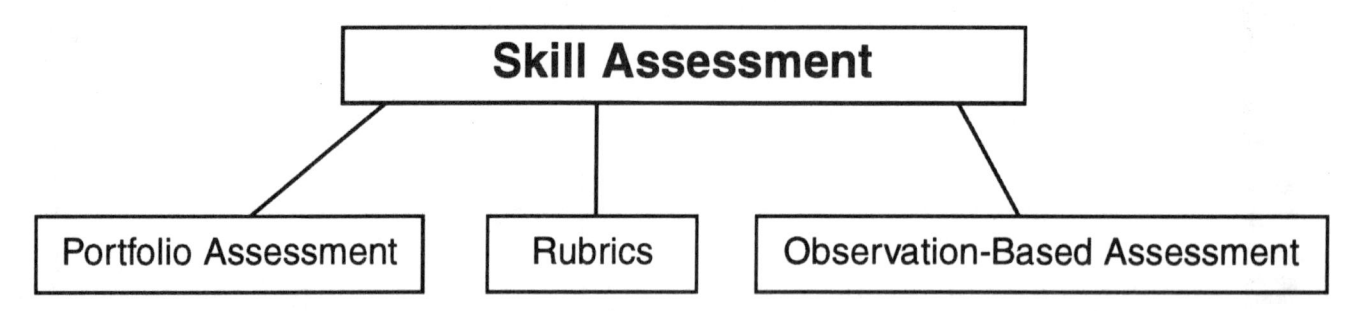

```
                    Skill Assessment
                   /       |        \
    Portfolio Assessment  Rubrics  Observation-Based Assessment
```

What is portfolio assessment?

Portfolios are collections of student work reviewed against criteria in order to assess students' progress over time. Portfolios were the first type of authentic assessment to gain ground. Portfolios represent a philosophy that demands we view assessment as an integral part of instruction, providing a vehicle for teachers to use as a guide for learning. They have gained popularity in the wake of the concept that assessment should be ongoing.

What are the types of portfolios I can use?

There are many kinds of portfolios. The type of portfolio you ultimately decide to use in your classroom depends on your particular assessment needs. It is important to remember that decisions regarding the type of portfolio to use in your classroom are not etched in stone. Many teachers try several different types of portfolios before settling on the one that works best for them and their students.

Although there are many types of portfolios, the most common fall into one of three categories: the *collection portfolio*, the *showcase portfolio*, and the *assessment portfolio*. The collection portfolio is a folder that holds an accumulation of a student's work. The showcase portfolio is a selection of work that represents a student's progress and achievement. The assessment portfolio is a collection of documentation used to support or supplement the student's report card grade. Ideas for what to include in each of the portfolios described are highlighted on page 29.

Assessment (cont.)

What do I include in a portfolio?

Collection Portfolio

- writing samples at all stages of the process
- skill checklists
- reading inventories
- responses to reading
- videotapes of the child reading

Showcase Portfolio

- items from the collection portfolio
- student self-reflections
- photos of projects

Assessment Portfolio

- samples of work showing growth
- anecdotal records
- student-teacher reports
- interest inventories
- conference reports

Assessment (cont.)

How do I evaluate the portfolio?

Take time to review the portfolio before doing your analysis. Perhaps note some comments about strengths and needs. Allow yourself time with the portfolio so a complete picture of the student can emerge. Review portfolio selections, using your knowledge of the subject area, and class expectations, along with your understanding of the strengths and needs of the particular student. Certainly, this process will be time consuming. For this reason, you may want to limit the number of items to include in the portfolio, at least at first.

In the process of reviewing portfolios and diagnosing individual strengths and needs, you may find that some students are having difficulty with a specific skill. You can then use this information when planning your curriculum. In this way your assessment procedures are guiding your instruction. After designing literature-based lessons to assist students in the acquisition of the specific skill, you can collect a new sample from students. Now you can compare the two samples and review students' progress over time.

A portfolio checklist sheet is included on page 32 for your convenience.

What is observation-based assessment?

Observation-based assessment is a new name for something teachers have already been doing for years. We have always carefully observed our students, making mental and written notes about their progress. In the past, however, we kept these notes private and did not really consider them assessment per se. Recently, this has changed. Teachers are now trusting their judgments more than ever.

There are two types of observations teachers can make: objective and interpretive. When using the objective style, you simply record what you are seeing as if you are a camera. Checklists are an objective form of observation because they simply require you to check off the skills you observe. Anecdotal records, on the other hand, can be either objective or interpretive. The interpretive style goes beyond mere recording. With it you actually evaluate and comment on the notes you have taken.

How do I use checklists?

Checklists are lists of skills to be checked off by the observer as a simple "yes-no" rating. The check indicates whether or not the skill was present. With the checklist there is no need to judge how well the skills are performed, only that they are present. This makes checklists fast and easy to use. Sample checklists can be found on pages 33 through 35.

Kindergarten Skills Checklist

Student's Name _____

Rating Scale
1=Rarely Observed   2= Occasionally observed   3=Often observed

Language Arts Skills	1st Quarter	2nd Quarter	3rd Quarter	4th Quarter
Identifies beginning consonants				
Identifies ending consonants				
Predicts story content				
Predicts outcomes				
Knows letter names				
Knows letter sounds				
Understands directionality				
Uses picture clues				
Understands opposites				
Compares stories				
Writes letters A–Z				
Writes first name				
Writes at least one-sentence stories				
Capitalizes first letter of name				

Assessment (cont.)

What are anecdotal records?

Anecdotal records are carefully documented notes of certain events, behaviors, and skills. When your anecdotal records are put together they tell an ogoing story about students' growth and progress. At the beginning of the year, it may be necessary to make more general entries as you start the process of becoming familiar with your students. As you get to know your students, your entries may become more specific, or the type of entry may change.

A simple way to record anecdotal records involves several copies of a recording form and a notebook. You may choose to have a form for each individual student or one form you can use for the whole class. Use either of these forms to note any observations you make of students throughout the course of the school day. Examples and blank forms of both types of anecdotal record forms can be found on pages 36 through 39.

What is a rubric?

A rubric is a set of criteria students see prior to engaging in a task. The rubric can be established for a single task or writing assignment or for several tasks that may be collected in a portfolio. The rubric identifies the qualities the teacher expects to see along several points on a scale. Each score on the rubric is matched to an example of a response. By viewing established criteria prior to the activity, students clearly know what is expected of them in order to receive a specific score.

How can I involve students in assessment?

Students can become involved in the assessment process by reflecting on certain assignments. Self-evaluation makes students aware of their own learning, progress, and growth throughout the school year. You can introduce students to the reflection process by having them complete reflection forms. If they are unable to complete student forms, you or a parent can sit down with students and ask them to talk about their performance on an assignment. The child's response can then be transcribed. Two sample reflection forms can be found on pages 40 and 41.

We cannot expect students to jump right into self-evaluation without training. Traditionally students do classroom work, then wait for the teacher to return it with a grade on top. Evaluating your own work is not easy, and taking responsibility for it is certainly a challenge. It will take awhile for students to begin to trust their own judgment, so be patient.

Portfolio Checklist

Name _____

_____

_____

My portfolio contains the following items:

Reading: _____

_____

_____

Writing: _____

_____

_____

This is how I feel about the work in my portfolio:

☺   😐   ☹

happy   not sure   sad

Kindergarten Skills Checklist

Student's Name _____

Rating Scale
1=Rarely Observed   2= Occasionally observed   3=Often observed

Language Arts Skills	1st Quarter	2nd Quarter	3rd Quarter	4th Quarter
Identifies beginning consonants				
Identifies ending consonants				
Predicts story content				
Predicts outcomes				
Knows letter names				
Knows letter sounds				
Understands directionality				
Uses picture clues				
Understands opposites				
Compares stories				
Writes letters A–Z				
Writes first name				
Writes at least one-sentence stories				
Capitalizes first letter of name				

©1995 Teacher Created Materials, Inc.　　　33　　　#791 Teaching Basic Skills through Literature: Phonics

First Grade Skills Checklist

Student's Name _____

Rating Scale
1=Rarely Observed   2= Occasionally observed   3=Often observed

Language Arts Skills	1st Quarter	2nd Quarter	3rd Quarter	4th Quarter
Knows short vowels				
Classifies				
Notes details				
Chooses best title				
Alphabetizes to first letter				
Identifies before/after				
Follows directions				
Understands synonyms				
Compares and contrasts				
Identifies rhyming sound				
Identifies the main idea				
Knows story patterns				
Understands plurals				
Writes complete sentences				

#791 Teaching Basic Skills through Literature: Phonics   ©1995 Teacher Created Materials, Inc.

Second Grade Skills Checklist

Student's Name _____

Rating Scale
1=Rarely Observed   2= Occasionally observed   3=Often observed

Language Arts Skills	1st Quarter	2nd Quarter	3rd Quarter	4th Quarter
Sequences stories				
Knows long vowels				
Understands cause/effect				
Can summarize				
Knows main ideas of stories				
Makes inferences				
Understands point of view				
Identifies prefixes/suffixes				
Knows antonyms/homonyms				
Can categorize information				
Identifies compound words				

©1995 Teacher Created Materials, Inc.

Individual Anecdotal Record—Example

This is an example of how to keep an individual record of observed behaviors. One of these pages is made for each student and kept in alphabetical order in a three-ring binder for convenient access. When the page is filled up, it can be replaced with a new page and the filled page placed in the student's portfolio.

Individual Anecdotal Record

Name: Marcie Wallace

Date	Comment
10/15/93	Having trouble with group skills— we talked about strategies she could try. I suggested some positive comments.
10/31/93	Marcie made several positive comments in her cooperative group today— "I like that" and "What a nice story."
11/1/93	Continues to be positive and helpful— shared today in oral language.

Individual Anecdotal Record—Form

Run off a stack of these forms and keep them— one for each student in your class — in a three-ring binder. Make your notes right on the appropriate form. When a page is filled up, it can be replaced with a new page and the filled page placed in the student's portfolio. No time is lost transcribing information!

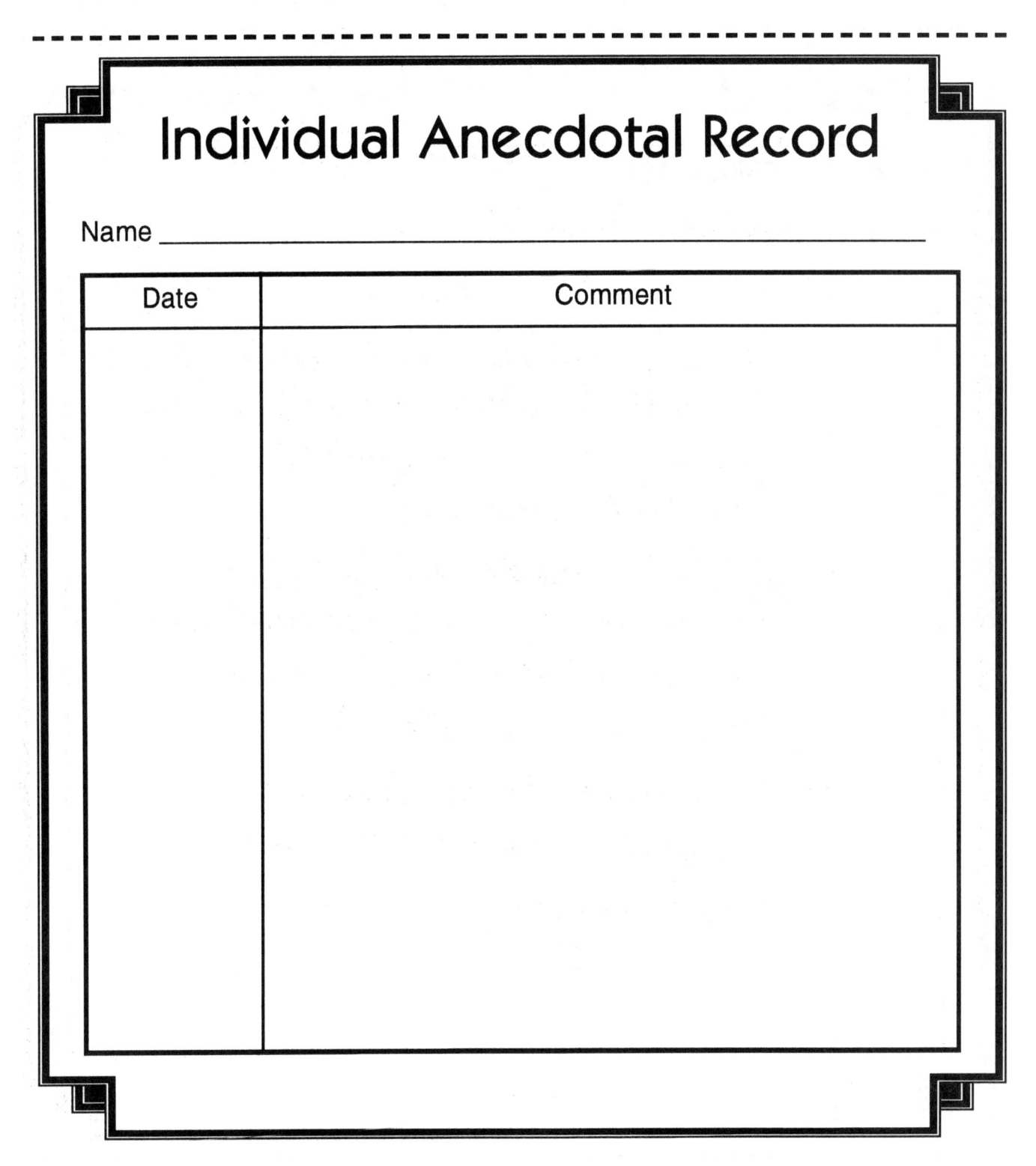

Individual Anecdotal Record

Name _____

Date	Comment

Classroom List Anecdotal Record—Example

This is an example of how to keep a running classroom list of observed behaviors. The comments are written with the idea of transferring them to individual forms, with elaborations perhaps, at the end of the day.

Record of Observed Behavior

Date	Child's Name	Comment
10/31/93	Raul L.	Holding up pretty well in spite of Halloween! Wrote a great "scary story."
10/31/93	Marcie W.	Made several positive comments in her coop. group—"I like that" and "What a nice story."
11/1/93	Joe S.	Needs help reading his new book—find parent helper
11/1/93	Marcie W.	Continues to be positive and helpful. Shared today in oral lang.

Classroom List Anecdotal Record— Form

Run off some of these classroom lists and carry them around on a clipboard to make moment-by-moment comments on what you observe in your classroom. Transfer the information to individual record forms at the end of the day.

- -

Record of Observed Behavior

Date	Child's Name	Comment

Assignment Self-Evaluation

Name: _____

Assignment: _____

1. How do you feel about this assignment? (Circle one.)

   happy   not sure   sad

2. What did you do best on this assignment?
   _____
   _____

3. What could you improve on this assignment?
   _____
   _____
   _____

Spelling Self-Evaluation

Name: _____

1. This is how I feel about my progress in spelling: (Circle one.)

   happy   not sure   sad

2. Here are some new words I have learned how to spell:
   _____
   _____

3. I have trouble spelling:
   _____
   _____

4. When I do not know how to spell a word, I usually...

   _____ ask the teacher.

   _____ ask a friend.

   _____ make a guess.

   _____ sound it out.

   _____ look in the dictionary.

©1995 Teacher Created Materials, Inc.   41   #791 Teaching Basic Skills through Literature: Phonics

Phonics Skills in Context: Letter "B"

Book: *Blueberries for Sal*
Author: Robert McCloskey
Publisher: Scholastic, New York, 1976
Summary: Little Sal and her mother have an adventurous day picking blueberries.
Recommended Grade Level: K–2
Related Poetry: "Backward Bill" by Shel Silverstein, *A Light in the Attic* (Harper & Row, New York, 1974). For additional titles see page 384.

Skill Activity
Students will name "b" words and then bounce a ball or toss a beanbag to the teacher.

Materials
- ball or beanbag
- blueberries in a bag
- chart paper

Lesson
Introduce the Literature: Ask students to guess what you have in the bag. Give them clues such as "They are round," "You can eat them," "The word begins with the sound of B." Allow time for them to guess. Show students the blueberries and give each one a taste. Show the cover of the book and tell students they will hear a story called *Blueberries for Sal*.

Read the Literature: Read the literature selection. Allow time for discussion of the story.

Introduce the Skill Lesson:

1. Ask students if they can think of any words in the story that began with "b." Reread the story as needed to help students recall the "b" words. Brainstorm other "b" words as well.
2. Write all the "b" words on chart paper. Display the list in the room as a word bank.
3. Have students form a circle with the teacher in the middle. The teacher bounces a ball to a student. That students must name a "b" word before bouncing it back to the teacher. Older students may enjoy having a turn in the middle.

Learning Center Activity: Students use the "b" picture cards on page 45 to complete the phrase "a _____ for _____" (example: a block for Billy). Have students copy their ideas onto the activity sheet on page 46 and illustrate. Pages can be collated into a class book and made available at the class library for independent reading.

Cooperative Learning Activity: Have students work in small cooperative groups to build "b" objects with blocks. Allow time for groups to share their "b" buildings with the rest of the class.

Across the Curriculum: Science
Have students make butter. Pour half pint (240 mL) of whipping cream, a dash of salt, and yellow food coloring (optional) into a medium-sized jar. Let students take turns shaking the jar vigorously until set. Spread the butter on bread, biscuits, bagels, or blueberry muffins.

Bb *Blueberries for Sal*

Extension Activities

Movement Activities
Stress the "b" sound as students participate in the following movements: backward walking, beanbag toss, basketball throw, fly like a butterfly, and blow bubbles.

Multisensory Activity
On 6" x 8" (15 cm x 20 cm) tagboard, have children glue buttons onto an upper-and lowercase "b." Patterns are provided on pages 47 and 48.

Creative Writing
Make a list of things that are bigger than a bread box. Illustrate the ideas using the activity sheet on page 49.

Handwriting
On 12" x 18" (30 cm x 46 cm) lined newsprint, ask children to copy this sentence: "B is for bear, boat, balloons, and a beautiful butterfly."

Cooking

Banana Kabobs

Ingredients
- half banana per child
- toothpicks
- knife
- cutting board

Directions
1. Peel banana.
2. Slice banana.
3. Skewer slices on toothpick.
4. Draw your recipe.
5. Clean up.

Interdisciplinary Topics

bears	George Bush	bones	butter
bees	babies	baths	broccoli
butterflies	banks	breakfast	Brussels sprouts
birds	beaches	body	biscuits
bats	bridges	blueberries	butterscotch
boa constrictors	bakeries	beans	berries
Black history	boats	bananas	beets
beavers	buildings		

©1995 Teacher Created Materials, Inc.

Blueberries for Sal Bb

Extension Activities (cont.)

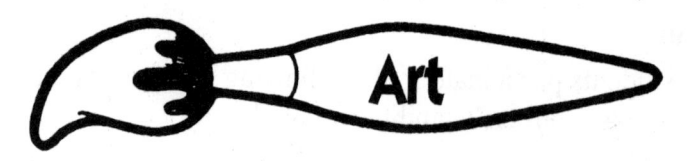

Art

Sponge Painted Bear
Materials
- bear pattern (page 50)
- brown paint
- bow spaghetti
- construction paper
- sponges
- buttons (eyes)
- scissors

Process
1. Trace pattern of bear onto paper and cut out.
2. Sponge paint entire bear.
3. Add bow and buttons while paint is wet.

Coffee Grounds Bear
Materials
- bear pattern (page 50)
- dried (used) coffee grounds
- scissors
- tagboard
- buttons (eyes)
- bow spaghetti
- water-thinned glue
- paintbrush

Process
1. Trace bear onto tagboard and cut out.
2. Spread water-thinned glue over the bear.
3. Add coffee grounds, eyes, and bow.

Butterfly
Materials
- butterfly wing patterns (pages 51 and 52)
- tissue paper 9" x 12" (23 cm x 30 cm)
- glue
- construction paper 9" x 12" (23 cm x 30 cm)
- black construction paper
- scissors

Process
1. Fold construction paper in half.
2. Place large butterfly pattern so that straight edge meets fold. Cut pattern out and open wings.
3. Fold tissue paper in half. Cut out small wing pattern following step 2 directions for large wing.
4. Glue small wing on top of large wing, matching center folds.
5. Cut two thin strips of black construction paper for antennae. Glue to body.
6. Decorate butterfly, if desired.

#791 Teaching Basic Skills through Literature: Phonics ©1995 Teacher Created Materials, Inc.

Bb *Blueberries for Sal*

"B" Picture Cards

bear	bat	book
bowl	bike	baby
bird	boat	bow
ball	balloon	boot

©1995 Teacher Created Materials, Inc. 45 #791 Teaching Basic Skills through Literature: Phonics

Blueberries for Sal Bb

"B" Activity Sheet

a _____ for _____

a _____ for _____

Bb *Blueberries for Sal*

"B" Pattern

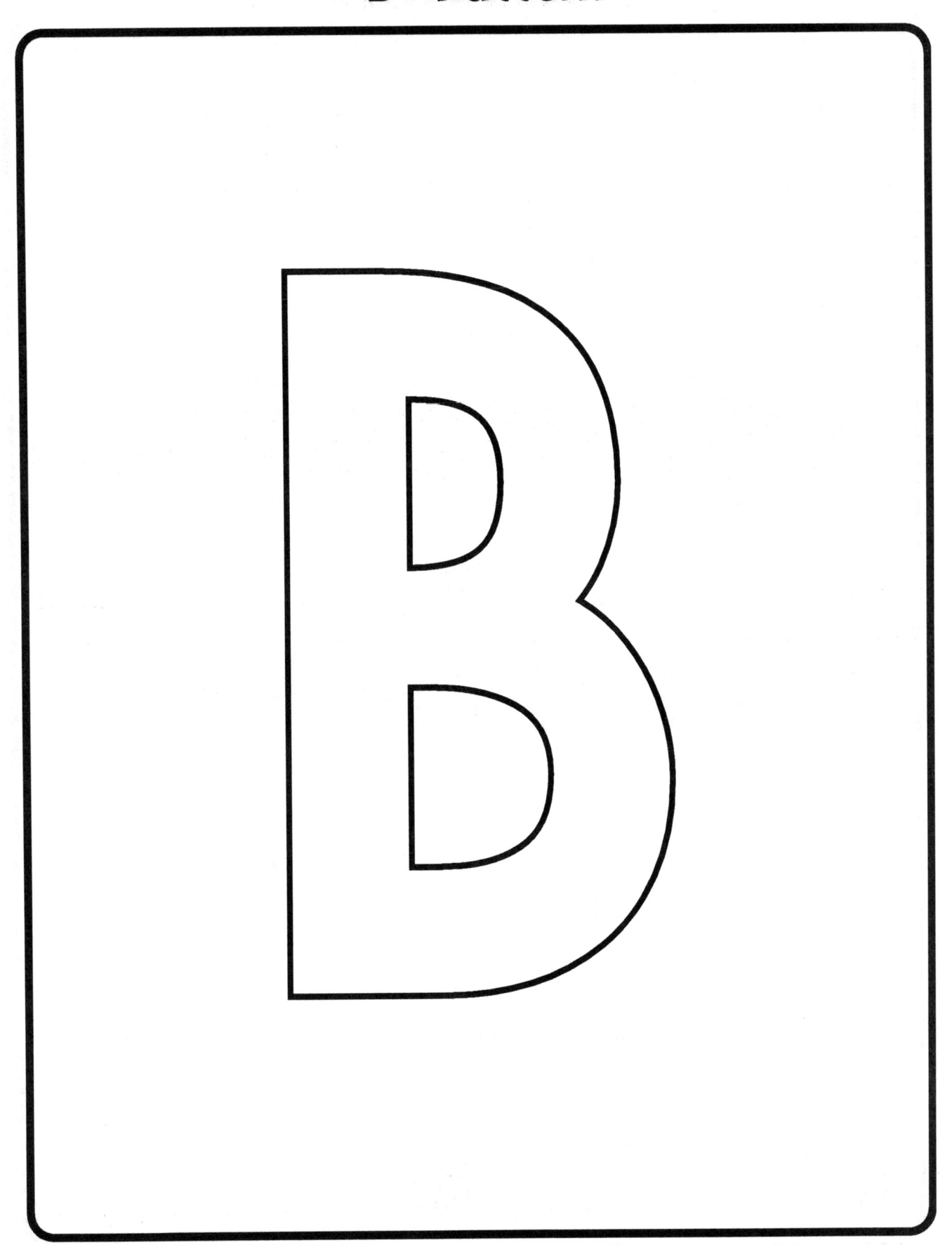

Blueberries for Sal   *Bb*

"b" Pattern

Bb *Blueberries for Sal*

Breadbox Pattern

I am bigger than a breadbox...

BREAD

©1995 Teacher Created Materials, Inc. 49 #791 Teaching Basic Skills through Literature: Phonics

Blueberries for Sal **Bb**

Bear Pattern

#791 Teaching Basic Skills through Literature: Phonics 50 ©1995 Teacher Created Materials, Inc.

Bb *Blueberries for Sal*

Large Butterfly Wing

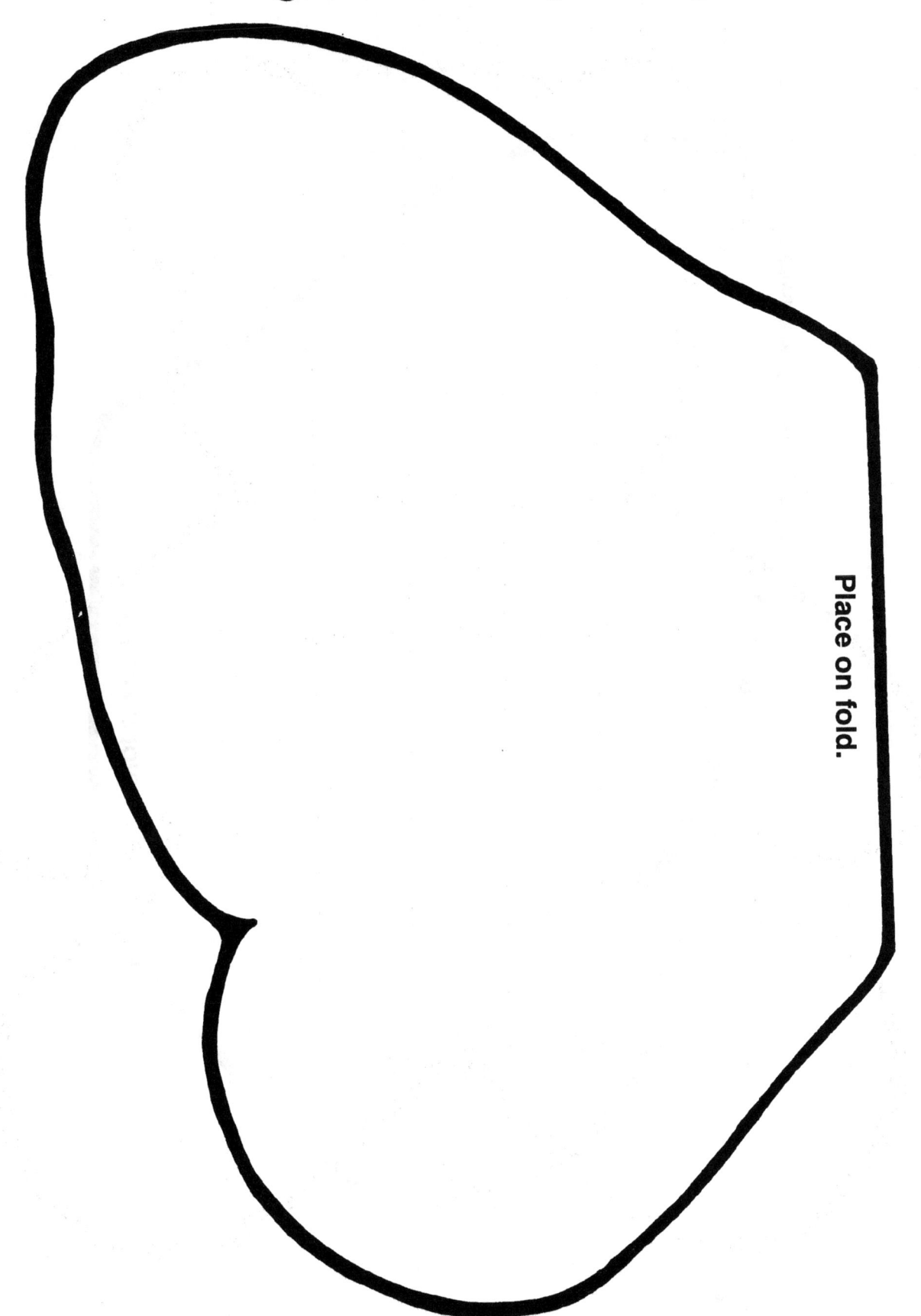

Place on fold.

©1995 Teacher Created Materials, Inc. 51 #791 Teaching Basic Skills through Literature: Phonics

Blueberries for Sal **Bb**

Small Butterfly Wing

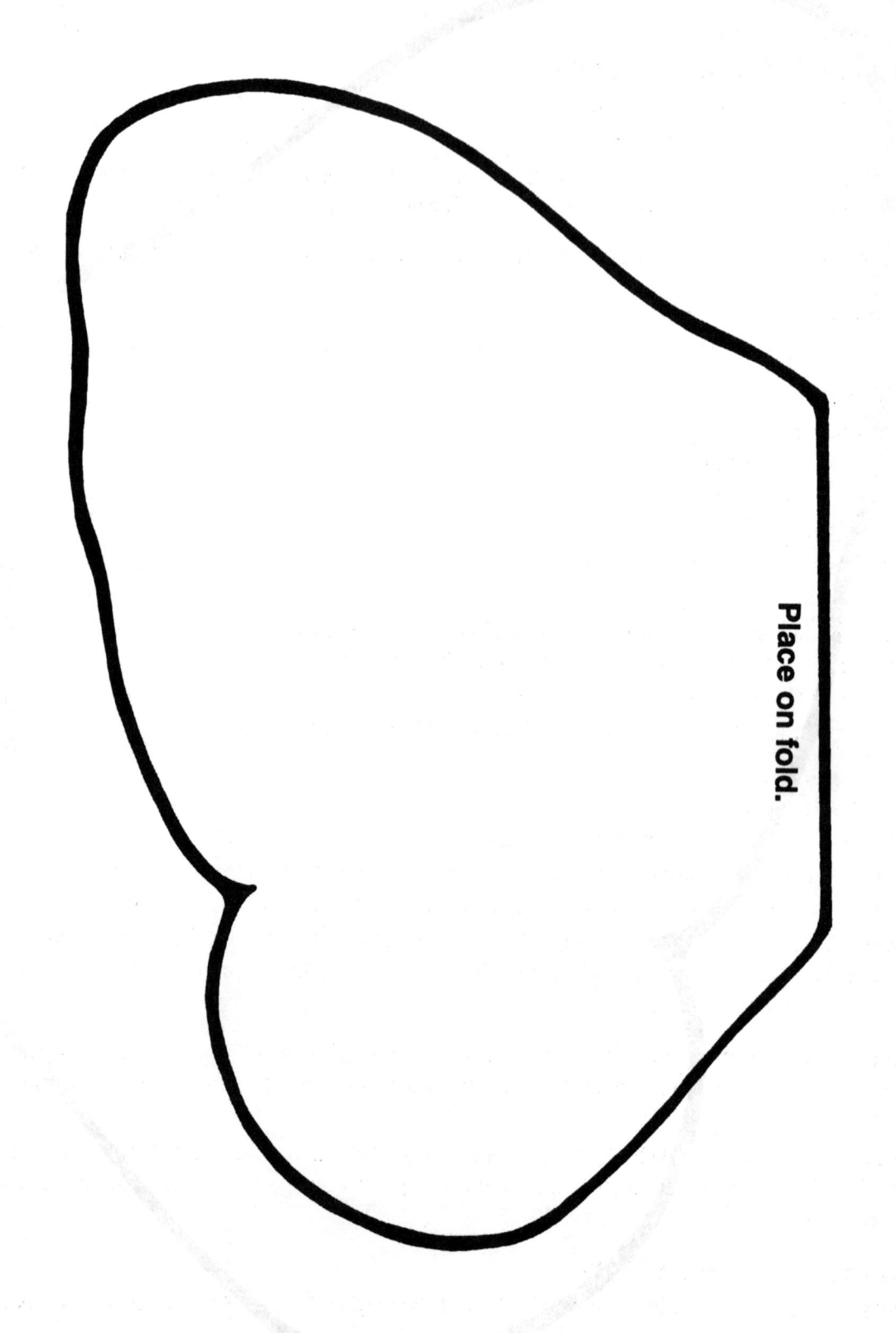

Place on fold.

#791 *Teaching Basic Skills through Literature: Phonics* 52 ©1995 *Teacher Created Materials, Inc.*

Phonics Skills in Context: Letter "C"

Book: *Corduroy*
Author: Don Freeman
Publisher: Puffin, New York, 1976
Summary: A toy bear finds what he always wanted most of all.
Recommended Grade Level: K–1
Related Poetry: "There was a Crooked Man" by Brian Wildsmith, *Brian Wildsmith's Mother Goose* (Scott Foresman, New York, 1964). For additional titles see page 384.

Skill Activity
Students will take turns playing "clerks and customers" by buying "c" toy pictures.

Materials
- chart paper
- "c" cards (page 56)
- clerk's badge (page 58)
- coins (page 58)
- customer wallet pattern (page 58)

Lesson
Introduce the Literature: Ask students if they have ever lost something and tell how they found it. Tell students this story is about looking for one thing, but finding something else. Allow time to make predications about what will be found in the story.

Read the Literature: Read the literature selection. Allow time for discussion of the story.

Introduce the Skill Lesson:
1. Have students brainstorm "c" words.
2. Put all "c" words on chart paper and display in the room as a word bank.
3. Show students the cards from page 56 and make sure they can name each one.
4. Have students pretend to go to the department store like Lisa did in the story.
5. Have students take turns role playing the "clerk" and "customer" and pretend to buy things. To make the role play more fun allow the clerk to wear a badge (page 58) and the customers to use coins and a wallet (page 58).

Learning Center Activity: Students will practice reading "c" words by matching the cupcake pieces together on page 59. Younger students could use a chart with the pictures and words to use as a reference.

Cooperative Learning Activity: Have students go on a "c" hunt. One student from the small group hides the letter "c" somewhere in the classroom, then gives clues as to its whereabouts. Use the "c" pattern from page 60.

Across the Curriculum: Math
Put prices on the picture cards on page 57. Cut out the cards. Then, have students choose two or more items and use calculators to add the prices.

Corduroy Cc

Extension Activities

Movement Activities
Stress the letter "c" as students participate in the following movements: chase a friend, crawl around the room, catch a ball, do cartwheels, and climb the jungle gym.

Multisensory Activity
On 6" x 8" (15 cm x 20 cm) tagboard, have children paste cotton balls onto an upper-and lowercase "c." Patterns are provided on pages 60 and 61.

Creative Writing
Have students complete the following: "I baked a cake for my _____. Here's the recipe." Then, have them write their favorite recipes on the cake pattern on page 62. These pages can be put together into a class cookbook.

Handwriting
On 12" x 18" (30 cm x 46 cm) lined newsprint, ask children to copy this sentence: "C is for camel, cake, corn, and crunchy carrots."

Cooking

Carrot-Top Crackers

Ingredients
- peanut butter
- crackers
- carrots
- knife
- shredder

Directions
1. Spread peanut butter on cracker with knife.
2. Shred carrots on top.
3. Draw your recipe.
4. Clean up.

Interdisciplinary Topics

cats	clothing	celery	coconuts
caterpillars	Christmas	cocoa	cantaloupe
crocodiles	Cinco de Mayo	cotton	cranberries
clams	cowboys	cactus	corn
colors	California	candy	cauliflower
clouds	careers		

#791 Teaching Basic Skills through Literature: Phonics © 1995 Teacher Created Materials, Inc.

Cc   Corduroy

Extension Activities (cont.)

Art

Cat
Materials
- cat pattern (page 63)
- black construction paper
- white crayon
- scissors
- glue

Process
1. Trace cat head pattern from page 63.
2. Cut out and turn upright to glue.
3. Use scraps from head to cut a spiral for tail.
4. Glue tail and add facial details with white crayon.

Caterpillar
Materials
- egg cartons
- green paint
- hole punch
- pipe cleaners
- glue
- construction paper scraps

Process
1. Prior to the art activity, cut and glue together two 6-cup sections of an egg carton. Position one lower cup to look like mouth is open.
2. Have children paint the egg carton green.
3. When dry, punch out holes to add eyes and decorate sides.
4. Glue on small pieces of pipe cleaners for antennae.

Paper Chain Caterpillar
Materials
- construction paper
- felt tip pens
- scissors

Process
1. Cut several 3" x 9" (8 cm x 23 cm) strips from construction paper. Paste strips into chain.
2. Cut a 4" (10 cm) construction paper square.
3. Draw face on square.
4. Paste square to front of chain.

©1995 Teacher Created Materials, Inc.   55   #791 Teaching Basic Skills through Literature: Phonics

Corduroy Cc

"C" Cards

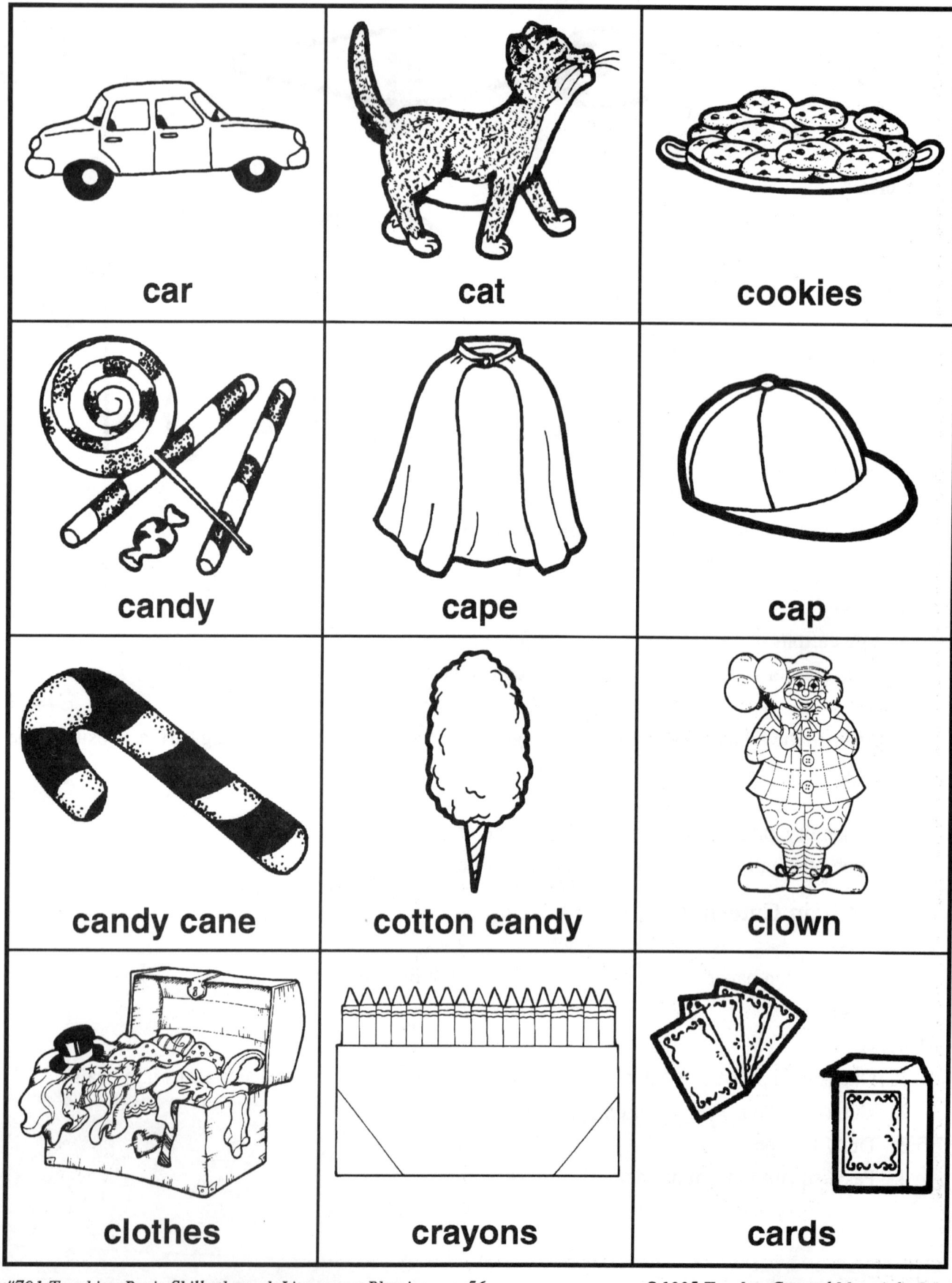

car	cat	cookies
candy	cape	cap
candy cane	cotton candy	clown
clothes	crayons	cards

#791 Teaching Basic Skills through Literature: Phonics 56 ©1995 Teacher Created Materials, Inc.

Cc Corduroy

Store Activities

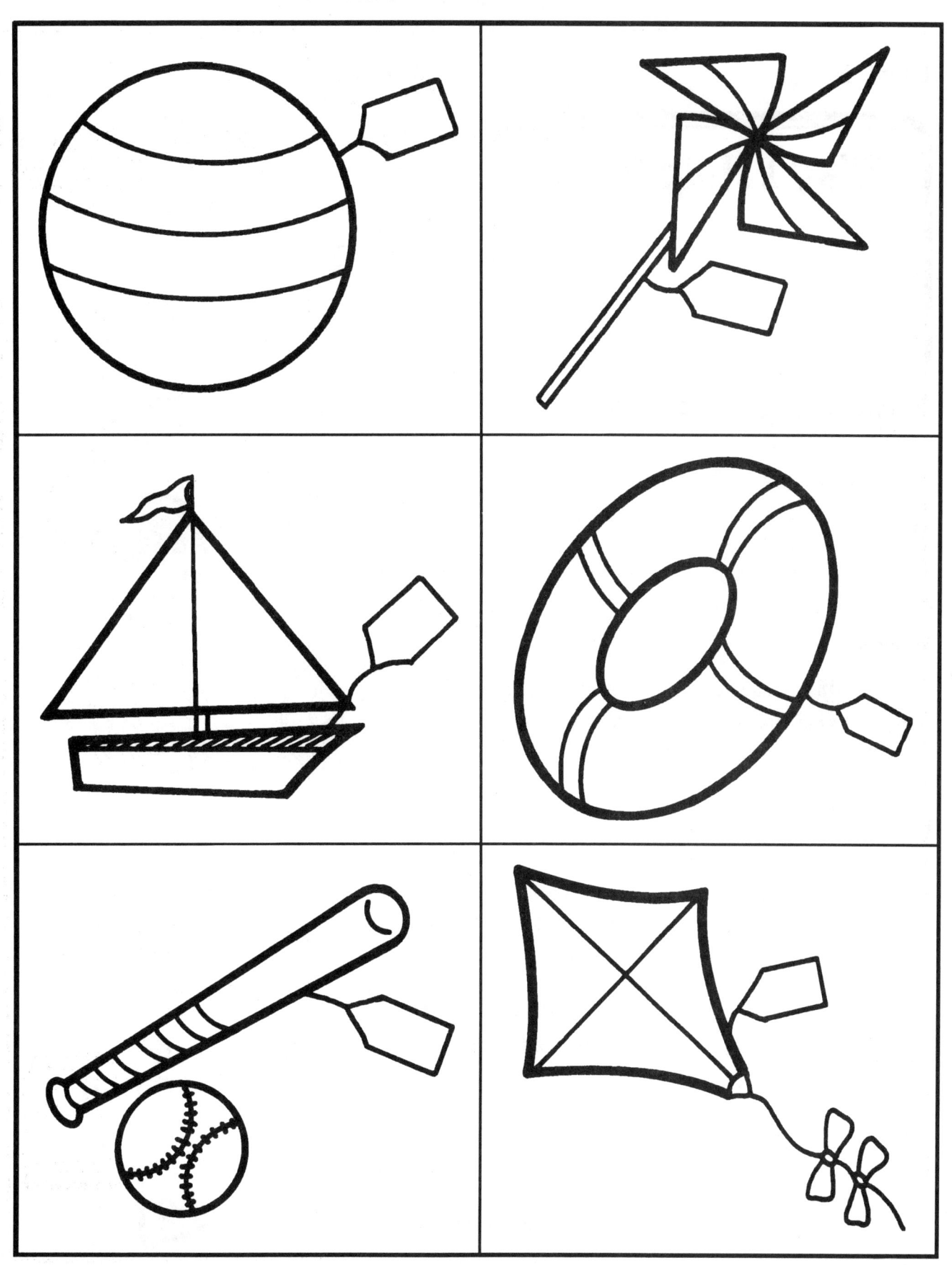

©1995 Teacher Created Materials, Inc. 57 #791 Teaching Basic Skills through Literature: Phonics

Corduroy   *Cc*

Store Activities (cont.)

Clerk Badge

May I Help You?

_____
Clerk

Corduroy's Department Store

Coins

Wallet

Make a wallet for customers to use in the deparment store.

Materials:

- 7" (18 cm) square piece of construction paper
- yarn (Put tape on one end to help with weaving.)
- play money

Process:

1. Fold paper in half.
2. Punch holes in the two side edges, leaving the long edge open for insertion of money.
3. Weave the yarn through the holes along one side. Tie at ends. Do the same on the opposite side.
4. Insert play money and fold wallet in half.

Cc   *Corduroy*

Cupcakes

camera	camel

cupcake	candle	clock	calendar

candy	carrot	cake	cloud

Corduroy *Cc*

"C" Pattern

#791 Teaching Basic Skills through Literature: Phonics ©1995 Teacher Created Materials, Inc.

"c" Pattern

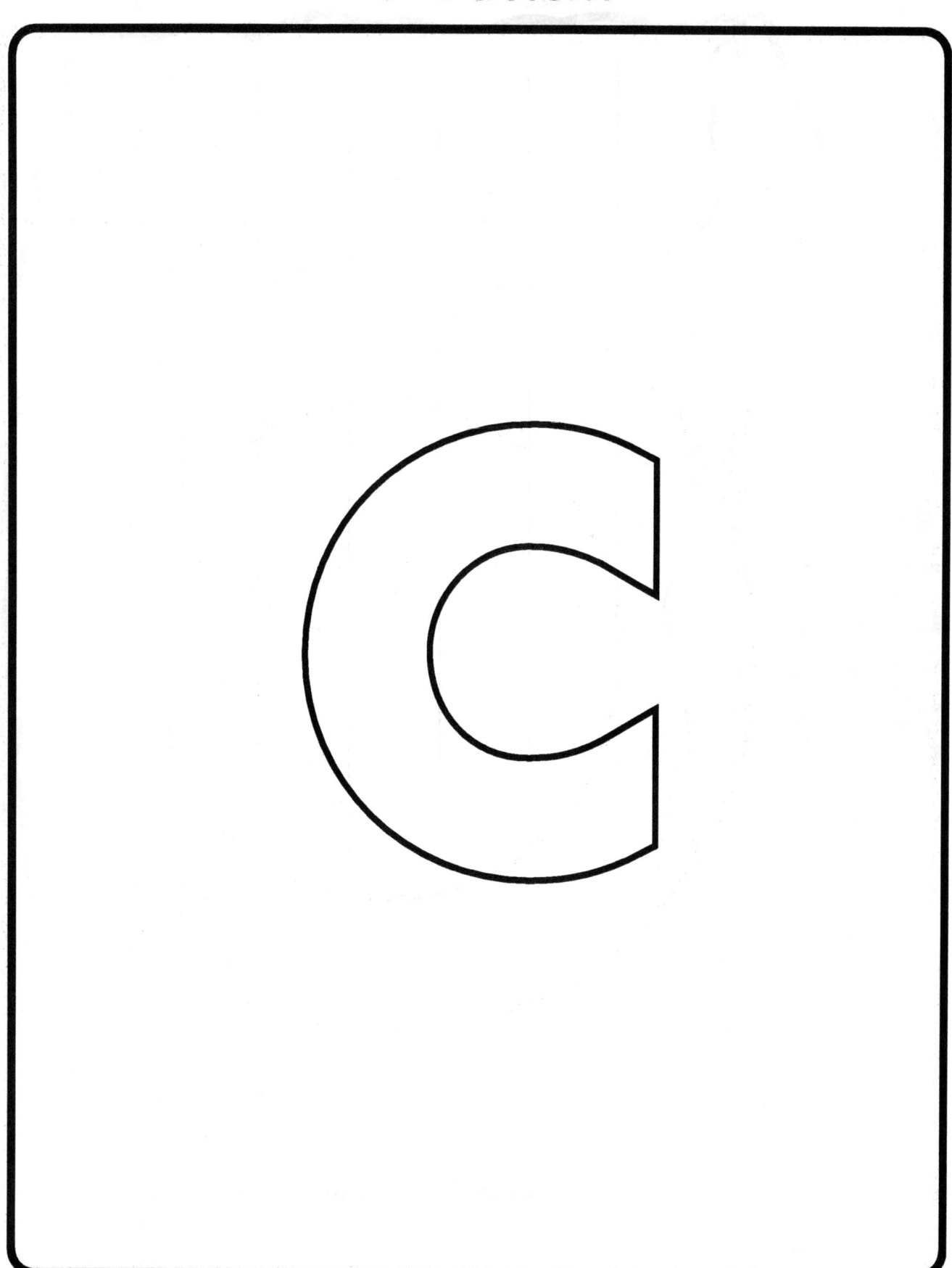

Corduroy Cc

Cake Pattern

I baked a cake for _____.

Here is the recipe:

by: _____

#791 Teaching Basic Skills through Literature: Phonics ©1995 Teacher Created Materials, Inc.

Cc   *Corduroy*

Cat Pattern

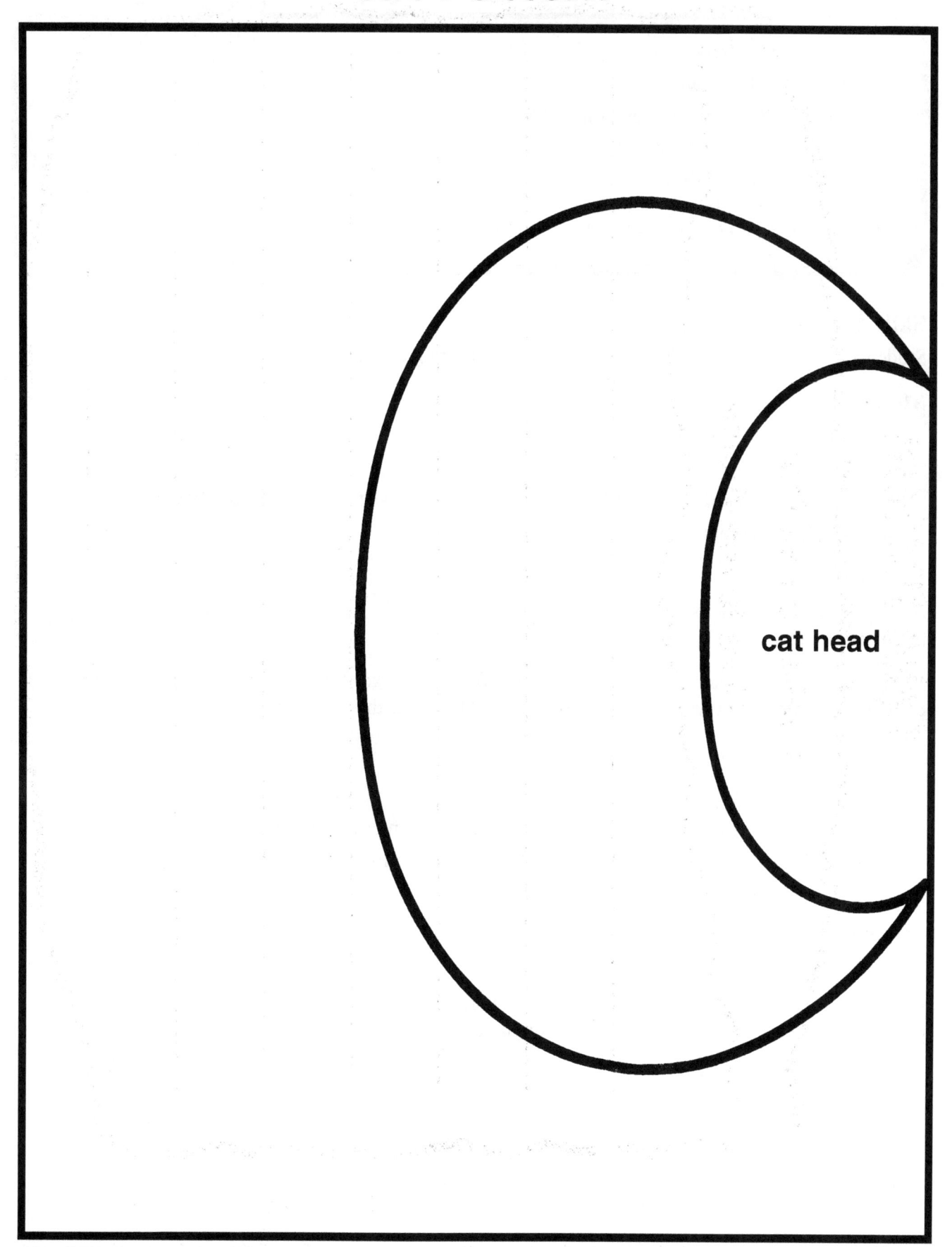

cat head

Phonics Skills in Context: Letter "D"

Book: *Ten Black Dots*
Author: Donald Crews
Publisher: Greenwillow, New York, 1986
Summary: This delightful counting book integrates dots into each illustration.
Recommended Grade Level: K–1
Related Poetry: "Hey, Diddle, Diddle" by Arnold Lobel, *The Random House Book of Mother Goose* (Random House, New York, 1986). For additional titles see page 384.

Skill Activity
Students will create an illustration of a "d" object utilizing dot stickers or ink dots.

Materials
- chart paper
- blank paper
- dot stickers or sponge-topped ink-bottle markers (such as those used in Bingo)
- crayons or markers

Lesson
Introduce the Literature: Show students the cover of the book. Ask them to predict what the story might be about.

Read the Literature: Read the literature selection. Read the pages for numbers one and two. Ask children to predict what will be on the next pages. Do this with each number.

Introduce the Skill Lesson:

1. Brainstorm with students words that begin with "d."
2. Write responses on chart paper and display in the room as a word bank.
3. Have students draw a "d" object incorporating one or more dots. Older students can label the picture or write a sentence.

Learning Center Activity: Have students create a dot design using various colors of paint or ink from Bingo markers.

Cooperative Learning Activity: Have students work in small groups to create a class big book of pictures with dots. See pattern pages 67 through 76.

Across the Curriculum: Math
Create dot patterns using different colors of stickers or Bingo markers.

Dd

Ten Black Dots

Extension Activities

Movement Activities
Stress the letter "d" as students participate in the following movements: dancing, digging in the dirt, drag your feet, dribble a ball, waddle like a duck, and deal cards.

Multisensory Activity
On 6" x 8" (15 cm x 20 cm) tagboard, have children paste dots onto an upper-and lowercase "d." Patterns are provided on pages 77 and 78.

Creative Writing
Give children the following story starter: "My pet dinosaur was so big..." They can write their stories on the dinosaur pattern on page 79.

Handwriting
On 12" x 18" (30 cm x 46 cm) lined newsprint, ask children to copy this sentence: "D is for dog, daisies, dirt, and dangerous dinosaurs."

Cooking

Dinosaur Dan's Delicious Dip

Ingredients
- plain yogurt
- dip package
- celery sticks
- tablespoon
- teaspoon
- plate or bowl

Directions
1. Mix together 1 tablespoon (15 mL) yogurt with ¼ teaspoon (1.25 mL) dip mix.
2. Use a celery stick to dip and eat.
3. Draw your recipe.
4. Clean up.

Interdisciplinary Topics

dinosaurs	daisies	danger	disaster drills
dragons	dogs	December	dress up
ducks	doctor	dates	dried fruit
daffodils	dentist	doughnuts	divers

Ten Black Dots   Dd

Extension Activities *(cont.)*

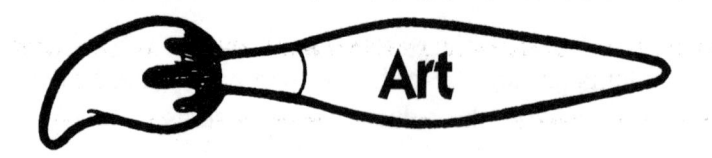

Art

Dip and Doodle
Materials
- food coloring
- water
- paper towels
- shallow containers

Process
1. Mix food coloring and small amounts of water in shallow containers.
2. Have children dip paper towels into different colors and lay the towel out to dry.

Disguise
Materials
- egg cartons
- construction paper
- scissors
- pipe cleaners
- tape
- mask patterns (page 80)

Process
1. Cut two egg carton cups and attach pipe cleaners for glasses. (Cut openings at bottoms of cups for eyeholes.)
2. Cut one egg carton section for nose.
3. Cut out mustache and beard on page 80.
4. Curl beard strands with pencil.
5. Tape nose, mustache, and beard to child's face.

Diver
Materials
- diver suit and flipper patterns (page 81)
- crayons
- construction paper
- plastic wrap
- glue
- scissors

Process
1. Cut waves at the top of paper.
2. Paste on diver suit.
3. Add legs, arms, and head.
4. Glue oval-shape from plastic wrap to make a face mask.
5. Glue on flippers.
6. Add details such as bubbles, sea life, weight belt, and yarn hair.

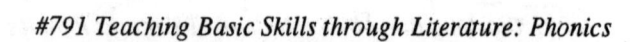

#791 *Teaching Basic Skills through Literature: Phonics*   ©1995 Teacher Created Materials, Inc.

Dd

Ten Black Dots

Dot Pictures

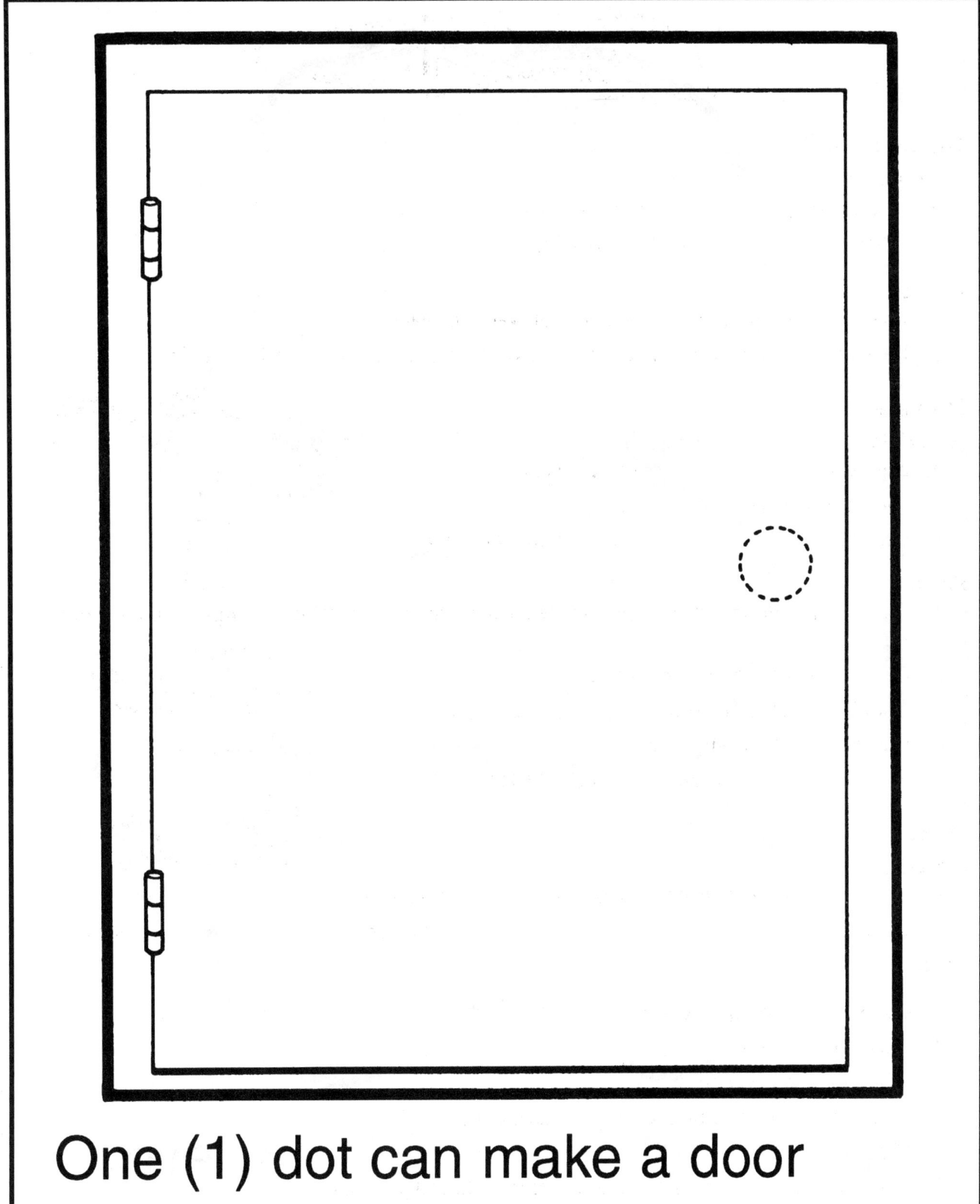

One (1) dot can make a door knob on a door.

Ten Black Dots   Dd

Dot Pictures *(cont.)*

Two (2) dots can make two eyes on a doll.

Dd ***Ten Black Dots***

Dot Pictures (cont.)

Three (3) dots can make the eyes and nose on a deer.

Ten Black Dots   Dd

Dot Pictures (cont.)

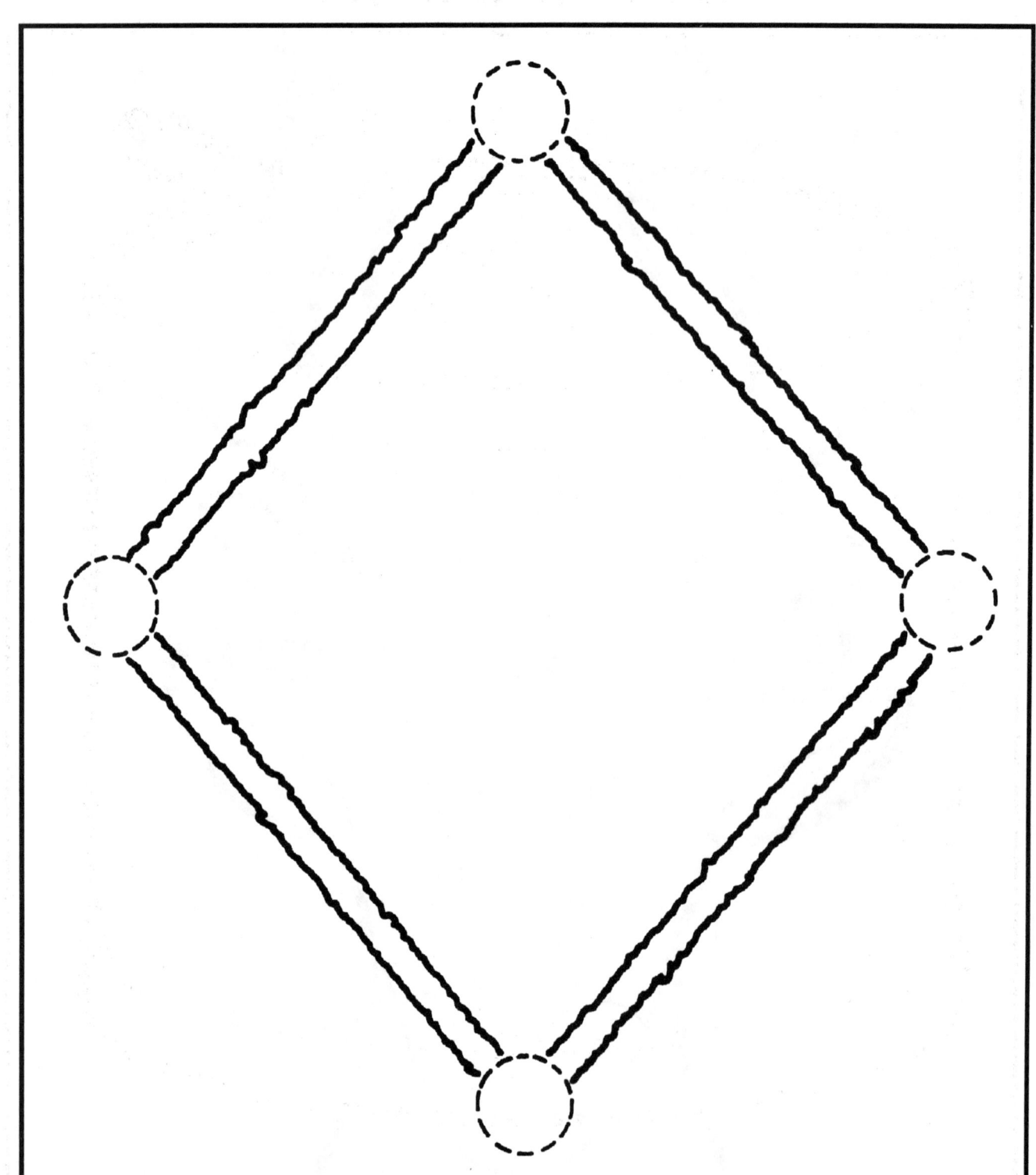

Four (4) dots can make the bases on a baseball diamond.

Dd Ten Black Dots

Dot Pictures (cont.)

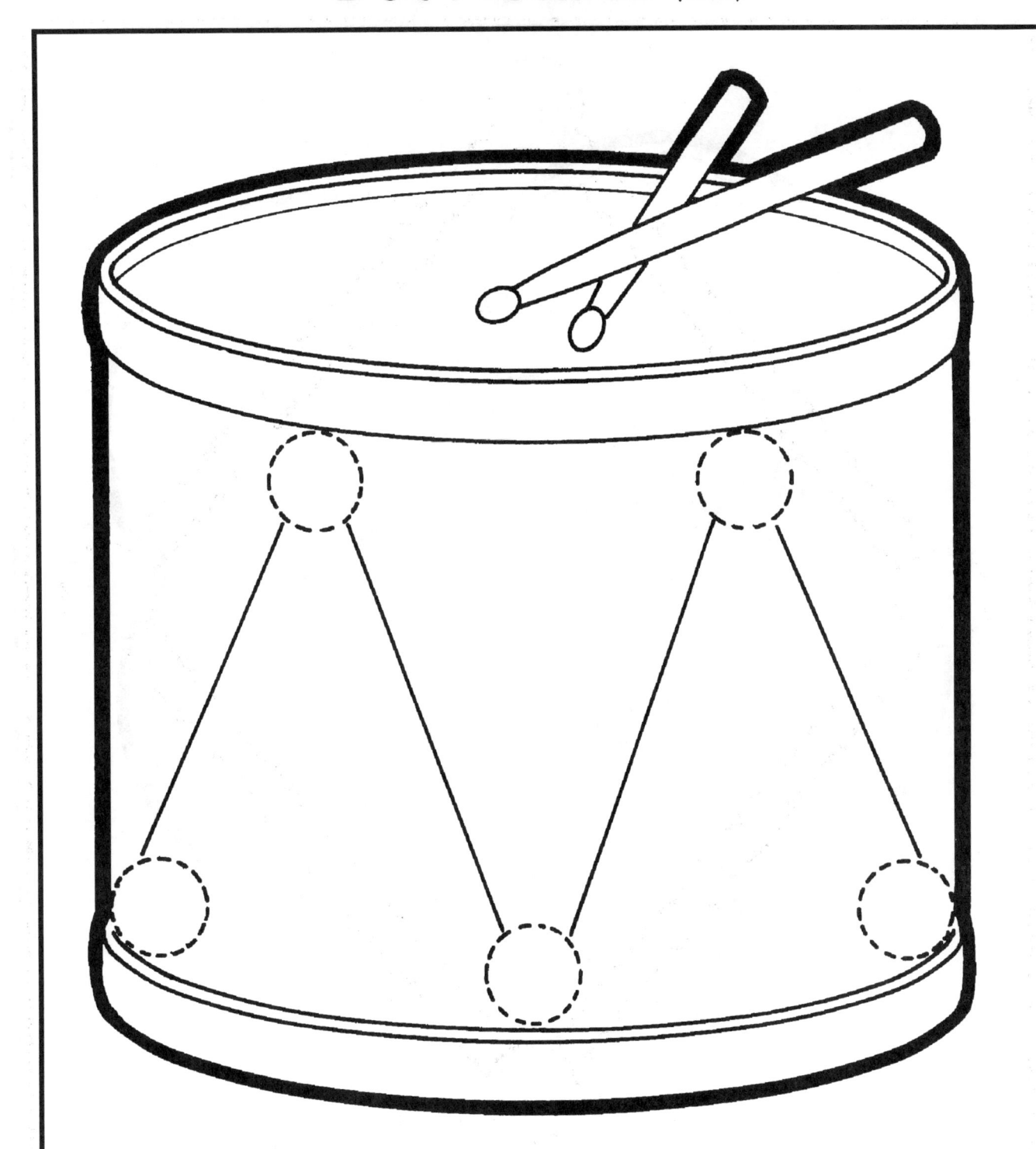

Five (5) dots can make the points on a drum.

©1995 Teacher Created Materials, Inc. 71 #791 Teaching Basic Skills through Literature: Phonics

Ten Black Dots   **Dd**

Dot Pictures (cont.)

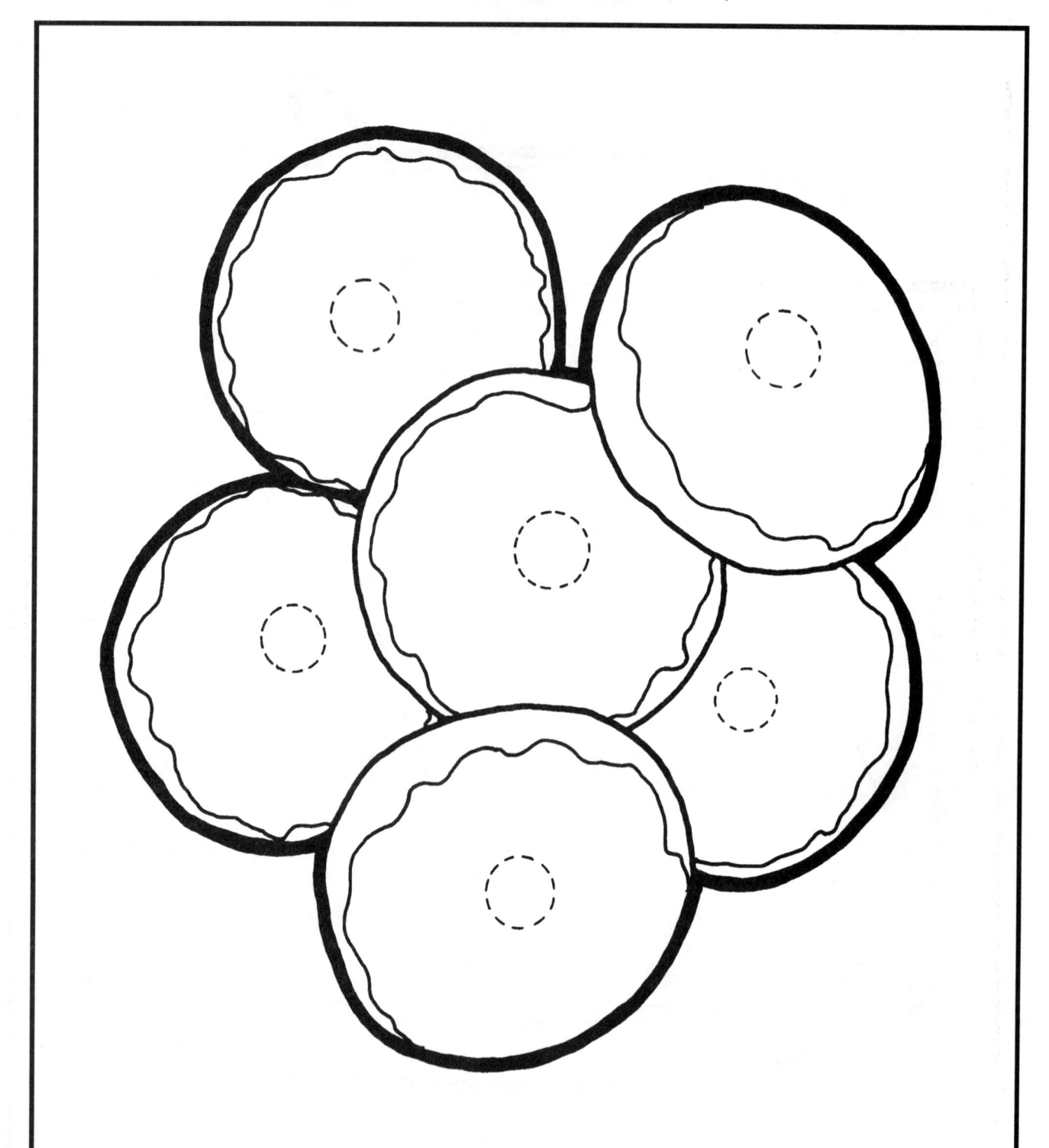

Six (6) dots can be the holes in doughnuts.

Dd   *Ten Black Dots*

Dot Pictures (cont.)

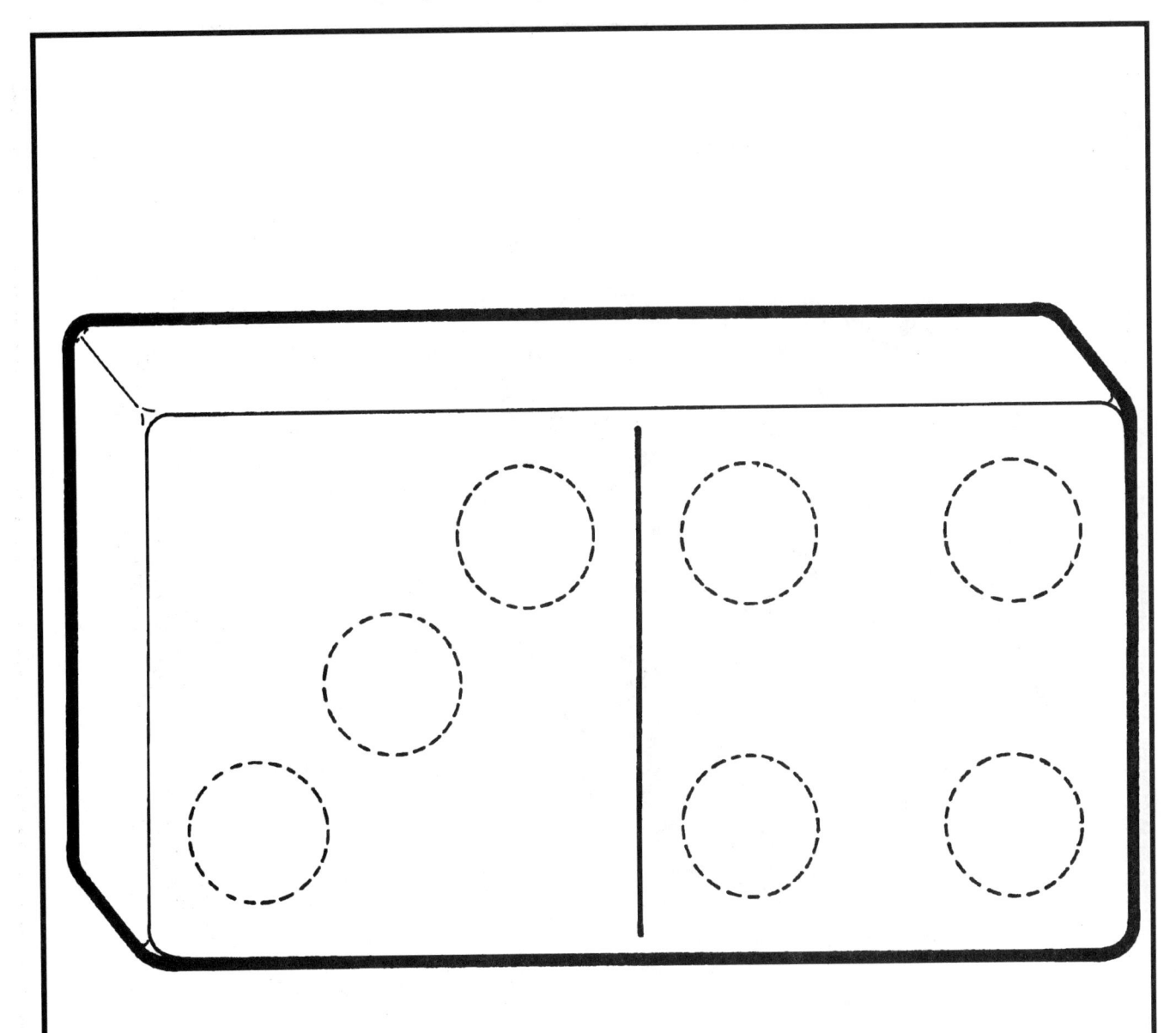

Seven (7) dots can be the spots on a domino.

Ten Black Dots — Dd

Dot Pictures (cont.)

Eight (8) dots can be the centers of daisies.

Dd Ten Black Dots

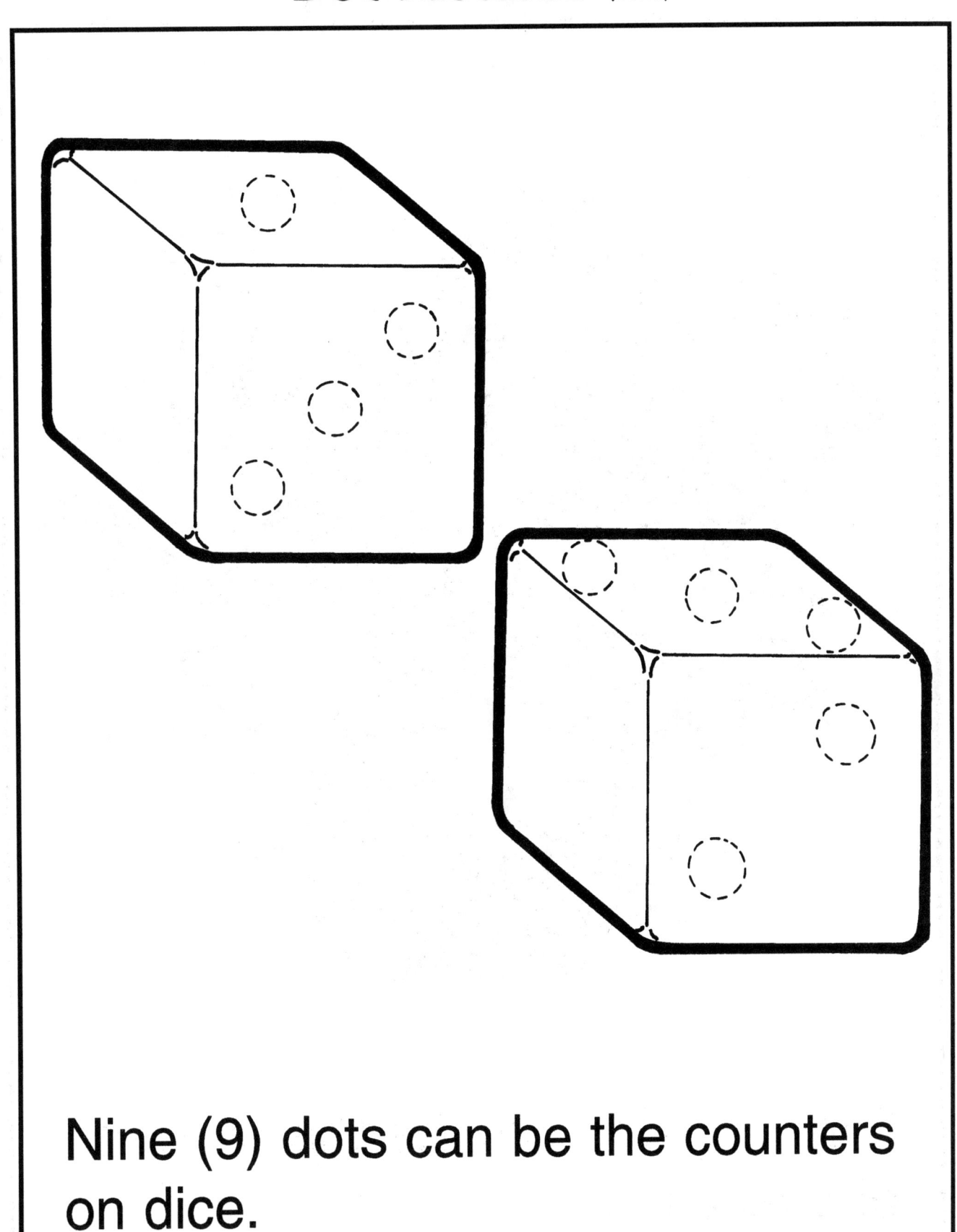

Dot Pictures (cont.)

Nine (9) dots can be the counters on dice.

Ten Black Dots — Dd

Dot Pictures (cont.)

Ten (10) dots can be the spots on a Dalmatian.

Dd Ten Black Dots

"D" Pattern

Ten Black Dots   *Dd*

"d" Pattern

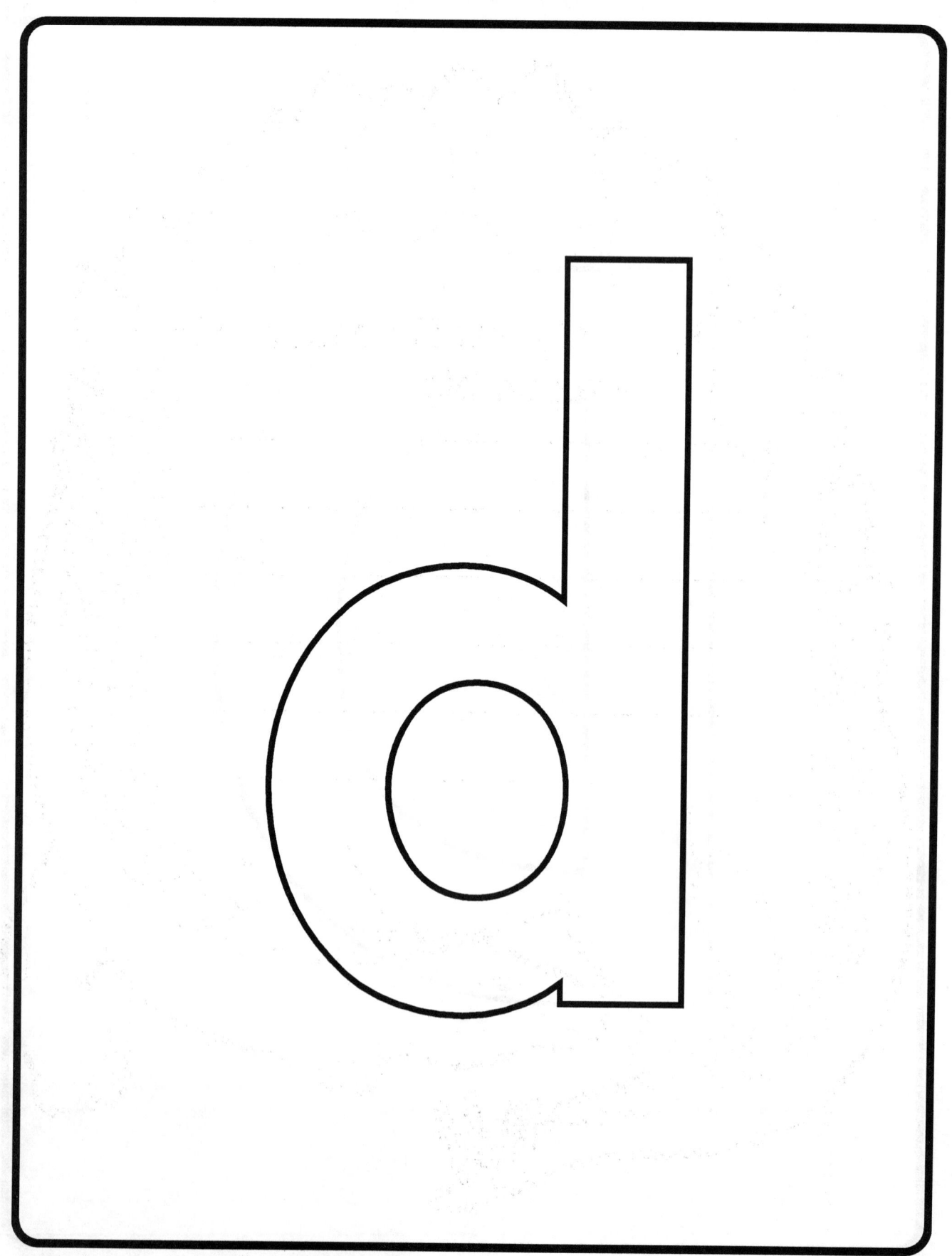

#791 Teaching Basic Skills through Literature: Phonics   ©1995 Teacher Created Materials, Inc.

Dd   *Ten Black Dots*

Dinosaur Pattern

My Pet Dinosaur was so big...

_____

_____

_____

_____

_____

©1995 Teacher Created Materials, Inc.   79   #791 Teaching Basic Skills through Literature: Phonics

Ten Black Dots   Dd

Mask Patterns

disguise beard

disguise mustache

Cut to end of lines. Then curl strips around pencil.

#791 Teaching Basic Skills through Literature: Phonics

Dd   *Ten Black Dots*

Diver Patterns

diver suit

glue   glue

Fold here and glue to suit.

©1995 Teacher Created Materials, Inc.   81   #791 Teaching Basic Skills through Literature: Phonics

Phonics Skills in Context: Letter "F"

Book: *Fish is Fish*
Author: Leo Lionni
Publisher: Pantheon, New York, 1970
Summary: The story of two friends, a fish and a frog, and their discoveries of being just who they are.
Recommended Grade Level: K–2
Related Poetry: "Fish" by Mary Ann Hoberman, *Yellow Butter, Purple Jelly, Red Jam, Black Bread* (Viking Press, New York, 1981). For additional titles see page 384.

Skill Activity

Students will create a class pop-up book of "f" words using the pattern from the title *Fish is Fish*.

Materials

- construction paper
- crayons or markers
- chart paper
- scissors
- glue

Lesson

Introduce the Literature: Show the book to students and read the title. Ask if any students have pet fish.

Read the Literature: Read the literature selection. Allow time for discussion.

Introduce the Skill Lesson:

1. Have students compile a list of "f" words. Use the pattern from the title of the book. For example, when making the list write "Frog is frog."
2. Write the sentences on chart paper and display in the classroom as a word bank.
3. Have students select one of the sentences to copy onto the bottom of a pop-up page. (See page 168 for directions on how to make a pop-up page or card.) Students then illustrate their ideas, cut them out, and glue them to the pop-up section.
4. Collate the pages into a class book titled "F is F" by attaching the students' pages together.

Learning Center Activity: Have students create funny fish figures like those in the book, using crayons, markers, or watercolors.

Cooperative Learning Activity: Have students play "fish and frogs." Use a playground circle as the water. Divide the group into two teams: fish and frogs. The fish cannot leave the water, but the frogs can. The frogs try to run through the circle without being tagged by the fish. If the frog is tagged, he or she becomes a tadpole and tries to tag other frogs.

Across the Curriculum: Social Studies

Discuss the concept of feelings with the class. Brainstorm the ways a person can feel and ways to express those feelings. Have students complete this sentence: "When I feel _____, I _____."

Ff   Fish is Fish

Extension Activities

Movement Activities

Stress the letter "f" as students participate in the following movements: flying, follow-the-leader, frog hops, move forward, fishing, finger plays, and freeze tag.

Multisensory Activity

On 6" x 8" (15 cm x 20 cm) tagboard, have children paste feathers onto an upper-and lowercase "f". Patterns are provided on pages 85 and 86.

Creative Writing

Have students make a list of five furry animals they would like to have as friends. Then, have them tell stories about their friends. They can use the activity sheet on page 87 for their stories.

Handwriting

On 12" x 18" (30 cm x 46 cm) lined newsprint, ask children to copy this sentence: "F is for football, flowers, four fish, and five furry foxes."

Cooking

Friendship Fruit Salad

Ingredients
- pieces of fruit
- knife
- plates

Directions
1. Cut fruit into different shapes.
2. Arrange on a plate.
3. Draw your recipe.
4. Clean up.

Interdisciplinary Topics

fish	farm animals	fire trucks	flour
frogs	families	flags	frankfurters
fossils	friends	food	fingerprints
flowers	feelings	fruit	floats
fire safety	firemen	five	four

©1995 Teacher Created Materials, Inc.   83   #791 Teaching Basic Skills through Literature: Phonics

Fish is Fish *Ff*

Extension Activities (cont.)

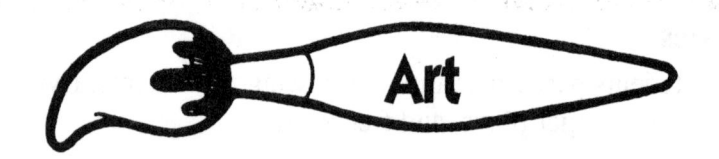

Art

Fence

Materials
- construction paper
- yarn
- twist ties cut into thirds
- craft sticks
- crayons or markers
- glue

Process
1. Draw the ground on a piece of construction paper.
2. Color craft sticks and glue onto paper as fence posts.
3. Twist ties on yarn to look like barbed wire.
4. Glue yarn to look like wire fence.

Fingerprint pictures

Materials
- construction paper
- stamp pads
- markers

Process
1. Using stamp pad, put fingerprints on construction paper to form bodies or heads of people or animals.
2. Draw in the rest of the characteristics and background.

Fish

Materials
- paper plates
- markers or crayons
- glue
- scissors

Process
1. Cut small triangular section from plate.
2. Save to use as tail.
3. Draw in eyes and scales.
4. Glue on tail.

Flowers

Materials
- large pieces of multicolored construction paper
- glue
- scissors

Process
1. Cut several open-fingered hand tracings and glue to form petals.
2. Add circle to middle of flower.
3. Cut strip of paper for stem.
4. Cut out 2 or 3 closed-finger hand tracings for leaves. Glue to stem.
5. Curl flower petals for 3-D effect.
6. Glue flower on construction paper background.

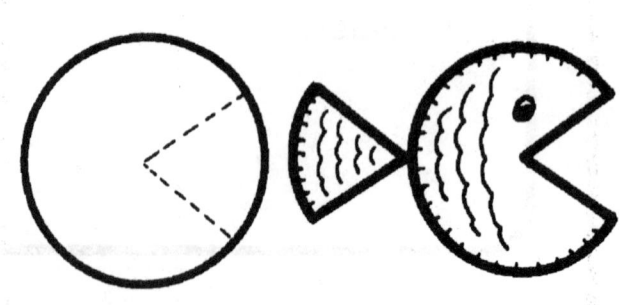

#791 Teaching Basic Skills through Literature: Phonics ©1995 Teacher Created Materials, Inc.

Ff *Fish is Fish*

"F" Pattern

Fish is Fish *Ff*

"f" Pattern

Ff

Fish is Fish

Five Furry Friends

Five Furry Friends

by:_____

I have five furry friends.

They are _____
(tell who)

_____

_____

One _____
(tell when)

the five furry friends went_____
(tell where)

_____

Here is what happened: _____

_____

_____

_____

_____

©1995 Teacher Created Materials, Inc.   87   #791 Teaching Basic Skills through Literature: Phonics

Phonics Skills in Context: Letter "G"

Book: *The Three Billy Goats Gruff*
Author: Paul Galdone
Publisher: Seabury Press, New York, 1973
Summary: This is the familiar tale of the three billy goats who outsmart the troll while crossing the bridge to the grassy hill.
Recommended Grade Level: K–2
Related Poetry: "Gazelle" by Mary Ann Hoberman, *Yellow Butter, Purple Jelly, Red Jam, Black Bread* (Viking Press, New York, 1981). For additional titles see page 384.

Skill Activity
Students will be able to cross over the bridge if they successfully identify the "g" sound.

Materials
- "g" and non-"g" picture cards (page 91)
- chart paper

Lesson
Introduce the Literature: Show students the book and read the title.

Read the Literature: Read the literature selection. Allow time for discussion of the story.

Introduce the Skill Lesson:

1. Read the story again and ask students to listen for "g" words.
2. Write the words on chart paper and post in the classroom as a word bank.
3. Have students line up at the beginning of the bridge (use a low table for students to walk across).
4. One at a time, show students a picture card (page 91) and ask if the word begins with the "g" sound.
5. If the student answers correctly, he/she may walk across the bridge. If not, he or she must go to the end of the line and try again.

Learning Center Activity: Allow students to grow green grass. Provide each student with a cup, soil, and grass seeds. Have students poke a small hole into the bottom of the cup and then fill it with soil. Sprinkle grass seeds on the soil and sprinkle with more soil. Water as needed. Grass seeds should sprout within a week.

Cooperative Learning Activity: Play the "Three Billy Goats Gruff" game. Provide each group with a game board (pages 92 and 93), spinner (page 94), and small objects to use as markers. Have groups decorate the game board and tape the two parts together. Players take turns saying a "g" word and then spin to determine the number of moves. The first one to the grassy hill is the winner.

Across the Curriculum: Physical Education
Play a variation of "Duck, Duck, Goose" by calling it "Goat, Goat, Troll."

Gg   *The Three Billy Goats Gruff*

Extension Activities

Movement Activities

Stress the letter "g" as students participate in the following movements: grasshopper hops, gallop, groan, chew gum, walk like a gorilla, and wave good-bye.

Multisensory Activity

On 6" x 8" (15 cm x 20 cm) tagboard, have children paste glitter onto an upper-and lowercase "g". Patterns are provided on pages 95 and 96.

Creative Writing

Have students complete the following story starter: "The reason giraffes have such long necks is..." They can use the pattern on page 97 as covers for their books.

Handwriting

On 12" x 18" (30 cm x 46 cm) lined newsprint, ask children to copy this sentence: "G is for ghost, gate, gumballs, and green goblins."

Cooking

Gorp

Ingredients
- assorted nuts
- dried fruits
- seeds
- baggies
- teaspoon

Directions
1. Mix 1 teaspoon (5 mL) of each ingredient into a baggy.
2. Draw your recipe.
3. Clean up.

Interdisciplinary Topics

gorillas	grizzly bears	gravity	grapes
goats	Groundhog Day	galaxy	grapefruit
goldfish	globe	gold	gingerbread
guinea pigs	gardening	grass	granola
grasshoppers	games	grandparents	

©1995 Teacher Created Materials, Inc.

The Three Billy Goats Gruff   Gg

Extension Acitivities (cont.)

Art

Gingerbread Man
Materials
- gingerbread pattern (page 98)
- yarn
- large brown grocery bags
- hole punch
- scissors
- glue
- decorations such as: glitter, fabric, spices, buttons
- stuffing such as: newspaper, cotton, paper towels

Process
1. Cut two gingerbread men from grocery bags.
2. Add facial features with decorations.
3. When dry, hole punch around both men and lace with yarn.
4. When it is almost completely laced, stuff.
5. Complete lacing.

Giraffe
Materials
- giraffe pattern (page 99)
- crayons or markers
- scissors
- construction paper
- hole punch
- yarn
- glue

Process
1. Trace and cut out patterns onto construction paper.
2. Paste on 9" x 12" (23 cm x 30 cm) construction paper.
3. Use hole punch to cut out designs for giraffe body.
4. Draw ears, horns, feet, and facial features.
5. Use yarn for tail.

Glue Pictures
Materials
- construction paper
- pencil
- glue
- paint

Process
1. Draw a picture with a pencil.
2. Trace over the picture with glue.
3. Allow to dry.
4. Apply paint over picture.
5. Place another sheet of paper over picture, rub, then remove carefully.

Gg *The Three Billy Goats Gruff*

"G" and non-"G" Cards

©1995 Teacher Created Materials, Inc. 91 #791 Teaching Basic Skills through Literature: Phonics

The Three Billy Goats Gruff   Gg

Game

#791 Teaching Basic Skills through Literature: Phonics   ©1995 Teacher Created Materials, Inc.

Gg   *The Three Billy Goats Gruff*

Board

The Three Billy Goats Gruff   Gg

Spinner

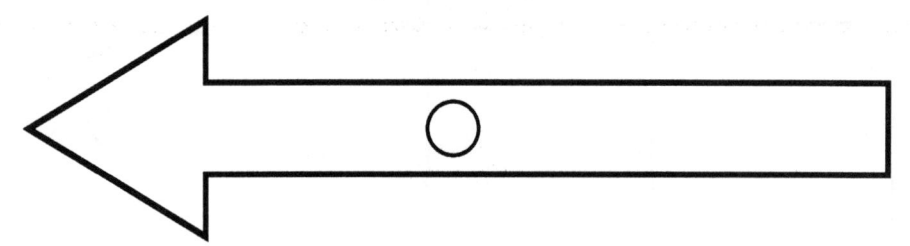

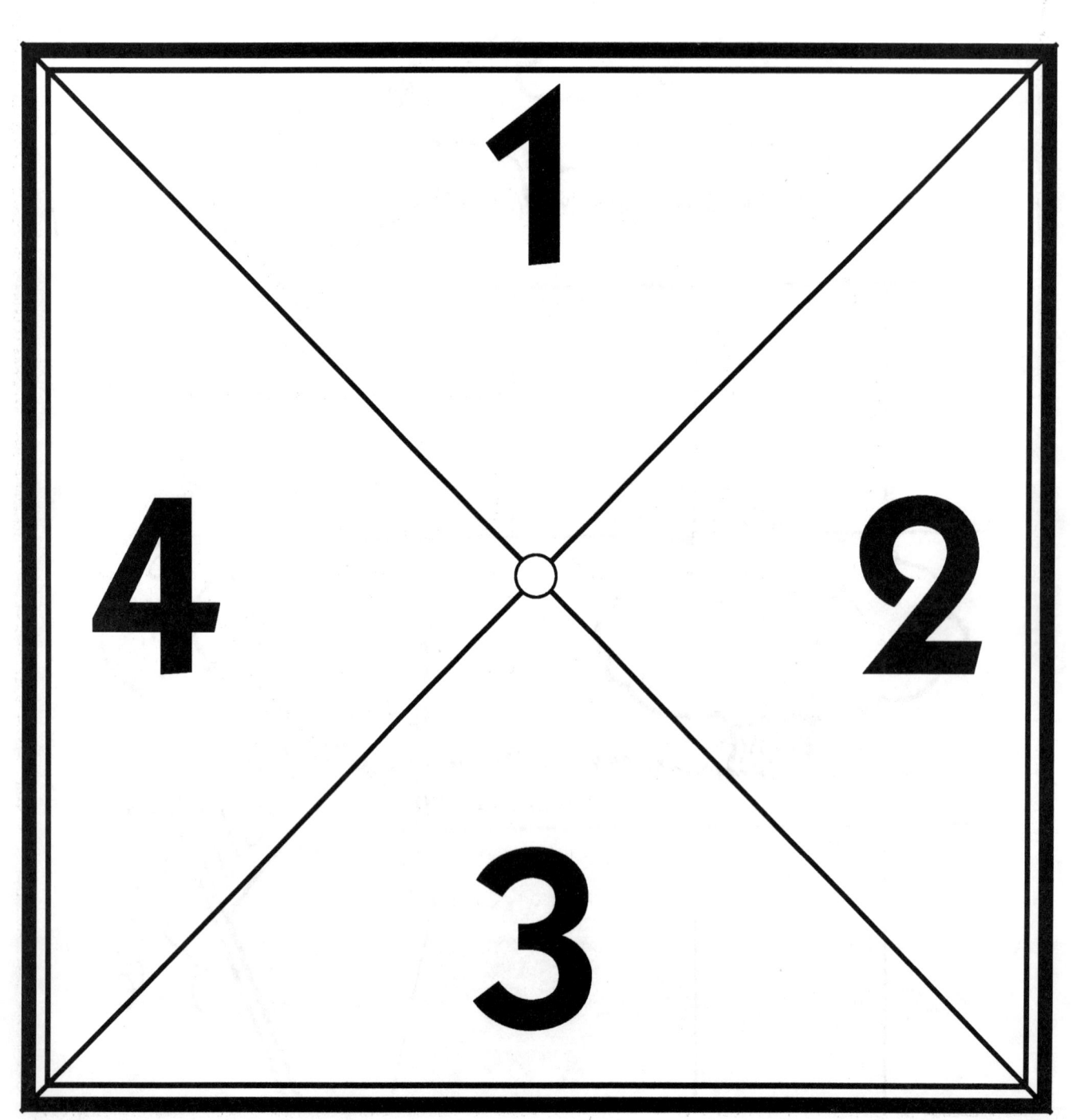

1

4   **2**

3

The Three Billy Goats Gruff

#791 Teaching Basic Skills through Literature: Phonics   94   ©1995 Teacher Created Materials, Inc.

Gg *The Three Billy Goats Gruff*

"G" Pattern

©1995 Teacher Created Materials, Inc. #791 Teaching Basic Skills through Literature: Phonics

The Three Billy Goats Gruff   Gg

"g" Pattern

#791 Teaching Basic Skills through Literature: Phonics   96   ©1995 Teacher Created Materials, Inc.

Gg   *The Three Billy Goats Gruff*

Story Cover

The reason giraffes have long necks is

_____

_____

By: _____

Date: _____

The Three Billy Goats Gruff   *Gg*

Gingerbread Man Pattern

Gg   *The Three Billy Goats Gruff*

Giraffe Pattern

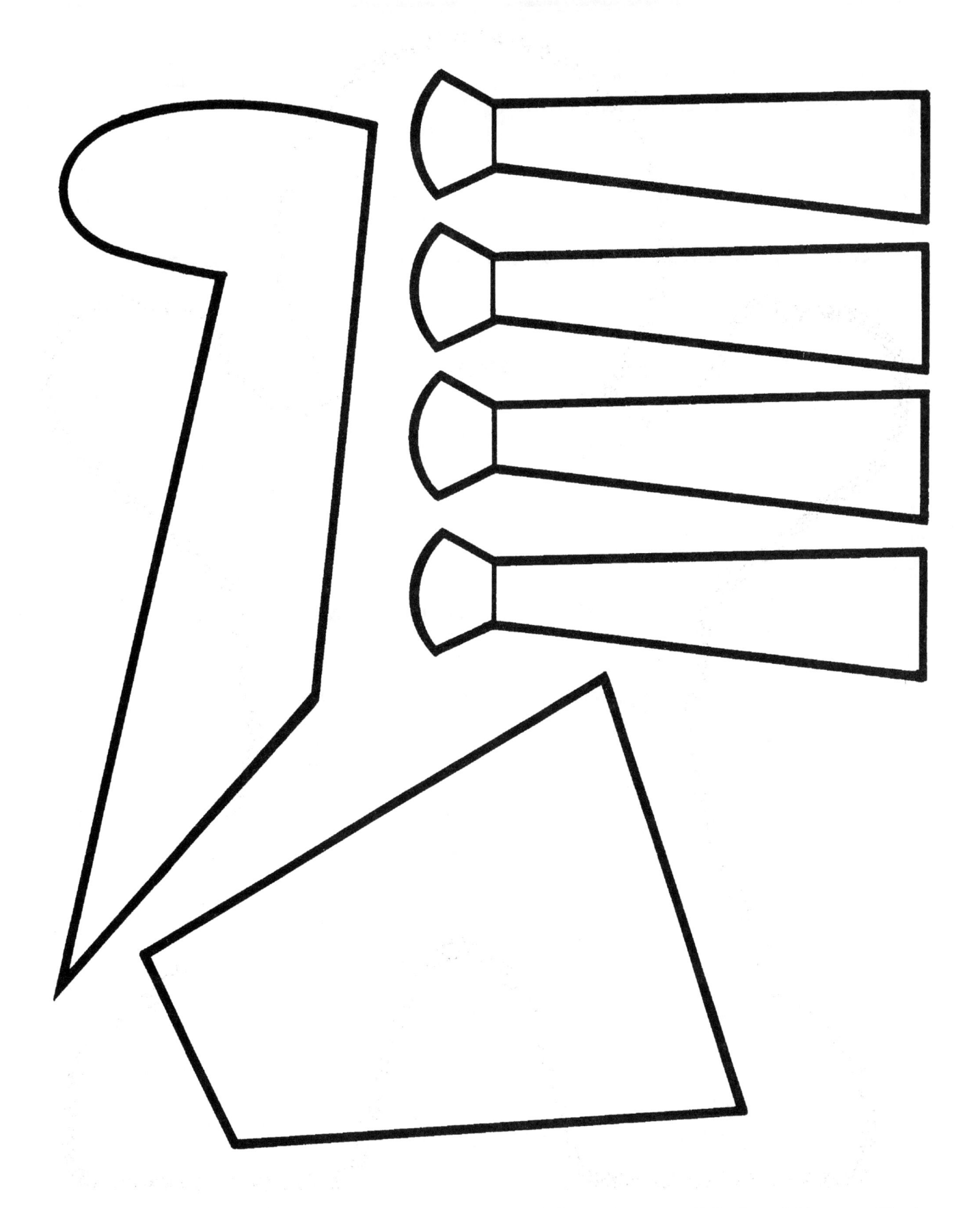

©1995 Teacher Created Materials, Inc.   99   #791 Teaching Basic Skills through Literature: Phonics

Phonics Skills in Context: Letter "H"

Book: *A House is a House for Me*
Author: Mary Ann Hoberman
Publisher: Scholastic, New York, 1978
Summary: This book lists in rhyme the dwellings of various animals and other things.
Recommended Grade Level: K–2
Related Poetry: "Hippopotamus" by Mary Ann Hoberman, *Yellow Butter, Purple Jelly, Red Jam, Black Bread* (Viking Press, New York, 1981). For additional titles see page 384.

Skill Activity

Students match their "h" word cards to other members in the class. Then, partners work together to think of other "h" words to compile a class word bank.

Materials

- two sets of "h" word cards (pages 103 and 104)
- chart paper

Lesson

Introduce the Literature: Show students the cover of the book and ask them what they think it will be about.

Read the Literature: Read the literature selection. Allow time for discussion.

Introduce the Skill Lesson:

1. Pass out two sets of the "h" word cards from pages 103 and 104 to the class.
2. Have students read their word cards and then find the other classmates with the same words.
3. Once they find their partners, have students think of other "h" words together.
4. Ask groups to share their "h" words while you write them on chart paper. Display the chart paper for students to use as a word bank.

Learning Center Activity: Have students create "A House is a House" class book. Each student writes an idea to complete this sentence: "A _____ is a house for _____." They can write and draw their ideas on the pattern on page 105. Students can choose ideas from the book or use an original idea. The pages can be bound together for a class book.

Cooperative Learning Activity: Have students work in small groups to create a mural modeled after the last page of the book "And the earth is a house for us all." Divide the class into five cooperative groups and assign one of the following topics to each group: animals, shelter, plants, clothing, and ideas. Each group is to brainstorm ideas that fit their topic. These ideas can be illustrated on the mural.

Across the Curriculum: Social Studies

Use the book as an introduction to the study of houses around the world or animals' houses.

Hh   *A House is a House for Me*

Extension Activities

Movement Activities

Stress the letter "h" as students participate in the following movements: hanging on the bars, hide and seek, hopping, walking like a hippo, trotting like a horse, and playing hopscotch.

Multisensory Activity

On 6" x 8" (15 cm x 20 cm) tagboard, have children paste hole-punched holes onto an upper and lowercase "h." Patterns are located on pages 106 and 107.

Creative Writing

Have students design their ideal houses. Students can illustrate the interiors of the houses using the pattern on page 108. Then, on a separate sheet of paper, they can write about what special things will happen in each room.

Handwriting

On 12" x 18" (30 cm x 46 cm) lined newsprint, ask children to copy this sentence: "H is for horse, heart (paste on paper heart or heart sticker), house, and happy hippo."

Cooking

"Hole" Wheat Sandwich

Ingredients
- a round cookie cutter
- whole-wheat bread
- peanut butter
- knife
- plate

Directions
1. Cut a hole in the bread with the cookie cutter.
2. Spread peanut butter on the bread.
3. Draw your recipe.
4. Clean up.

Interdisciplinary Topics

horses	holidays	habitats	hurricanes
hamsters	honey	hibernation	heart
hummingbirds	Halloween	helicopters	hospital
hippopotamus	Hanukkah		

©1995 Teacher Created Materials, Inc.   101   #791 Teaching Basic Skills through Literature: Phonics

A House is a House for Me   Hh

Extension Activities (cont.)

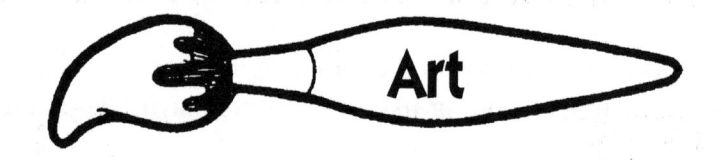

Art

"H" Mobile
Materials
- construction paper
- hangers
- yarn or string
- crayons or markers
- tape
- scissors

Process
1. Students draw and cut out a house, hat, and heart and trace and cut out hand prints on construction paper.
2. Tape yarn of differing lengths to each cutout.
3. Tie the opposite ends of the yarn to the hanger.

House of Sticks
Materials
- 6 craft sticks per child
- construction paper
- crayons or markers

Process
1. Place sticks in house shape.
2. Glue onto paper.
3. Decorate.

House of Paper
Materials
- construction paper
- crayons or markers
- scissors

Process
1. Fold paper so ends meet in middle.
2. Cut pointed top for roof.
3. Open "door" to decorate inside of house.
4. Decorate outside of house.

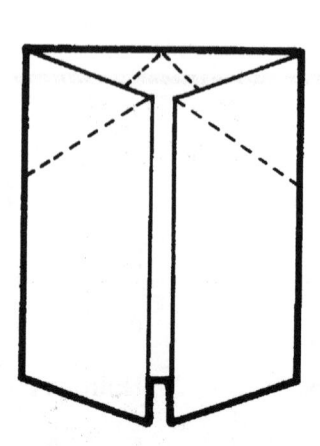

"H" Word Cards

hat	hop
hen	ham
her	his
house	home
hot	hay
here	have

A House is a House for Me

"H" Word Cards (cont.)

happy	hello
head	heart
horse	hand
hippo	hero
hammer	honey
hexagon	helicopter

Hh A House is a House for Me

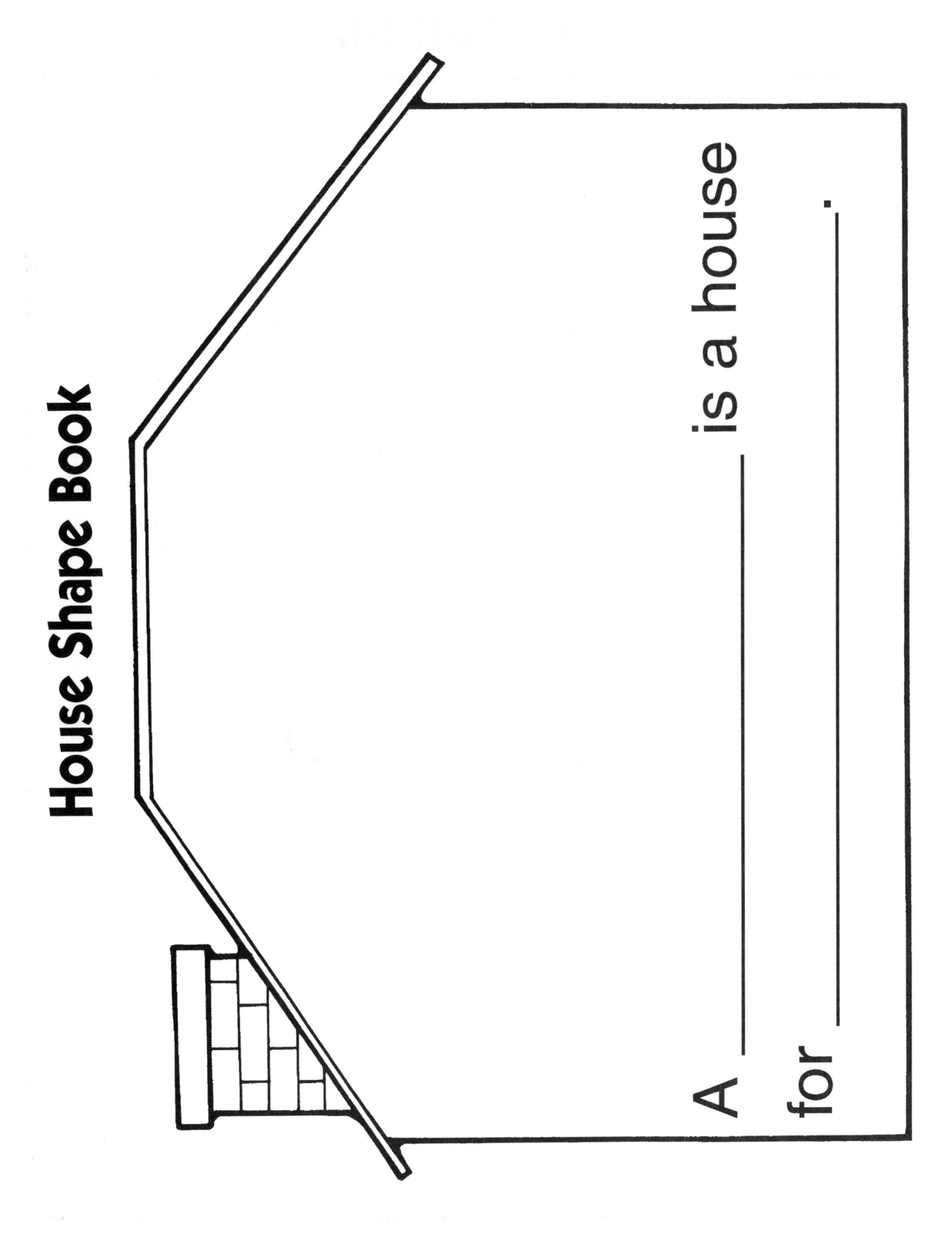

House Shape Book

A _____ is a house for _____.

©1995 Teacher Created Materials, Inc.

A House is a House for Me

Hh

"H" Pattern

#791 Teaching Basic Skills through Literature: Phonics   106   ©1995 Teacher Created Materials, Inc.

"h" Pattern

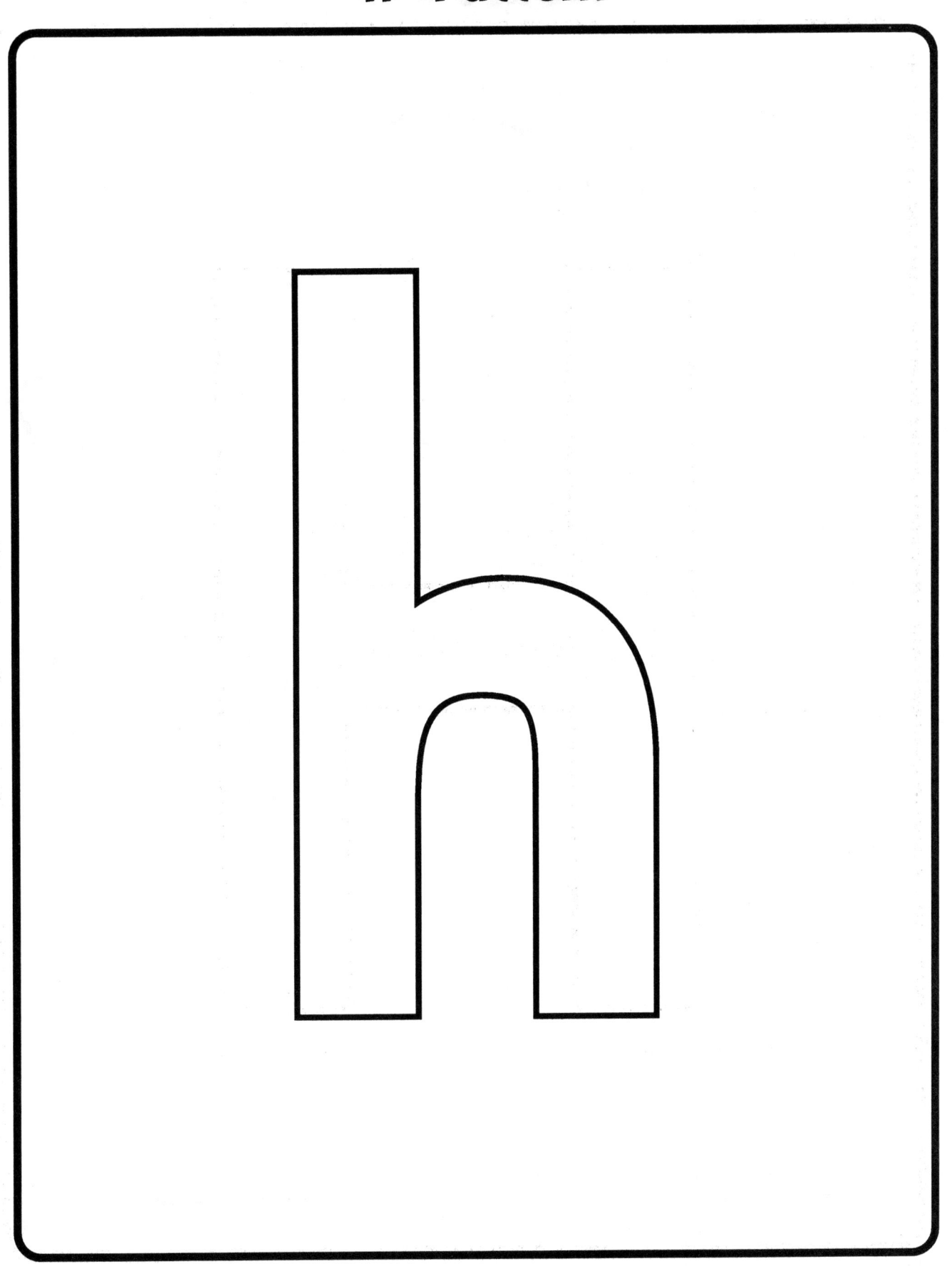

A House is a House for Me Hh

House Story

Phonics Skills in Context: Letter "J"

Book: *Jump, Frog, Jump!*
Author: Robert Kalan
Publisher: Greenwillow, New York, 1989
Summary: This cumulative pattern story is about a frog's escape from a multitude of dangers.
Recommended Grade Level: K–1
Related Poetry: "Jump or Jiggle" by Josette Frank, *Poems to Read to the Very Young* (Random House, New York, 1982). For additional titles see page 385.

Skill Activity
Students will jump each time they hear a "j" word as the teacher reads from a list of "j" and non-"j" words.

Materials
- "j" and non-"j" word list (page 112)
- chart paper

Lesson
Introduce the Literature: Show the cover of the book and ask students to jump up and down.

Read the Literature: Read the literature selection. Allow time for discussion.

Introduce the Skill Lesson:

1. Ask students to think of as many "j" words as they can.
2. Write these words on chart paper to use as a word bank.
3. Read the word list from page 112.
4. Ask students to jump up each time they hear a "j" word.

Learning Center Activity: Allow students to make a jack-in-the-box. Directions are on page 111.

Cooperative Learning Activity: In a small group, challenge the students to think of other animals that jump. Children illustrate their animals and complete the sentences on page 113. These can be put together into a class book.

Across the Curriculum: Physical Education/Math
Have students compete in four jumping events: running jump, high jump (two people hold the ends of a jump rope), standing broad jump, jump rope. Incorporate math skills by measuring the distances children jump or how long they jump (time).

Jump, Frog, Jump! Jj

Extension Activities

Movement Activities
Stress the letter "j" as students participate in the following movements: jumping jacks, jump high, shake like jelly, join hands, juggle, jog, jiggle your arms, and play jacks.

Multisensory Activity
On 6" x 8" (15 cm x 20 cm) tagboard, have children paste jelly beans onto an upper and lowercase "j." Patterns are provided on pages 114 and 115.

Creative Writing
Give students this story starter: "One day I was jumping rope, when all of a sudden the rope turned into . . . ." They can write their stories using page 116.

Handwriting
On 12" x 18" (30 cm x 46 cm) lined newsprint, ask children to copy this sentence: "J is for jack-in-the-box, jump rope (glue on yarn), jeep, and jolly jack-o-lantern."

Cooking

Juice

Ingredients
- oranges
- juicer
- knife
- cups

Directions
1. Cut oranges in half.
2. Push oranges onto juicer and push. Pour into cup.
3. Draw your recipe.
4. Clean up.

Interdisciplinary Topics

jungle animals	Jewish holidays	janitors	January
jellyfish	journals	jam	June
jaguars	Japanese holidays	juice	July
Jupiter	jack-o-lanterns	jelly beans	junk

Jj *Jump, Frog, Jump!*

Extension Activities (cont.)

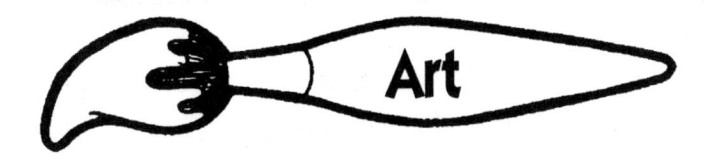

Art

Jack-in-the-Box
Materials
- milk carton (Remove two sides of top and make slit in bottom.)
- Jack pattern (page 117)
- construction paper
- glue
- scissors
- craft sticks
- crayons or markers

Process
1. Copy the jack-in-the-box pattern onto construction paper.
2. Color and cut out.
3. Glue a different color paper around milk carton.
4. Glue jack to the craft stick.
5. Slip the stick through the slit in the carton.
6. Make jack jump out of the carton.

Jaguar
Materials
- jaguar pattern (page 118)
- scissors
- crayons or markers
- brown paint
- yellow construction paper
- small sponges

Process
1. Reproduce or trace jaguar pattern onto yellow construction paper.
2. Sponge paint brown spots all over body. Allow to dry.
3. Cut out pattern.

Jet
Materials
- jet pattern (page 119)
- paper clips
- Styrofoam meat trays
- crayons or markers

Process
1. Using pattern and Styrofoam tray, trace and cut out jet pieces.
2. Assemble jet and add details.
3. Put a paper clip on the nose of the plane to help it fly better.

©1995 Teacher Created Materials, Inc.

"J" and non-"J" Word List

jar	jelly	jaguar
gum	jam	make
jeep	play	jet
jump	give	desk
rope	jog	juggle

Jj *Jump, Frog, Jump!*

Book Pattern

Jump, _____, jump!

Jump, _____, jump!

©1995 Teacher Created Materials, Inc. 113 #791 *Teaching Basic Skills through Literature: Phonics*

Jump, Frog, Jump!   Jj

"J" Pattern

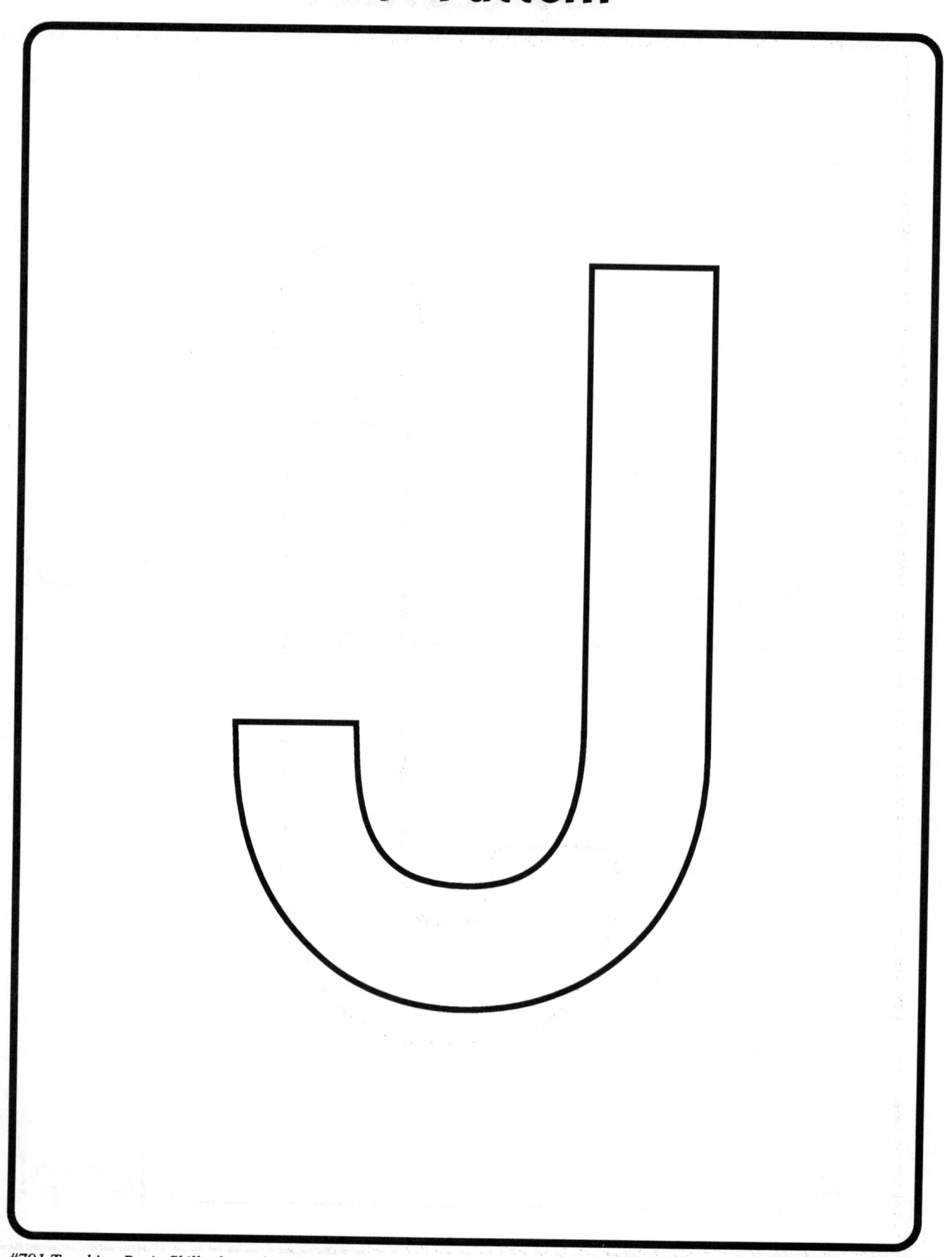

Jj *Jump, Frog, Jump!*

"j" Pattern

©1995 Teacher Created Materials, Inc. 115 #791 Teaching Basic Skills through Literature: Phonics

Jump, Frog, Jump!   Jj

My Jump Rope Story

by:_____

One day I was jumping rope, when all of a sudden the rope turned into _____

_____

_____

_____

_____

_____

_____

_____

_____

_____

Jj *Jump, Frog, Jump!*

Jack Pattern

©1995 Teacher Created Materials, Inc. 117 #791 Teaching Basic Skills through Literature: Phonics

Jump, Frog, Jump!   Jj

Jaguar Pattern

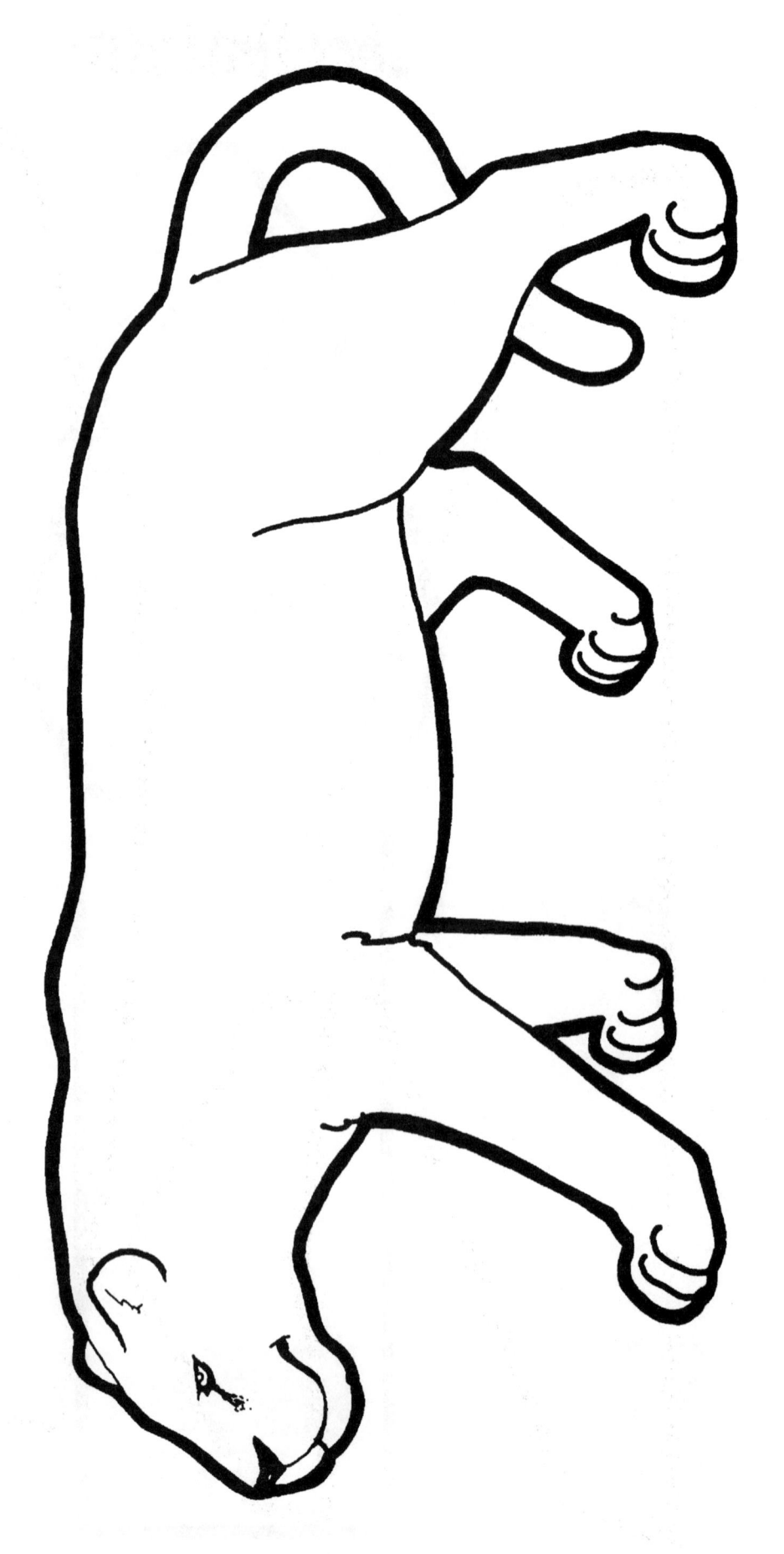

#791 Teaching Basic Skills through Literature: Phonics   118   ©1995 Teacher Created Materials, Inc.

Jj *Jump, Frog, Jump!*

Jet Pattern

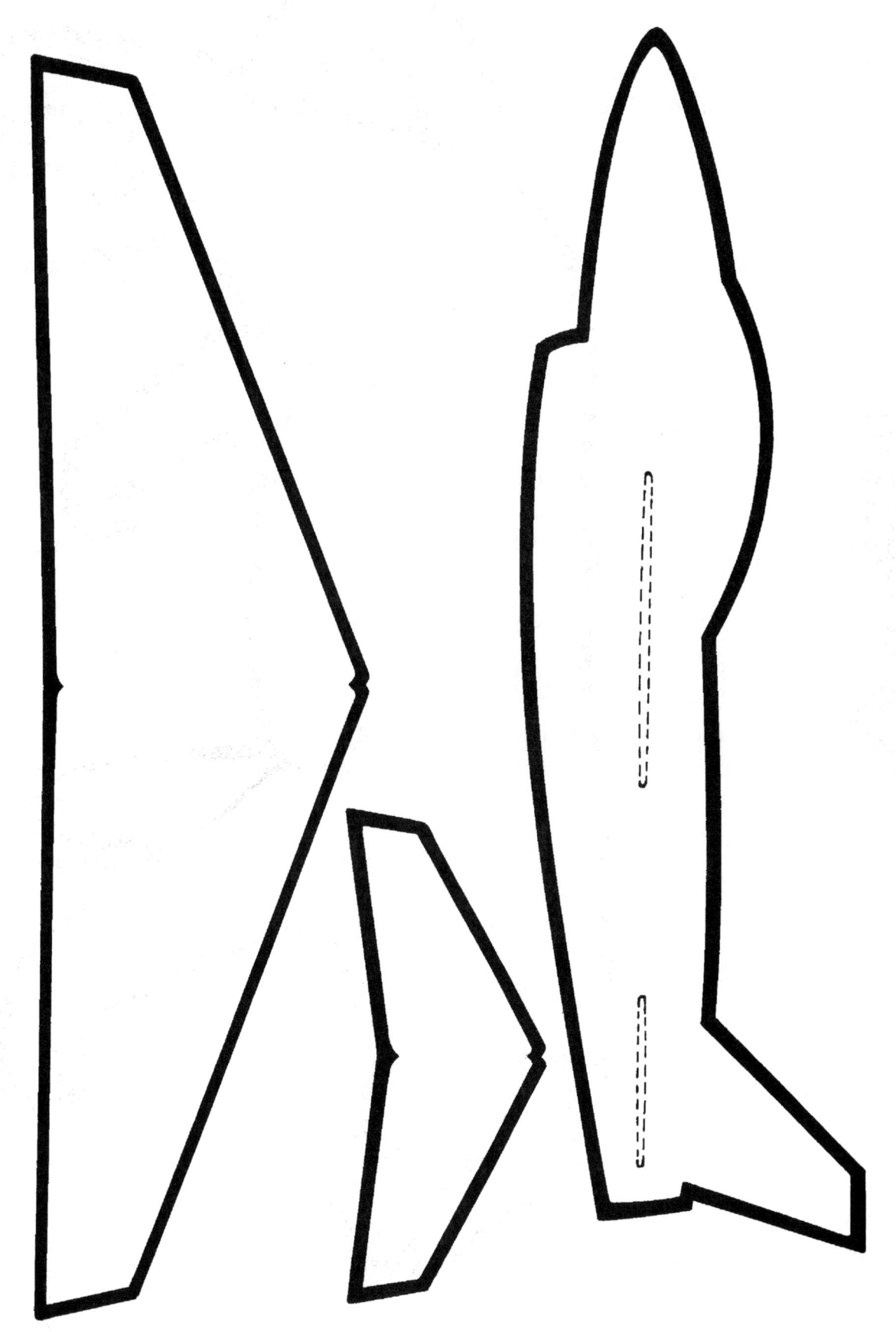

Phonics Skills in Context: Letter "K"

Book: *Koala Lou*
Author: Mem Fox
Publisher: Harcourt, San Diego, 1988
Summary: Koala Lou misses her mother's affection until she proves to herself that her mom has loved her and always will love her.
Recommended Grade Level: K–2
Related Poetry: "A Kite" by Frank D. Sherman, *A Child's Book of Poems* (Grosset & Dunlap, New York, 1972). For additional titles see page 385.

Skill Activity
Students match "k" words and picture cards. Then, they select from a list to write and illustrate their "k" words in a "Koala Lou Shape Book."

Materials
- Koala Lou pattern (page 123)
- crayons or markers
- chart paper
- "k" word cards and picture cards (pages 124 and 125)
- pocket chart

Lesson
Introduce the Literature: Show students where Australia is on a globe. Tell the students that the animals in the book are from Australia.

Read the Literature: Read the literature selection. Allow time for discussion.

Introduce the Skill Lesson:
1. Brainstorm "k" words as a class.
2. Write the words on chart paper to use as a word bank.
3. Pass out the "k" picture cards and word cards to the class. Have students match their pictures to the corresponding words. When all the cards have been matched, place them on a pocket chart for all to see.
4. Provide each student with a Koala Lou shape book (page 123). Students should select several "k" words to illustrate and write in their books.
5. Older students can write sentences for their "k" words.

Learning Center Activity: Make seven copies of the kangaroo pattern (page 126). For each kangaroo, cut and paste a word and its matching picture (page 127) on the boxes in the kangaroo pattern. Students choose a kangaroo and read its word.

The students then use the letter cards on page 128 to spell the "k" word shown on the kangaroo. (Cut out letter cards in advance.) Letter cards are stored in the kangaroo's pouch. Provide alphabet stamps for students to copy each of the words onto a separate piece of paper.

Cooperative Learning Activity: Talk about the Bush Olympics in the story. Have students form teams to compete in various races such as the "koala climb" and the "kangaroo kickoff." Brainstorm with students for other possible events.

Across the Curriculum: Science
Develop a unit on koalas, kangaroos, kookaburras, and other animals of Australia.

Extension Activities

Movement Activities
Stress the letter "k" as students participate in the following movements: kangaroo hopping, kicking a ball, playing keep away, playing king of the hill, flying a kite, and kneading bread.

Multisensory Activity
On 6" x 8" (15 cm x 20 cm) tagboard, have students glue kidney beans onto an upper and lowercase "k." Patterns are provided on pages 129 and 130.

Creative Writing
Kangaroos have pouches. Have students make a list of the good things and the not-so-good things about life in a pouch if people their age had to live in pouches. For fun, students can draw pictures of themselves, glue them to craft sticks, then put them in the pouch of the kangaroo pattern on page 126.

Handwriting
On 12" x 18" (30 cm x 46 cm) lined newsprint, ask children to copy this sentence: "K is for key, kid, kite (glue on a paper kite) and kind king."

Cooking

Katy Kangaroo Kabobs

Ingredients
- assorted fruit
- toothpicks
- knife

Directions
1. Cut fruit into chunk size pieces.
2. Skewer onto toothpicks.
3. Draw your recipe.
4. Clean up.

Interdisciplinary Topics

kangaroos	Martin Luther King, Jr.	ketchup
kiwi	kaleidoscopes	kale
kitten	kites	kumquats
John F. Kennedy	kidney beans	koalas

Koala Lou   *Kk*

Extension Activities (cont.)

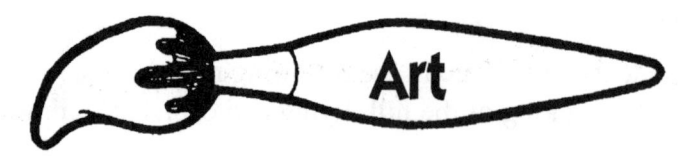

Art

Kangaroo Crayon Can
Materials
- crayon can kangaroo pattern (page 131)
- construction paper
- scissors
- juice cans
- glue

Process
1. Trace pattern and cut pieces.
2. Assemble kangaroo around can.
3. Store crayons in pouch.

Kazoo
Materials
- cardboard tubes
- rubber bands
- crayons or markers
- wax paper
- pencils

Process
1. Decorate tube.
2. Punch three holes in top of tube with pencil point.
3. Cover one end of tube with waxed paper.
4. Secure with rubber band and play a tune!

Koalas
Materials
- koala pattern (page 132)
- crayons or markers
- green tissue paper
- construction paper
- paste
- scissors
- craft stick or small branch

Process
1. Children color and cut out koalas. Paste baby on back of mother, then glue mother to a stick or branch.
2. Glue all to construction paper.
3. Cut out and glue on green tissue-paper leaves.

Kk *Koala Lou*

Koala Lou Shape Book

"K" Word Cards

king	kitten
kite	koala
kangaroo	key
kettle	keyboard
kitchen	kayak

Kk   Koala Lou

"K" Picture Cards

©1995 Teacher Created Materials, Inc.   125   #791 Teaching Basic Skills through Literature: Phonics

Koala Lou *Kk*

Kangaroo Pattern

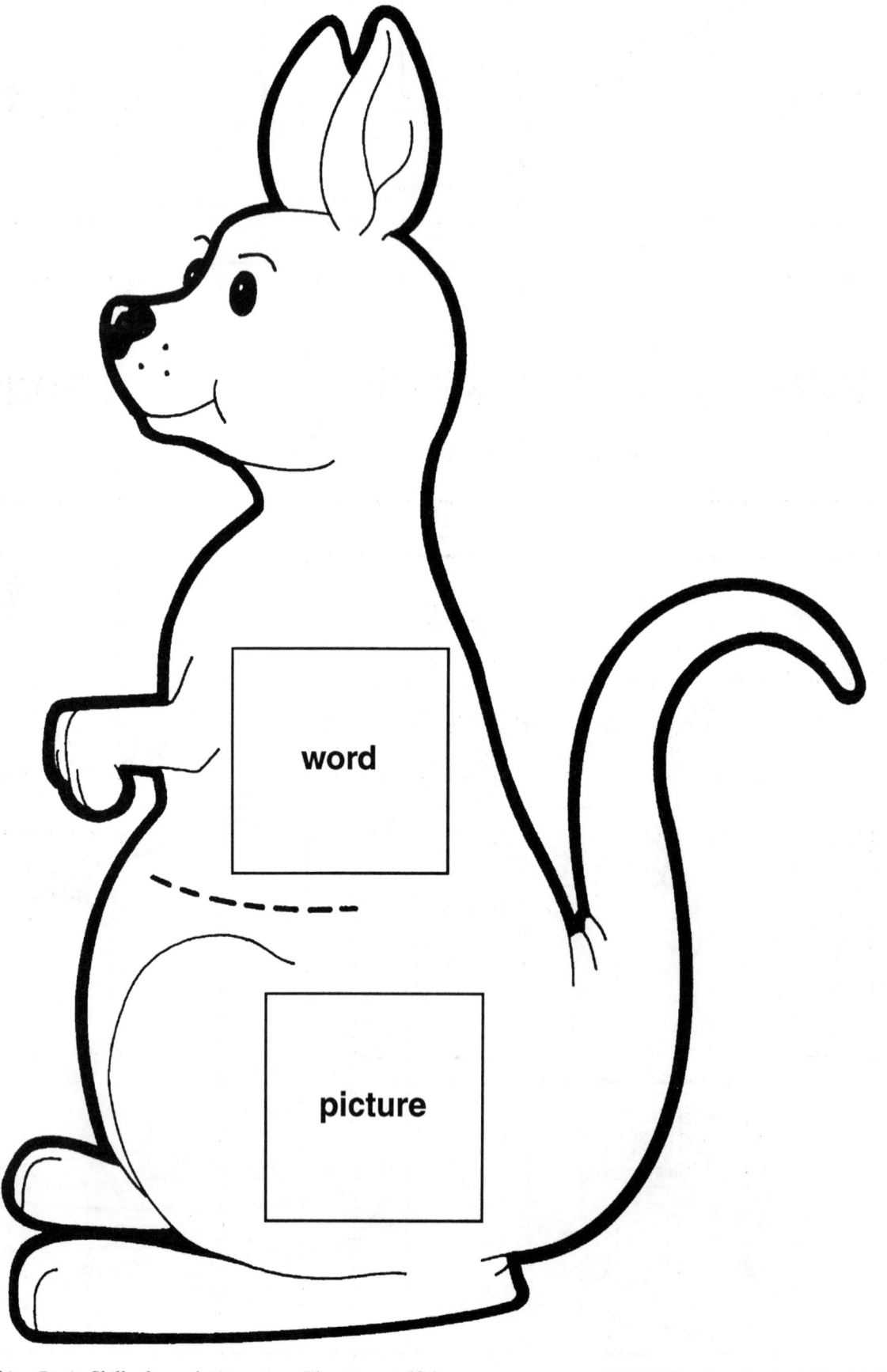

word

picture

Kk   *Koala Lou*

Kangaroo Word Cards

key	king	kitten
kite	kettle	kangaroo
koala		

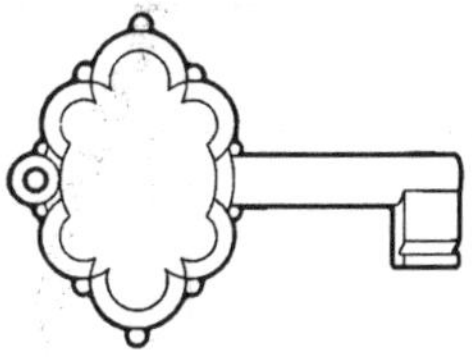

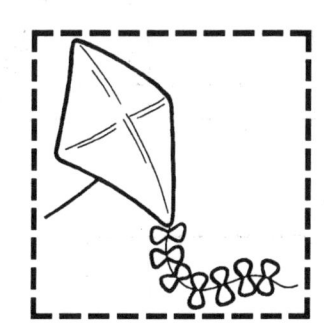

©1995 Teacher Created Materials, Inc.   127   #791 Teaching Basic Skills through Literature: Phonics

Koala Lou   Kk

Letter Cards

k	e	y	k
i	n	g	k
i	t	t	e
n	k	i	t
e	k	e	t
t	l	e	k
a	n	g	a
r	o	o	k
o	a	l	a

Kk *Koala Lou*

"K" Pattern

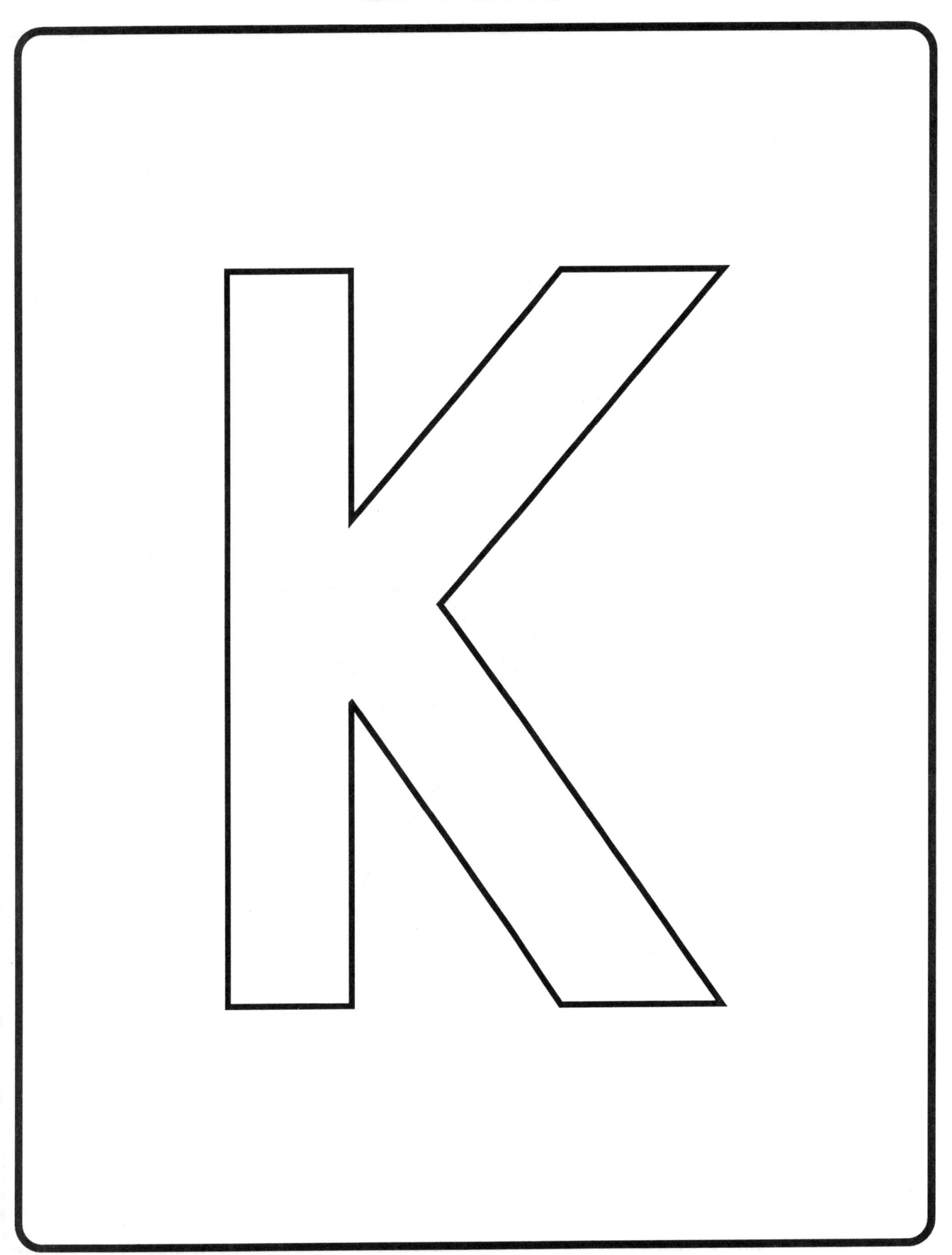

Koala Lou   *Kk*

"k" Pattern

Kk *Koala Lou*

Crayon Can Pattern

©1995 Teacher Created Materials, Inc. 131 #791 Teaching Basic Skills through Literature: Phonics

Koala Lou   Kk

Koala Pattern

Phonics Skills in Context: Letter "L"

Book: *Leo the Late Bloomer*
Author: Leo Lionni
Publisher: Scholastic, New York, 1971
Summary: Leo the tiger and his parents wait for the day that Leo will "bloom" by being able to do all the things that his friends can do.
Recommended Grade Level: K–1
Related Poetry: "Late One Night" by Jack Prelutsky, *Ride a Purple Pelican* (Greenwillow, New York, 1986). For additional titles see page 385.

Skill Activity
Students play lineup when they can correctly identify an "l" word.

Materials
- chart paper

Lesson
Introduce the Literature: Read the title of the book to the class. Explain what a late bloomer is.

Read the Literature: Read the literature selection. Allow time for discussion.

Introduce the Skill Lesson:

1. Students are asked to name a word that begins with the letter "l." After each student names a word, he or she lines up.
2. Write each word on chart paper to display as a word bank.
3. Continue the activity, having students line up in an "l" shape.

Learning Center Activity: Students can make a "Things I Like to Do" booklet. Have students brainstorm "l" words that are actions. Students write one of the "l" words to complete the sentence "I like to _____." This prompt can be found on page 136. Illustrations are then added to the sentences. You may want students to use the cover pattern on page 137.

Cooperative Learning Activity: Make a class book modeled after the page in the book with the heading "Then one day, in our own good time, we bloomed." Have them complete the sentence "Once I couldn't _____, but then one day, in my own good time, I bloomed!" This sentence can be found on page 138 to be copied for students. Discuss with students their sense of pride when they accomplished their goals.

Across the Curriculum: Science
Have students collect different types of leaves. Students can study about the different types of leaves and do leaf rubbings and collages.

©1995 Teacher Created Materials, Inc.

Leo the Late Bloomer   Ll

Extension Activities

Movement Activities

Stress the letter "l" as students participate in the following movements: lion leaps, climb a ladder, stretch long and low, hop on your left foot, and laugh.

Multisensory Activity

On 6" x 8" (15 cm x 20 cm) tagboard, have students glue leaves to an upper and lowercase "l." Patterns are provided on pages 139 and 140.

Creative Writing

Have students finish these sentences: "I love to...", I love it when...", and "I love..." Story page patterns are located on pages 141 and 142.

Handwriting

On 12" x 18" (30 cm x 46 cm) lined newsprint, ask children to copy this sentence: "L is for letters (use letter stamps), lady, leaves, and large lion."

Cooking

Leo Lion's Lettuce Lunch

Ingredients
- lettuce
- peanut butter
- raisins
- apricots
- pretzel sticks
- plates
- peaches

Directions
1. Put a piece of lettuce on a plate. Add a peach on top.
2. Add raisins for eyes, nose, and mouth. Add pretzel sticks for whiskers. Cut an apricot in half for ears.
3. Draw your recipe.
4. Clean up.

Interdisciplinary Topics

ladybugs	leprechaun	lighthouses	limes
lizards	Abraham Lincoln	liquids	lemonade
lobster	Labor Day	lettuce	licorice
lion	lifeguard	lemons	lollipops
lake	lantern		

Ll   *Leo the Late Bloomer*

Extension Activities (cont.)

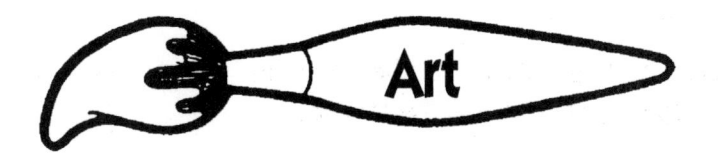

Art

Ladybug

Materials
- ladybug pattern (page 143)
- red, white, and black construction paper
- glue
- paper fasteners
- scissors

Process
1. Trace and cut out body from black paper.
2. Cut out 2 wings from red paper and attach with fastener.
3. Use scraps to cut out ladybug's spots.
4. Use black strips to make legs and antennae.
5. Add white eyes with black pupils.

Lamb

Materials
- white and black construction paper
- cotton
- glue

Process
1. Cut out two white ovals, one large and one small.
2. Use black paper to make floppy ears and legs.
3. Draw facial features on small oval and attach ears.
4. Glue cotton to large oval.
5. Attach head and legs.

Lion

Materials
- brown, orange, black, and white construction paper
- brown and orange tissue paper
- lion pattern (page 144)
- black crayon or marker
- scissors
- pencil
- glue

Process
1. Using patterns, cut out an orange mane and brown face.
2. Paste face on mane. Add black eyes and nose tip. Draw in rest of facial features.
3. To make mane fluffy, glue on small squares of tissue, allowing it to stand up by wrapping tissue over the end of a pencil, dipping it in glue, and attaching it to mane.

Leo the Late Bloomer Ll

Book Pages

I like to _____.

I like to _____.

Ll *Leo the Late Bloomer*

Book Cover

Things I Like to Do

by: _____

Things I Like to Do

by: _____

Leo the Late Bloomer Ll

Late Bloomer Page

Once I couldn't _____

_____

_____

_____

_____

_____

_____,

but then one day, in my own good time, I bloomed!

by: _____

Ll   *Leo the Late Bloomer*

"L" Pattern

Leo the Late Bloomer   Ll

"l" Pattern

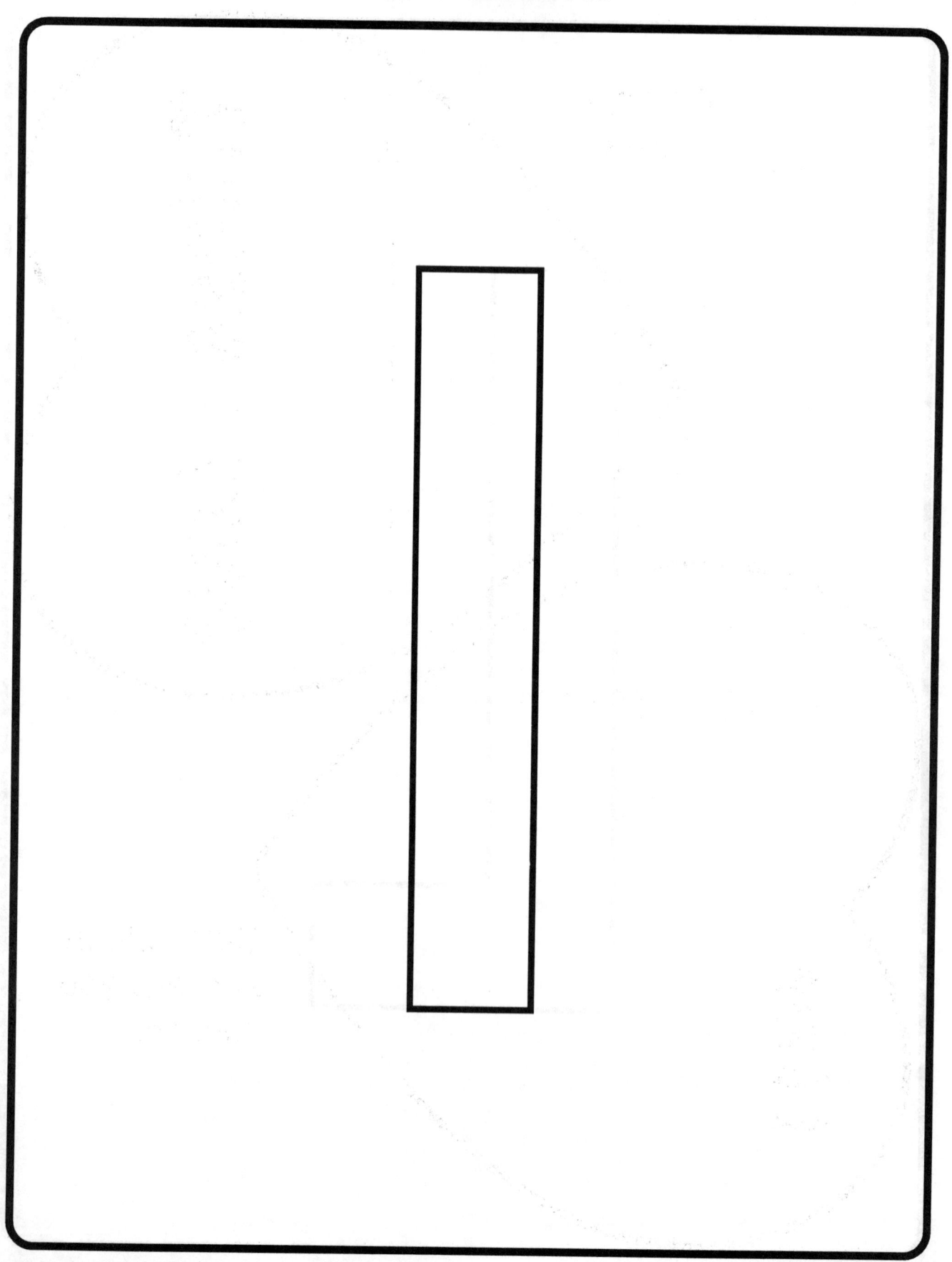

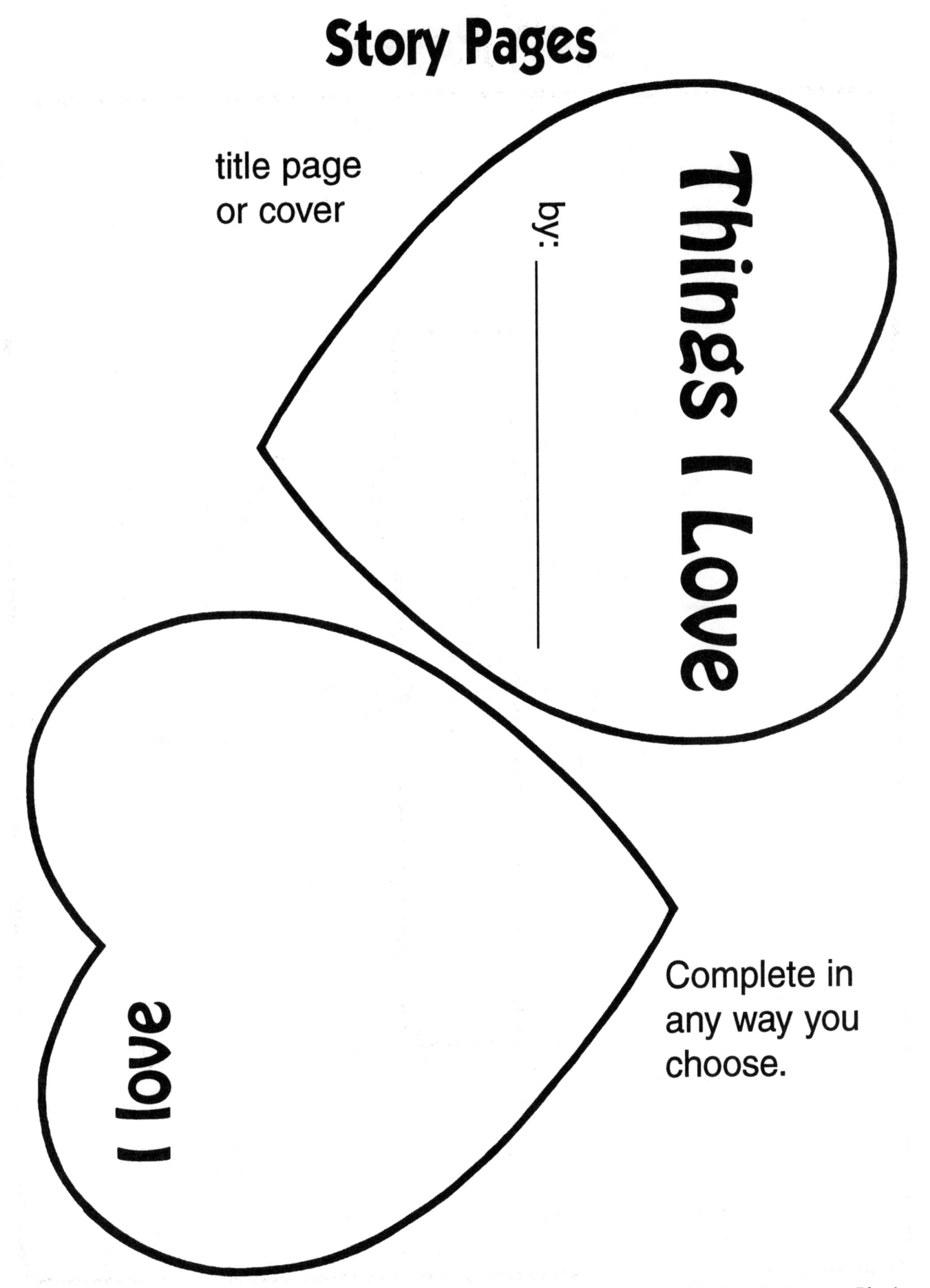

Ll Leo the Late Bloomer

Story Pages

title page or cover

Things I Love

by: _____

I love

Complete in any way you choose.

©1995 Teacher Created Materials, Inc. 141 #791 Teaching Basic Skills through Literature: Phonics

Leo the Late Bloomer

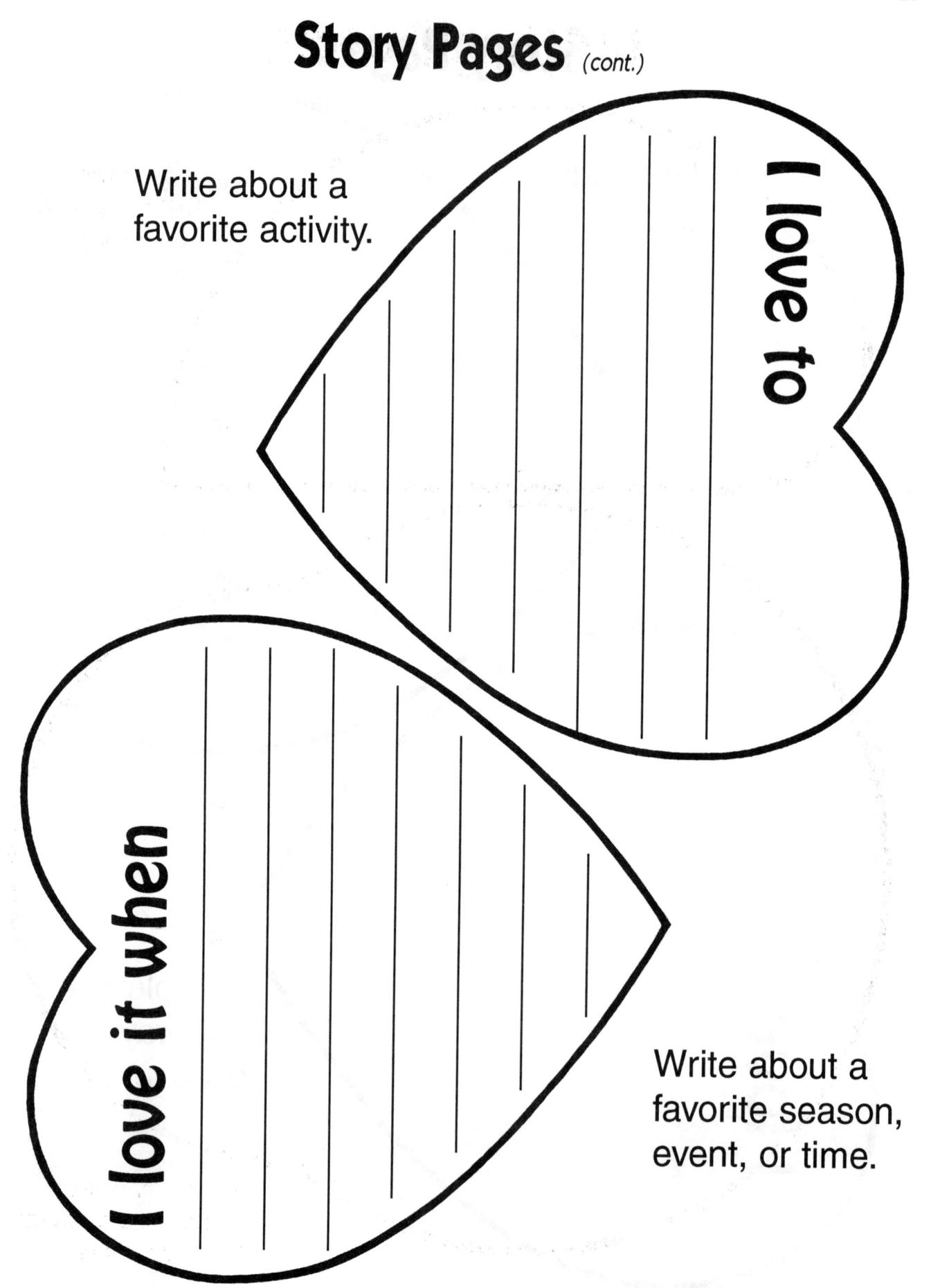

Story Pages (cont.)

Write about a favorite activity.

I love to

I love it when

Write about a favorite season, event, or time.

Ll

Leo the Late Bloomer

Ladybug Pattern

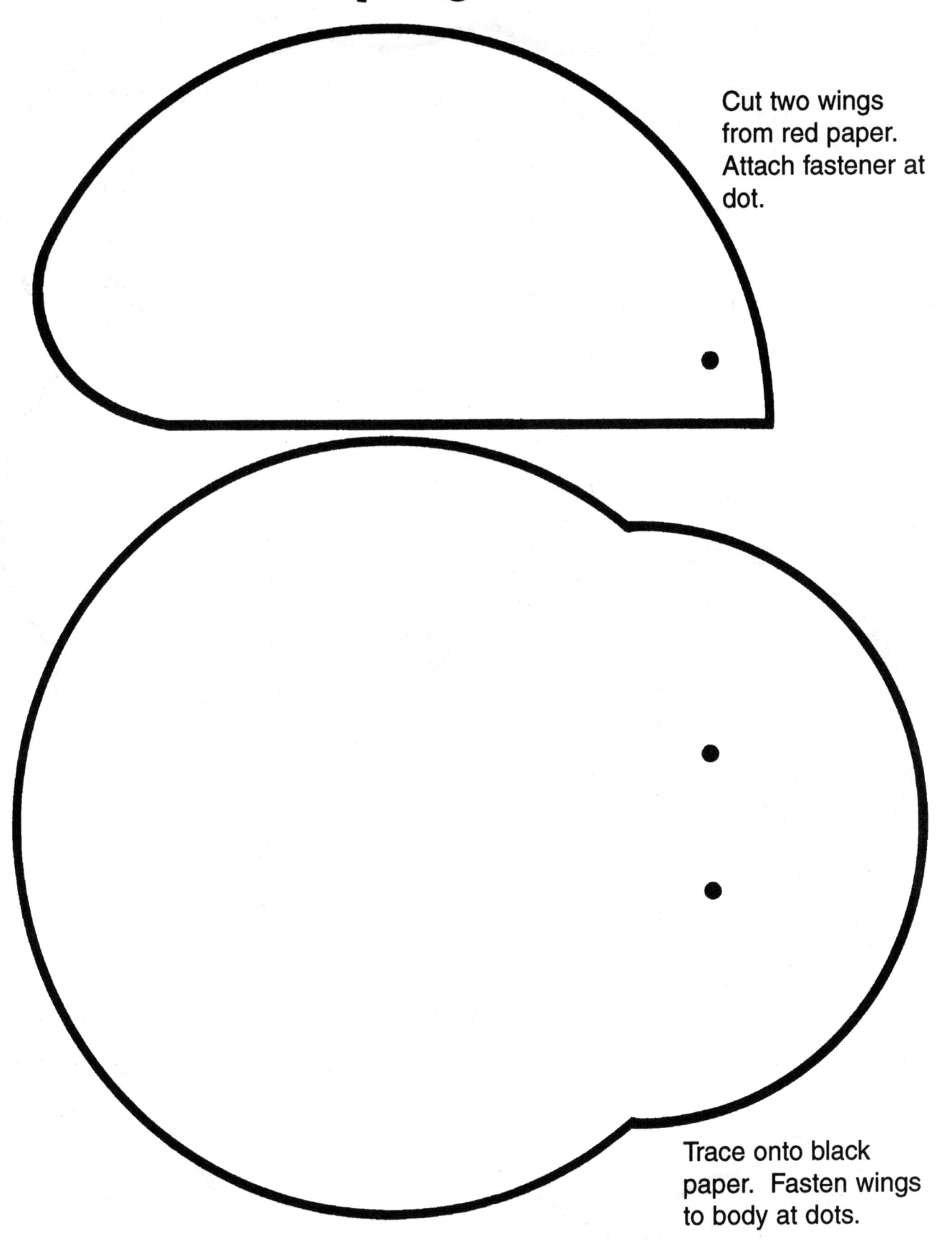

Cut two wings from red paper. Attach fastener at dot.

Trace onto black paper. Fasten wings to body at dots.

Leo the Late Bloomer   *Ll*

Lion Pattern

Phonics Skills in Context: Letter "M"

Book: *Happy Birthday, Moon*
Author: Frank Asch
Publisher: Prentice-Hall, New York, 1982
Summary: When a bear discovers that the moon shares his birthday, he buys the moon a beautiful hat as a present.
Recommended Grade Level: K–1
Related Poetry: "The Man in the Moon" by Arnold Lobel, *The Random House Book of Mother Goose* (Random House, New York, 1986). For additional titles see page 385.

Skill Activity
Students brainstorm "m" words and create a book titled "M is for Moon."

Materials
- chart paper
- crayons or markers
- "M is for Moon" shape book (page 148)
- plain paper

Lesson
Introduce the Literature: Show students the cover of the book. Ask them if they have ever seen the moon.

Read the Literature: Read the literature selection. Allow time for discussion.

Introduce the Skill Lesson:
1. Write the word "moon" on chart paper. Underline the "m."
2. Read selected pages from the book and ask students to listen for "m" words. List the "m" words on chart paper. Display the list as a word bank.
3. Have each student make an "M is for Moon" shape book. (A cover is provided on page 148.)
4. Give all students three pieces of paper cut in the shape of the book cover. On each page they should write an "m" word and illustrate it. Older students can write a sentence for each word.

Learning Center Activity: Have students create "Me on the Moon." Provide each student with a paper plate, black construction paper, drawing paper, glue, white chalk or crayon, scissors, and gold or silver stars. Students cut off the edges of the paper plates leaving the circles to form the moons. Glue the moons onto black construction paper. Students then draw and cut out pictures of themselves and glue them on the moons. Use chalk or crayon to draw a space scene. Stars can be added as well.

Cooperative Learning Activity: Have students work in groups to play "Match the Mittens" game. Provide students with the mitten patterns (page 149). Have them select an "m" word, write it on both mittens, and cut the mittens out. When all mittens are complete, the group lays all mittens face down. Students take turns selecting two mittens and reading both words. If they match, the student keeps them; if not, they are turned over and the game continues.

Across the Curriculum: Science
Develop a study unit about the moon which could include facts about the moon, the monthly phases of the moon, and other information.

Happy Birthday, Moon   Mm

Extension Activities

Movement Activities
Stress the letter "m" as students participate in each of the following movements: marching, playing motor boat, scrambling like a mouse, playing Mother May I?, and moving like a monkey.

Multisensory Activity
On 6" x 8" (15 cm x 20 cm) tagboard, have students glue magazine pieces to an upper and lowercase "m." Patterns are provided on pages 150 and 151.

Creative Writing
Ask students to make a list of all the things they would buy if they had all the money in the world. Then, they can illustrate their ideas, using page 152.

Handwriting
On 12" x 18" (30 cm x 46 cm) lined newsprint, ask children to copy this sentence: "M is for mountains, mop, money, and many mice."

Cooking

Mice

Ingredients
- apples
- raisins
- string cheese
- peanut butter
- knife
- plates

Directions
1. Cut apples into quarters.
2. Use peanut butter as glue to add raisins as eyes, nose, ears, and mouth.
3. Use a strand of string cheese for the tail.
4. Draw your recipe.
5. Clean up.

Interdisciplinary Topics

mammals	manners	magic	March
monkeys	May Day	mountains	measurement
mice	Monday	museums	money
me	Memorial Day	*Mayflower*	magnet
mothers	months	microscope	moon

#791 Teaching Basic Skills through Literature: Phonics   ©1995 Teacher Created Materials, Inc.

Mm   **Happy Birthday, Moon**

Extension Activities

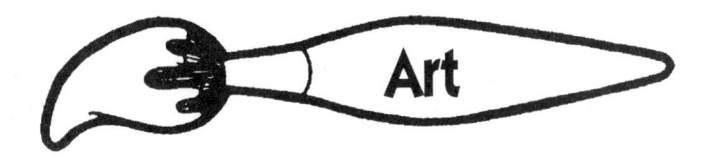

Art

Mailbox
Materials
- cardboard strips
  1" x 12" (3 cm x 30 cm) for post
  ½" x 4" (1.5 cm x 10.5 cm) for flagpole
- mailbox pattern (page 153)
- construction or heavy index paper
- letters in envelopes (optional)
- paper flag 2" x 3" (5 cm x 8 cm)
- glue
- fasteners (brads)
- scissors
- address labels

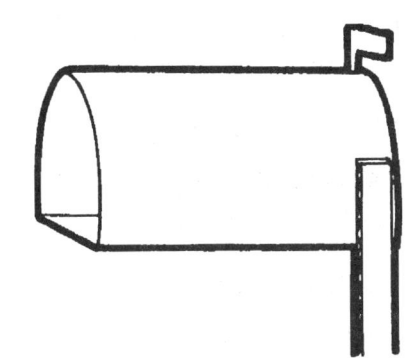

Process
1. Reproduce mailbox pattern on construction or index paper.
2. Fold under along dashed lines, "arch" paper and glue bottom of mailbox together.
3. Glue flag to small strip of cardboard. Attach cardboard with brad to side of mailbox.
4. Glue cardboard strip (post) on side of mailbox.
5. Children copy their names and addresses on front of mailing labels.
6. Pretend letters can be mailed.

Marble Painting
Materials
- construction paper cut to fit pan
- several colors of paint
- pie pan
- marbles

Process
1. Put paper circle into bottom of pie pan and drop different colors of paint onto paper.
3. Roll marble around pan, allowing it to track paint to make a design.

Mouse
Materials
- circle pattern
- glue
- scissors
- red, white, and black construction paper
- rubber bands cut in half
- crayons or markers

Process
1. Using pattern, trace and cut out 1 white, 1 red, and 2 black circles.
2. Draw facial features on white circle.
3. Attach black ears and red body.
4. Glue on rubber band for tail.

©1995 Teacher Created Materials, Inc.

Happy Birthday, Moon   *Mm*

Moon Shape Book Cover

"M" is for Moon

by: _____

Mm

Happy Birthday, Moon

Mitten Patterns

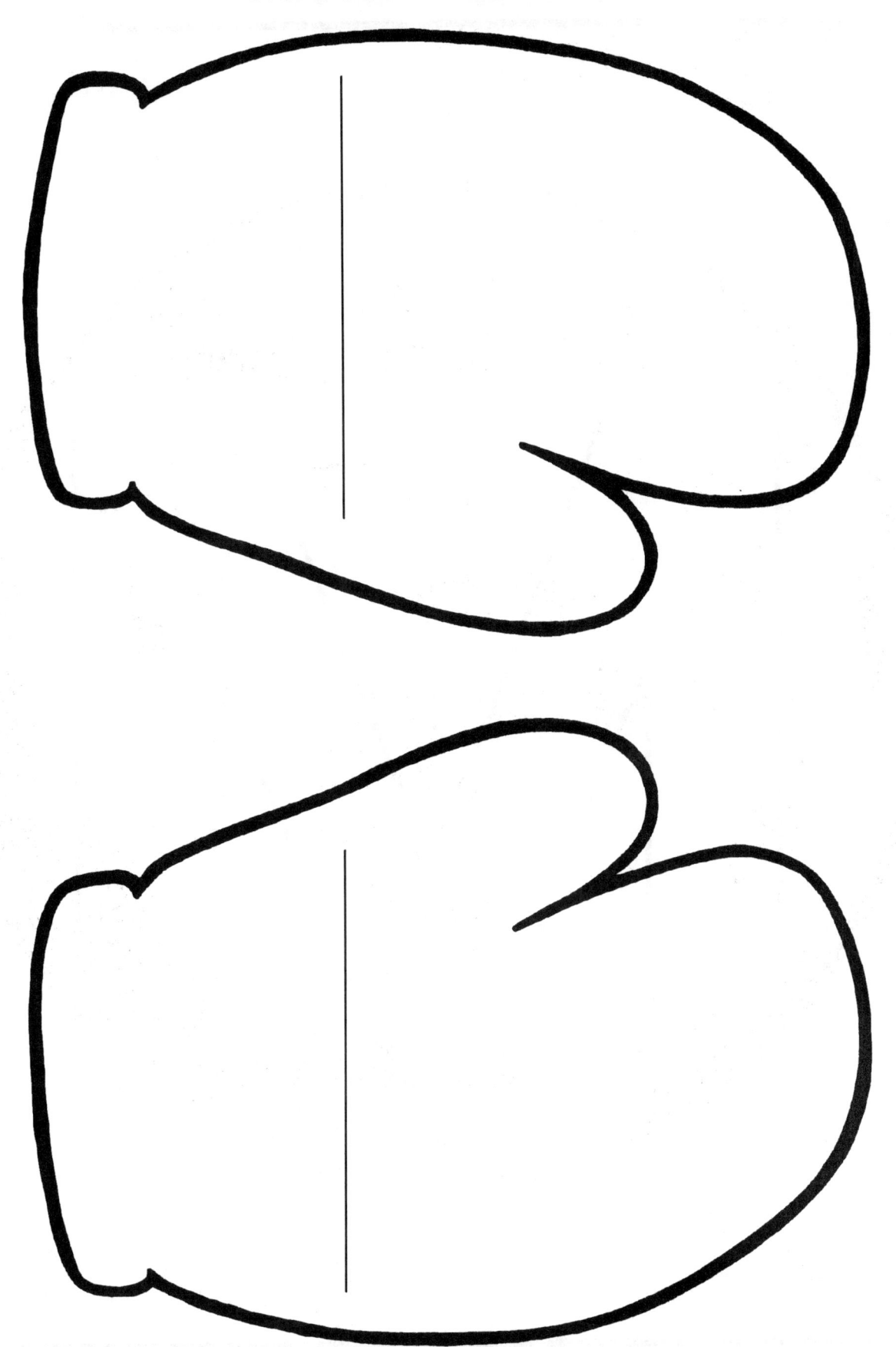

©1995 Teacher Created Materials, Inc. 149 #791 *Teaching Basic Skills through Literature: Phonics*

Happy Birthday, Moon   Mm

"M" Pattern

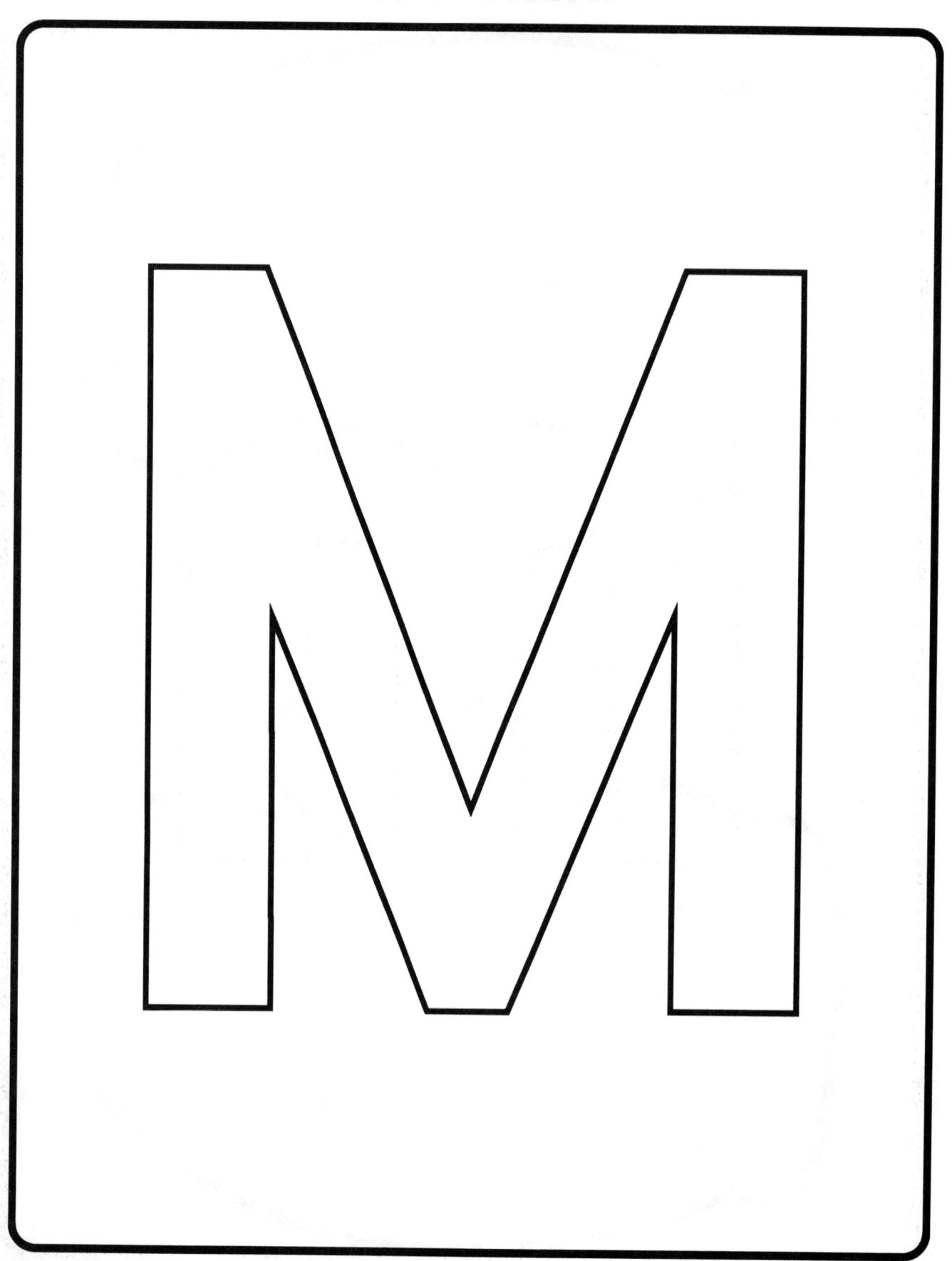

#791 Teaching Basic Skills through Literature: Phonics   ©1995 Teacher Created Materials, Inc.

Mm   *Happy Birthday, Moon*

"m" Pattern

©1995 Teacher Created Materials, Inc.   #791 Teaching Basic Skills through Literature: Phonics

Happy Birthday, Moon   *Mm*

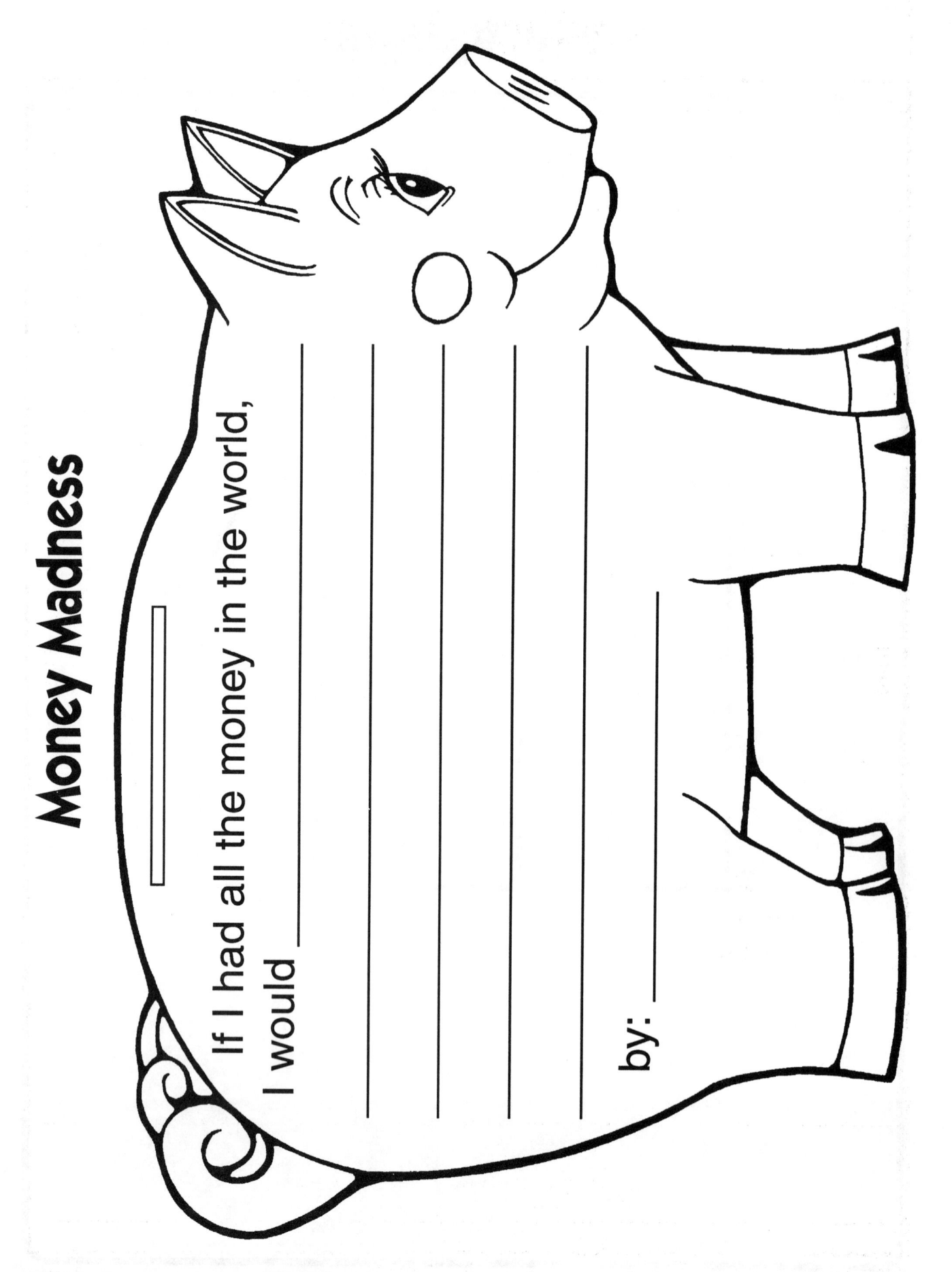

Money Madness

If I had all the money in the world, I would _____

by: _____

Mm *Happy Birthday, Moon*

Mailbox Pattern

Attach post here.

front

back

● Attach flag here.

glue

©1995 Teacher Created Materials, Inc.   153   #791 Teaching Basic Skills through Literature: Phonics

Phonics Skills in Context: Letter "N"

Book: *There's a Nightmare in My Closet*
Author: Mercer Mayer
Publisher: Dial, New York, 1968
Summary: This is a humorous bedtime story to chase away fears of the dark.
Recommended Grade Level: K–2
Related Poetry: "Wynken, Blynken, and Nod" by Eugene Field, *Poems for Young Children* (Doubleday, New York, 1986). For additional titles see page 385.

Skill Activity

Students create a closet which opens up to reveal an "n" word. Individual pages can be collated into a class "n" book, if desired.

Materials

- chart paper
- construction paper
- closet door pattern (page 157)
- crayons or markers
- glue
- scissors

Lesson

Introduce the Literature: Ask students to share a nightmare they have had. Ask students how they felt when they got scared. Show the cover of the book.

Read the Literature: Read the literature selection. Allow time for discussion.

Introduce the Skill Lesson:

1. Show the word "nightmare" in the title of the story. Ask children to listen for the "n" sound.
2. Brainstorm other "n" words and list them on chart paper to be displayed as a word bank.
3. Give each student construction paper and a closet door (page 157). Read the sentence on the door with the class.
4. Tell students they will color, cut, and paste the edge of the door onto the construction paper. Underneath the door they will write an "n" word and draw a picture of the word.

Learning Center Activity: Provide students with watercolor, paint brush, construction paper, and a small container of water. Ask students to use their imaginations to draw pictures of what they think the nightmare could have looked like. Then have students complete the activity sheet on page 158.

Cooperative Learning Activity: Have students work in cooperative groups to play the number game on page 159. Have students write the "n" words by substituting the correct letters from the code on page 160. Have students write their own names and other "n" words using the number code and trade words with the rest of the students in their group.

Across the Curriculum: Science

Develop a unit of study on nocturnal animals, nighttime community workers, and why we have night and day.

Nn　　　　　　　　　　　　　　　　　　　　　　　　　　There's a Nightmare in My Closet

Extension Activities

Movement Activities
Stress the letter "n" as students participate in the following movements: take a nap, jump nine times, wiggle your nose, hammer nails, be noisy, and crawl like a newt.

Multisensory Activity
On 6" x 8" (15 cm x 20 cm) tagboard, have students glue newspaper onto an upper and lowercase "n." Patterns are provided on pages 161 and 162.

Creative Writing
Have students write their names in fancy letters vertically on a sheet of paper. Challenge them to think of words that describe them that begin with each letter of their names.

Handwriting
On 12" x 18" (30 cm x 46 cm) lined newsprint, ask children to copy this sentence: "N is for nest, needle, noodles, and nine nickels (use coin stamps)."

Cooking

Nutty Bananas

Ingredients
- bananas
- chopped nuts
- peanut butter
- knife
- plates

Directions
1. Spread peanut butter on banana.
2. Roll in nuts.
3. Draw your recipe.
4. Clean up.

Interdisciplinary Topics

nature	newspaper	navy	numbers
nest	neighborhood	New Year's Day	nachos
Native American	nurse	nutrition	navy beans
nationalities	noise	nighttime	noodles
north	nylon	nectarines	newts
November	nicknames	nuts	

©1995 Teacher Created Materials, Inc.　　　155　　　#791 Teaching Basic Skills through Literature: Phonics

There's a Nightmare in My Closet Nn

Extension Activities *(cont.)*

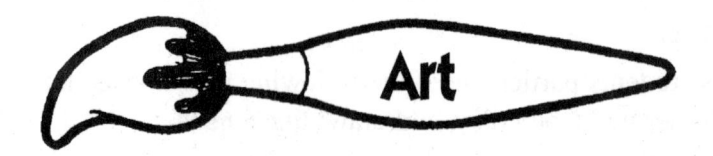

Art

Note Holder
Materials
- Styrofoam trays
- yarn
- needle
- construction paper
- glitter
- glue
- scissors

Process
1. Cut meat tray in half.
2. Place on bottom of another tray to form a pocket.
3. Lace yarn around trays to fasten. (If lacing is too difficult, they can be glued.)
4. Use glitter and glue to write "notes" on the bottom tray.

Nicky the Nut
Materials
- nut pattern (page 163)
- crayons or markers
- construction paper
- scissors
- paper strips
    2 strips per child 1" x 12" (3 cm x 30 cm)
    2 strips per child 1" x 24" (3 cm x 60 cm)
- yarn (optional)

Process
1. Draw or cut out facial features and paste on nut shape.
2. Accordion fold paper strips, attaching for arms and legs.
3. Children trace and cut out own hands and footprints, attaching to opposite ends.
4. Yarn can be added as shoelaces.

Nn

There's a Nightmare in My Closet

Closet Door Pattern

It's not a nightmare, it's only . . .

Fold back and glue onto construction paper.

There's a Nightmare in My Closet   Nn

Nightmare Book

If I saw a nightmare, I would _____

_____

_____

_____

_____

_____

_____.

by: _____

Nn

There's a Nightmare in My Closet

Number Game

Name _____

a	b	c	d	e	f	g	h	i	j	k	l	m	n
1	2	3	4	5	6	7	8	9	10	11	12	13	14

o	p	q	r	s	t	u	v	w	x	y	z
15	16	17	18	19	20	21	22	23	24	25	26

Can you decode the "n" words?

___ ___
14 15

___ ___ ___
14 15 20

___ ___ ___ ___
14 15 19 5

___ ___ ___ ___
14 1   9   12

___ ___ ___ ___
14 5   19 20

___ ___ ___
14 5   23

___ ___ ___ ___ ___
14 5   22 5   18

___ ___ ___ ___ ___ ___ ___ ___ ___
14 9   7   8   20 13 1   18 5

©1995 Teacher Created Materials, Inc.   159   #791 Teaching Basic Skills through Literature: Phonics

There's a Nightmare in My Closet   Nn

Number Game (cont.)

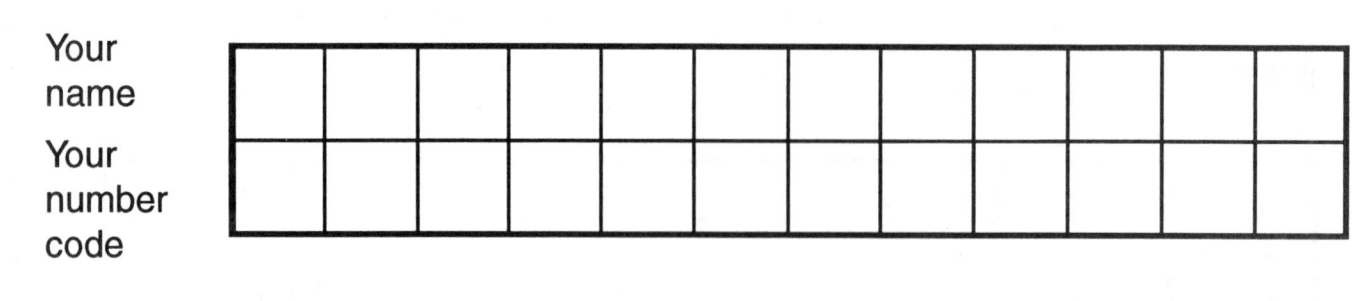

Your name

Your number code

a	b	c	d	e	f	g	h	i	j	k	l	m	n
1	2	3	4	5	6	7	8	9	10	11	12	13	14

o	p	q	r	s	t	u	v	w	x	y	z
15	16	17	18	19	20	21	22	23	24	25	26

Find your friends' number codes.

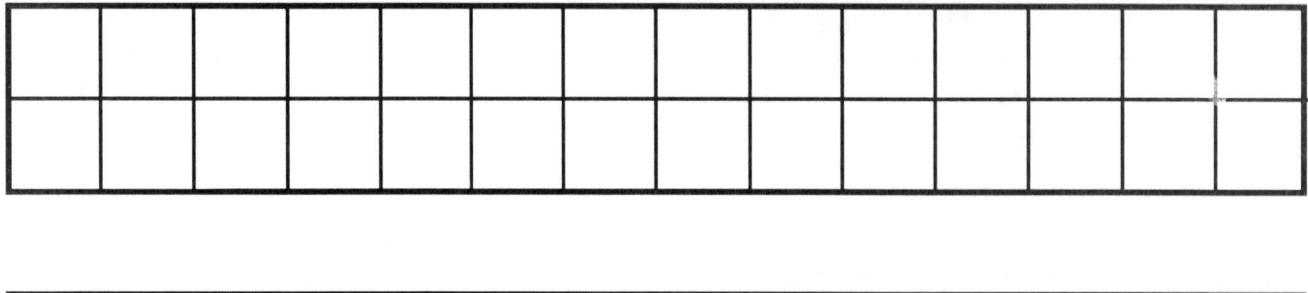

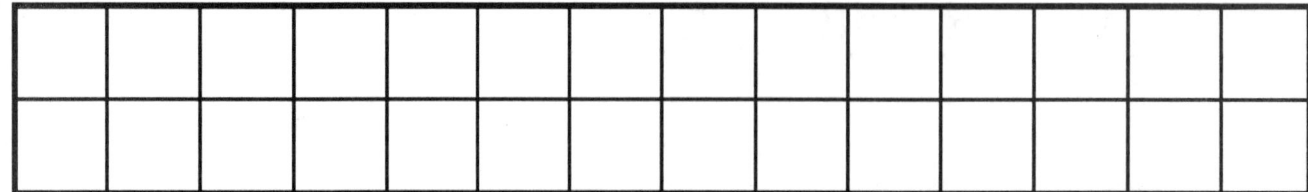

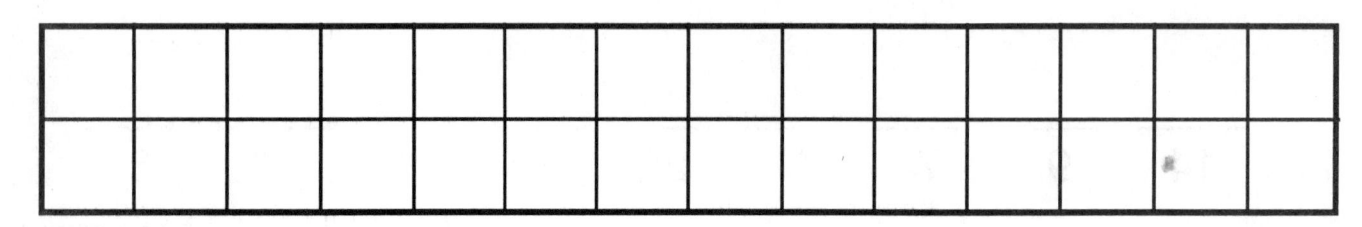

#791 Teaching Basic Skills through Literature: Phonics   160   ©1995 Teacher Created Materials, Inc.

Nn · *There's a Nightmare in My Closet*

"N" Pattern

There's a Nightmare in My Closet Nn

"n" Pattern

#791 Teaching Basic Skills through Literature: Phonics　　162　　©1995 Teacher Created Materials, Inc.

Nn

There's a Nightmare in My Closet

Nut Pattern

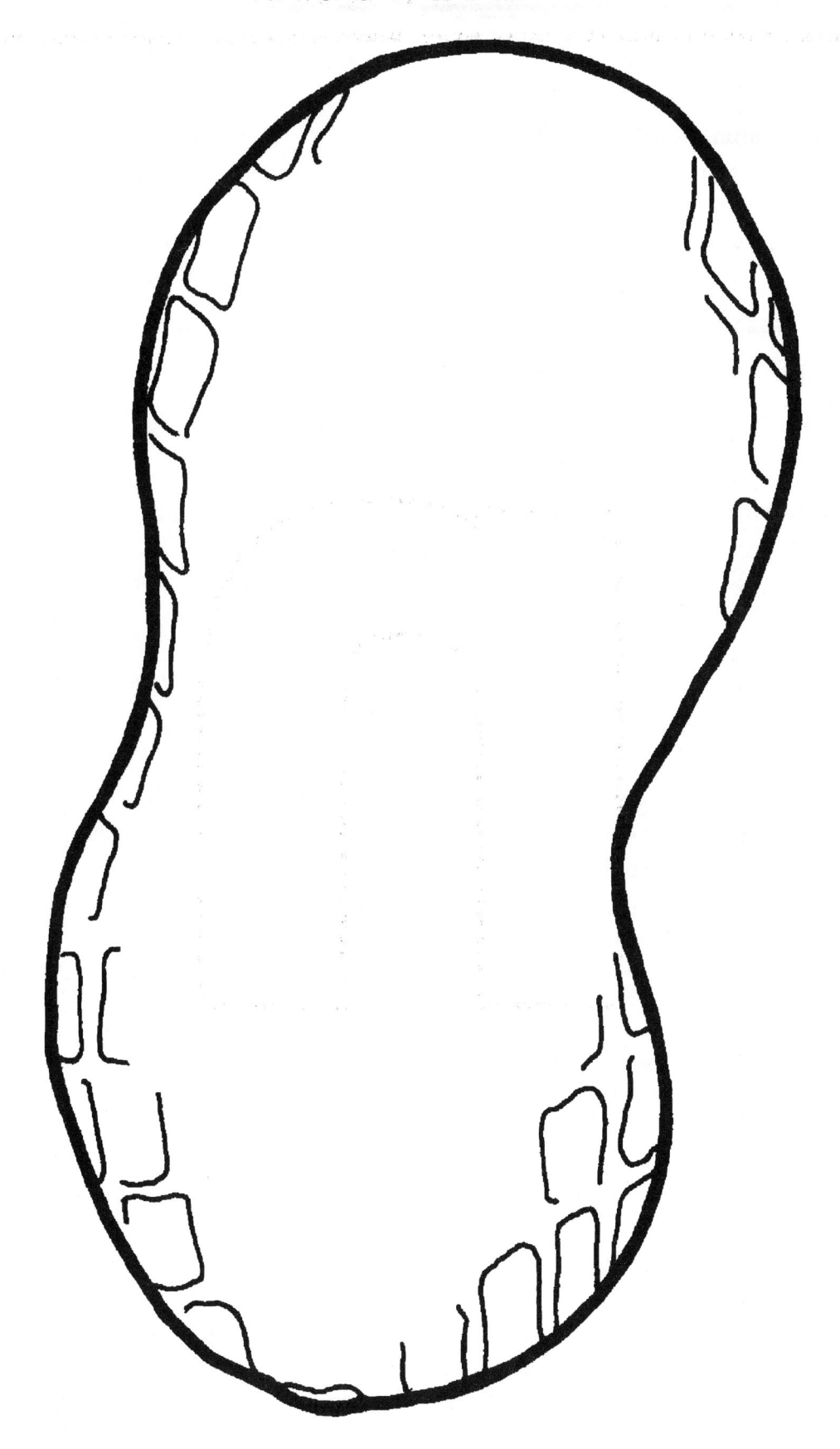

©1995 Teacher Created Materials, Inc. 163 #791 Teaching Basic Skills through Literature: Phonics

Phonics Skills in Context: Letter "P"

Book: *A Pocket for Corduroy*
Author: Don Freeman
Publisher: Puffin, New York, 1978
Summary: A toy bear has adventures as he searches for a pocket of his very own.
Recommended Grade Level: K–1
Related Poetry: "Penguin" by Mary Ann Hoberman, *Yellow Butter, Purple Jelly, Red Jam, Black Bread* (Viking, New York, 1981). For additional titles see page 385.

Skill Activity

Students create a little pocket to hold their "p" words and drawings.

Materials

- pocket pattern (page 167)
- crayons or markers
- construction paper
- 3" x 5" (8 cm x 13 cm) index cards
- pencil
- chart paper
- scissors

Lesson

Introduce the Literature: Show students the cover of the book and ask if anyone can identify the bear.

Read the Literature: Read the literature selection. Allow time for discussion.

Introduce the Skill Lesson:

1. Read the book again and ask students to listen for the "p" words such as pocket.
2. Make a list of the "p" words on chart paper and display them in the room as a word bank.
3. Make pockets out of construction paper using the pattern on page 167. Provide each student with several index cards, crayons or markers, and a pencil.
4. Ask students to write "p" words and illustrate them on the cards. Store all words in the students' pockets.

Learning Center Activity: Students will make pop-up cards for their families. Leave the instructions for how to make the card (page 168) at the learning center. Have students write messages to their families and seal the messages in their envelopes.

Cooperative Learning Activity: Have students work in small groups to count their pockets from the skill lesson and write an addition problem to show how many pockets are in their group.

Across the Curriculum: Math

Have students create paper chain patterns. Provide students with a 1" x 6" (3 cm x 15 cm) strips of colored construction paper and glue. Show them how to link the strips together to make a chain. Encourage them to create patterns with their paper chains.

Pp   A Pocket for Corduroy

Extension Activities

Movement Activities
Stress the letter "p" as students participate in each of the following movements: pitch pennies, do pull-ups, pat your head and stomach, pop like popcorn, and point.

Multisensory Activity
On 6" x 8" (15 cm x 20 cm) tagboard, have children paste curled paper onto an upper and lowercase "p." Patterns are provided on pages 169 and 170.

Creative Writing
Have students make an "All About Me" poster. Divide a piece of tagboard into four sections. Have students choose a topic that tells about them for each of the sections. Decorate each section with words, pictures, or magazine cutouts. Or, students can be given the activity sheets on pages 171 through 174 to paste onto their posters.

Handwriting
On 12" x 18" (30 cm x 46 cm) lined newsprint, ask children to copy this sentence: "P is for panda, pepper (sprinkle pepper onto glue), pickles, and precious puppy."

Cooking

Pita Pocket Sandwiches

Ingredients
- pita bread
- mayonnaise
- cheese
- knife
- grater

Directions
1. Cut pita bread in half.
2. Spread mayonnaise inside pita bread.
3. Stuff with grated cheese.
4. Draw your recipe.
5. Clean up.

Interdisciplinary Topics

panda	pig	pony	pumpkin
parrot	porcupine	poodle	Pacific Ocean
penguin	porpoise	plant	people
peacock	pigeon	pussy willow	pilgrim

A Pocket for Corduroy   **Pp**

Extension Activities *(cont.)*

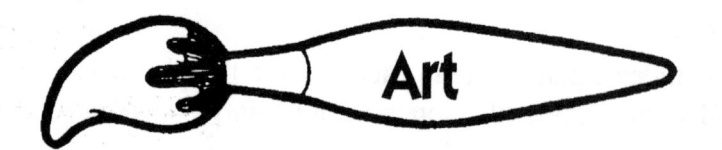

Art

Panda
Materials
- black paint
- three sectioned paper plates
- glue
- black and white construction paper
- scissors
- black marker

Process
1. Paint two smaller sections of plate black.
2. While drying, cut out two black ears and a black nose. Also cut two smaller white circles for eyes.
3. When paint is dry attach eyes, ears, and nose. Draw mouth lines.

Piggy Privacy Sign
Materials
- sign pattern (page 175)
- construction paper
- markers or crayons
- paste

Process
1. Cut out sign pattern, including center section.
2. Make eyes by either drawing with markers or cutting from scrap paper.
3. Add a small sign at bottom with child's name to identify his or her room.

Porcupine
Materials
- clay (2 colors)
- colored toothpicks

Process
1. Form clay into two ball shapes, one smaller than the other.
2. Add different color clay as eyes.
3. Join the balls and insert toothpicks as quills.

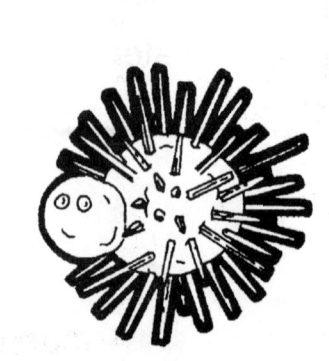

Pp *A Pocket for Corduroy*

Pocket Pattern

Top Section

Use as patterns.

Glue top section around sides and bottom, leaving top portion open.

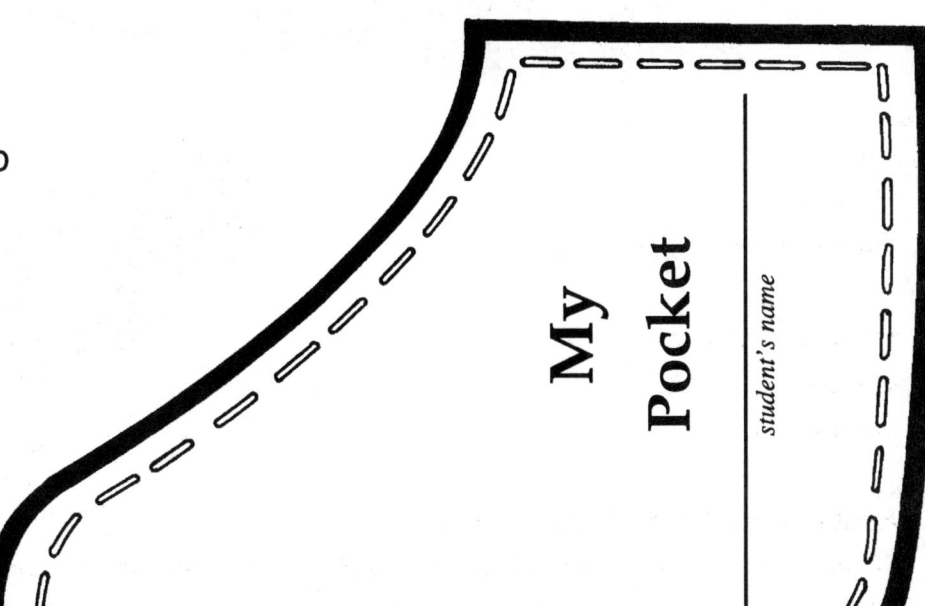

My Pocket
student's name

Bottom Section

Glue top section of pocket to bottom section, matching curves and edges.

Glue top of pocket here.

A Pocket for Corduroy Pp

Pop-Up Card

How to Make a Pop-Up Card

Materials

- two pieces of 9" x 12" (23 cm x 30 cm) white construction paper
- glue
- crayons, colored pencils, or markers
- scissors

Directions

1. Fold a piece of paper in half and cut a slit on the fold 3" (8 cm) in from each edge. Make slits about 2" (5 cm) long.

2. Open the fold, push it through, and crease it to form a pop-up section. (See picture.)

3. Fold the second piece of paper in half and glue it to the back of the card as shown.

4. Color and cut out a picture. Glue it on the pop-up section.

5. Write a message on the inside of the card. You may decorate the cover if you wish.

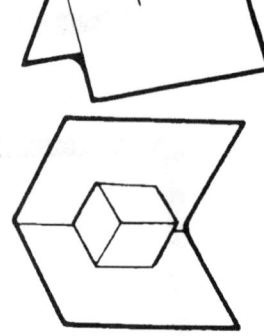

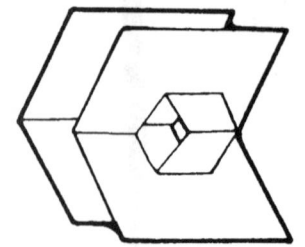

Pp A Pocket for Corduroy

"P" Pattern

A Pocket for Corduroy   Pp

"p" Pattern

Pp   *A Pocket for Corduroy*

Poster Page

When I grow up I will be . . .

_____

_____

_____

_____

picture of me

©1995 Teacher Created Materials, Inc.   #791 Teaching Basic Skills through Literature: Phonics

A Pocket for Corduroy Pp

Poster Page (cont.)

My Family

Attach picture here.

#791 Teaching Basic Skills through Literature: Phonics   172   ©1995 Teacher Created Materials, Inc.

Pp   *A Pocket for Corduroy*

Poster Page (cont.)

My Stats

Height _____

Age _____

Eye color _____

Hair color _____

My favorite food

_____

_____

©1995 Teacher Created Materials, Inc.   173   #791 Teaching Basic Skills through Literature: Phonics

A Pocket for Corduroy Pp

Poster Page (cont.)

Things to do with Friends

Pp *A Pocket for Corduroy*

Sign Pattern

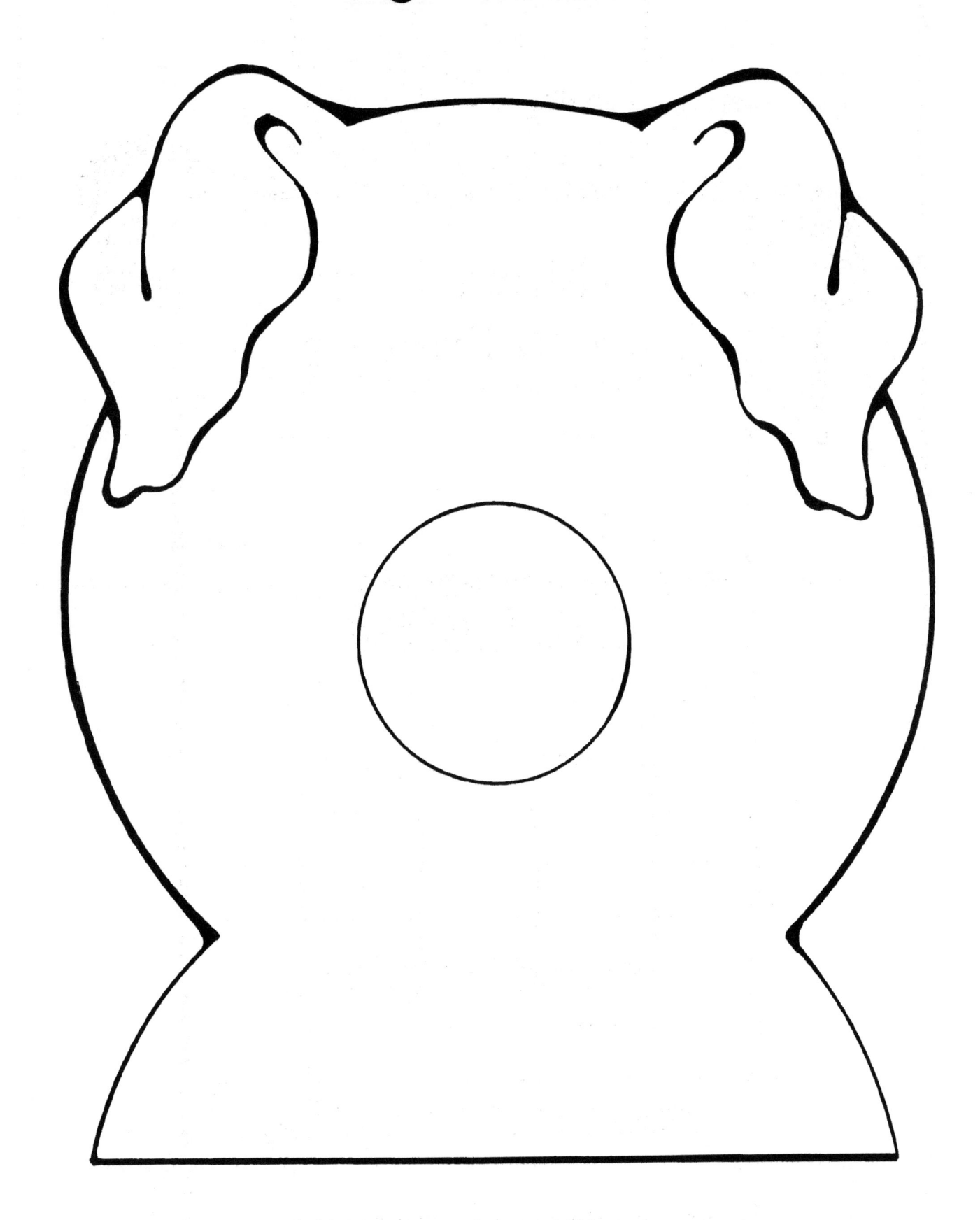

Phonics Skills in Context: Letter "Q"

Book: *Quick as a Cricket*
Author: Audrey Wood
Publisher: Child's Play, New York, 1989
Summary: A small child compares himself to all his favorite animals.
Recommended Grade Level: K–1
Related Poetry: "Question" by Mary Ann Hoberman, *Yellow Butter, Purple Jelly, Red Jam, Black Bread* (Viking, New York, 1981). For additional titles see page 386.

Skill Activity

Students will make pages for a class book titled "The Quick Book."

Materials

- book pages (page 179)
- pencil
- crayon or markers
- chart paper

Lesson

Introduce the Literature: Show students the cover of the book. Ask them to predict what it might be about.

Read the Literature: Read the Literature selection. Allow time for discussion.

Introduce the Skill Lesson:

1. Point out the "q" in the title of the story. Ask students to brainstorm other "q" words.
2. Write the "q" words on chart paper to use as a word bank.
3. Ask students to name things that are quick. Ask each student to complete the sentences on page 179. Have them add illustrations to the pages.
4. Collate pages into a class book.
5. Students can also write books about things that are quiet, using page 180.

Learning Center Activity: Students make a question board by drawing pictures of three "q" words and one non-"q" word in the boxes on page 181. Students then color and cut out the question doors on page 182 and glue the folded edges on top of their drawings. When the glue has dried, students ask their friends to guess which door has a "q" word behind it.

Cooperative Learning Activity: Make a class quilt by allowing students to make paper quilt squares. All squares can be tied together using yarn to form a large quilt.

Across the Curriculum: Physical Education

Play "How quick are you?" with the class. Using a stopwatch, students time themselves doing various movement activities such as running, hopping, jumping rope, skipping, etc. Have students compete against themselves by trying to beat their previous times. Students can record their times on the activity on page 183.

Qq   *Quick as a Cricket*

Extension Activities

Movement Activities

Stress the letter "q" as students participate in the following movements: quick walk, quiet walk, run like a quail, quiver, act like a queen, and quack like a duck.

Multisensory Activity

On 6" x 8" (15 cm x 20 cm) tagboard, have students glue cotton swabs onto an upper and lowercase "q." Patterns are provided on pages 184 and 185.

Creative Writing

Have students make a list of things that are quick. Then, they can be challenged to put them in order from least quick to quickest.

Handwriting

On 12" x 18" (30 cm x 46 cm) lined newsprint, ask children to copy this sentence: "Q is for queen, quilt, quills (glue on quills), and quacking quackers."

Cooking

Quarter Backs

Ingredients
- cheese
- crackers
- knife

Directions
1. Cut your cheese into quarters.
2. Put each quarter piece on a cracker.
3. Draw your recipe.
4. Clean up.

Interdisciplinary Topics

quails	quintuplets	quarts	quicksand
queen bees	quadruplets	quill	quarry
Quakers	quilts	quarrels	quiche
queens	quarters		

©1995 Teacher Created Materials, Inc.   177   #791 Teaching Basic Skills through Literature: Phonics

Quick as a Cricket

Qq

Extension Activities (cont.)

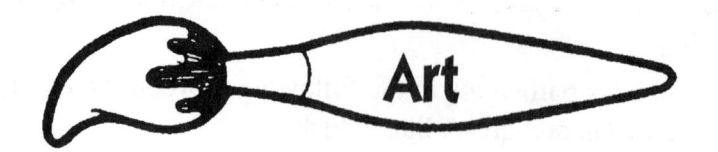

Art

Quail
Materials
- quail pattern (page 186)
- gray and blue construction paper
- glue
- scissors
- pipe cleaners cut into three sections
- crayons or markers

Process
1. Cut out quail pattern on gray paper.
2. Color eyes and beak.
3. Tear little pieces of blue paper and glue on as wings.
4. Curl pipe cleaner and attach to back of head.
5. Add pipe cleaner legs.

Quintuplets
Materials
- buggy pattern (page 187)
- blue and pink construction paper
- markers or crayons
- scissors
- macaroni pin wheels (optional)

Process
1. Trace and cut five buggy patterns.
2. Paste onto larger paper.
3. Wheels can be made from macaroni instead of paper.

Q-tip® Painting
Materials
- Q-tips®
- coffee filters
- paint
- pipe cleaners

Process
1. Children twist middle of coffee filter to make butterfly wings.
2. Secure wings with pipe cleaner and form antennae.
3. Dip Q-tip® into paint and dab on wings.

Qq "Quick as a Cricket"

"Quick" Book Pages

I am as quick as a_____.

I am as quick as a_____.

Quick as a Cricket

Qq

"Quiet" Book Pages

I am as quiet as a_____.

I am as quiet as a_____.

Qq Quick as a Cricket

Question Board

Quick as a Cricket Qq

Question Board *(cont.)*

Cut out the boxes. Fold them under as shown. Then, glue each folded section to the top of a box on page 181.

fold under	fold under
?	?

fold under	fold under
?	?

Qq   *Quick as a Cricket*

How Quick Are You?

Name _____

Event	1st try	2nd try	3rd try
_____	_____	_____	_____
_____	_____	_____	_____
_____	_____	_____	_____
_____	_____	_____	_____
_____	_____	_____	_____

Quick as a Cricket   Qq

"Q" Pattern

#791 Teaching Basic Skills through Literature: Phonics   184   ©1995 Teacher Created Materials, Inc.

Qq   *Quick as a Cricket*

"q" Pattern

Quick as a Cricket *Qq*

Quail Pattern

Qq   *Quick as a Cricket*

Buggy Pattern

buggy

handle   wheels

©1995 Teacher Created Materials, Inc.   #791 Teaching Basic Skills through Literature: Phonics

Phonics Skills in Context: Letter "R"

Book: *A Rainbow of My Own*
Author: Don Freeman
Publisher: Puffin, New York, 1966
Summary: A little boy discovers many things as he pretends and plays with rainbows.
Recommended Grade Level: K–1
Related Poetry: "It's Raining, It's Pouring" by Arnold Lobel, *The Random House Book of Mother Goose* (Random House, New York, 1986). For additional titles see page 386.

Skill Activity

Students make up riddles to use as clues for guessing "r" words.

Materials

- chart paper

Lesson

Introduce the Literature: Tell students "I have a riddle for you. If you can answer the riddle you will know what our story is about. It is something that begins with the letter 'r.' It is something you can see but you cannot touch. Sometimes you see it, sometimes you don't. It has many colors. What is it?" (Answer: a rainbow.)

Read the Literature: Read the literature selection. Allow time for discussion.

Introduce the Skill Lesson:

1. Brainstorm words that begin like rainbow. Add the words to the chart paper and display as a word bank.
2. Students can take turns making up riddles about the words.
3. Others in the group try to guess the answers.

Learning Center Activity: Play "Race Around the Rainbow" game. Give each student a blank gameboard (page 191) to color and picture cards to cut out (page 192). The game is played by stacking the cards face down in a pile. The students take turns flipping over a card and stating whether the picture begins with the letter "r." If a picture does, the player may roll a die and move a small marker the indicated number of spaces. The first one to get to the finish line is the winner.

Cooperative Learning Activity: Make a rainbow mural. Divide the class into five groups and assign each a color of the rainbow (orange, yellow, green, blue, and purple). Each group makes a print by dipping or painting their hands in their rainbow color. The handprints are arranged in the shape of a rainbow.

Across the Curriculum: Science

Allow students to experiment with prisms to make rainbows.

Rr   *A Rainbow of My Own*

Extension Activities

Movement Activities
Stress the letter "r" as students participate in the following movements: hop like a rabbit, raise their right hands, rest, run, row a boat, reach high, relax, and play "Red Rover."

Multisensory Activity
On 6" x 8" (15 cm x 20 cm) tagboard, have children paste red rectangles onto an upper and lowercase "r." Patterns are provided on pages 193 and 194.

Creative Writing
Have students use page 195 to write what they might find at the end of a rainbow instead of a pot of gold.

Handwriting
On 12" x 18" (30 cm x 46 cm) lined newsprint, ask children to copy this sentence: "R is for rainbow (design with markers), rabbit, rocking horse, and roaring rocket."

Cooking

Rocket Ships

Ingredients
- bananas
- cottage cheese
- pineapple slices
- plates
- knife
- fork

Directions
1. Put banana on plate.
2. Spread cottage cheese below banana for "flames."
3. Cut pineapple slice in half for rocket.
4. Draw your recipe.
5. Clean up.

Interdisciplinary Topics

reptiles	redwood	raft	reported
reindeer	rainbow	river	raisin
raccoon	rose	railroad	rice
rabbit	rock	responsibility	rhubarb
rattlesnake	rocket	rule	raspberry
robin	robot	relatives	radish
rat	radio		

©1995 Teacher Created Materials, Inc.   189   #791 *Teaching Basic Skills through Literature: Phonics*

A Rainbow of My Own   **Rr**

Extension Activities *(cont.)*

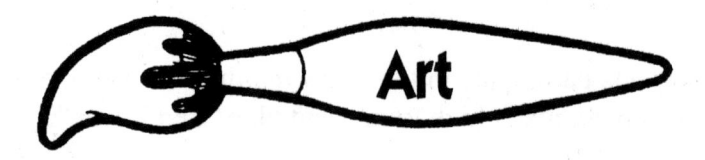

Art

Rainbow Hot Air Balloon
Materials
- tagboard
- baking cup
- hole punch
- watercolors
- crayons or markers
- yarn
- scissors

Process
1. Draw balloon shape on tagboard.
2. Draw a rainbow on the balloon shape.
3. When dry, cut out and attach with yarn to baking cup.
4. Draw and cut out a person to put inside the cup.

It's Raining
Materials
- blue and white construction paper
- paste
- crayons or markers
- scissors

Process
1. Trace and cut out handprint from blue and white paper.
2. Tear the fingers from the palm of hand to form raindrops.
3. Paste onto other paper.
4. Draw a rain scene.

Rocking Horse
Materials
- large paper plates
- scissors
- yarn
- glue
- horse head pattern (page 196)
- construction paper
- crayons or markers

Process
1. Add details to both sides of the horse head, color and cut out. Color other side.
2. Fold paper plate. Slit one end to fit head and attach.
3. Make a saddle. Color both sides and paste on back of horse.
4. Glue yarn in back for tail.

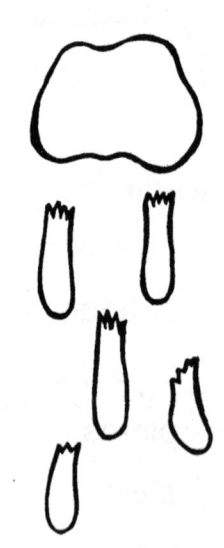

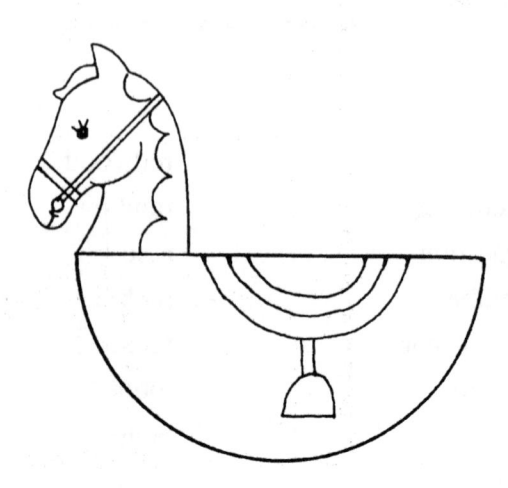

Rr

A Rainbow of My Own

Race Around the Rainbow

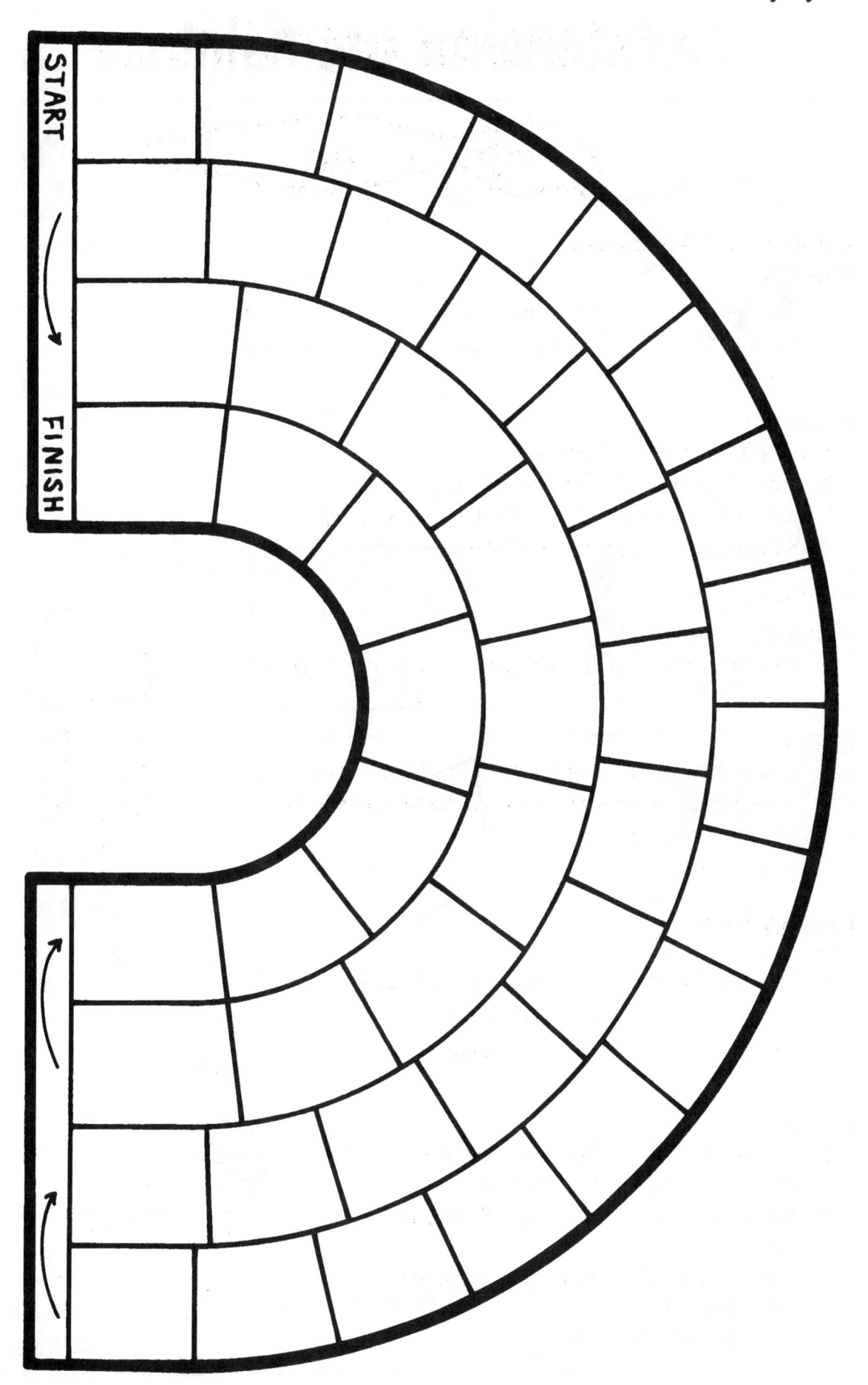

START

FINISH

©1995 Teacher Created Materials, Inc. 191 #791 Teaching Basic Skills through Literature: Phonics

A Rainbow of My Own   Rr

Race Around the Rainbow (cont.)

#791 Teaching Basic Skills through Literature: Phonics   192   ©1995 Teacher Created Materials, Inc.

Rr   *A Rainbow of My Own*

"R" Pattern

A Rainbow of My Own Rr

"r" Pattern

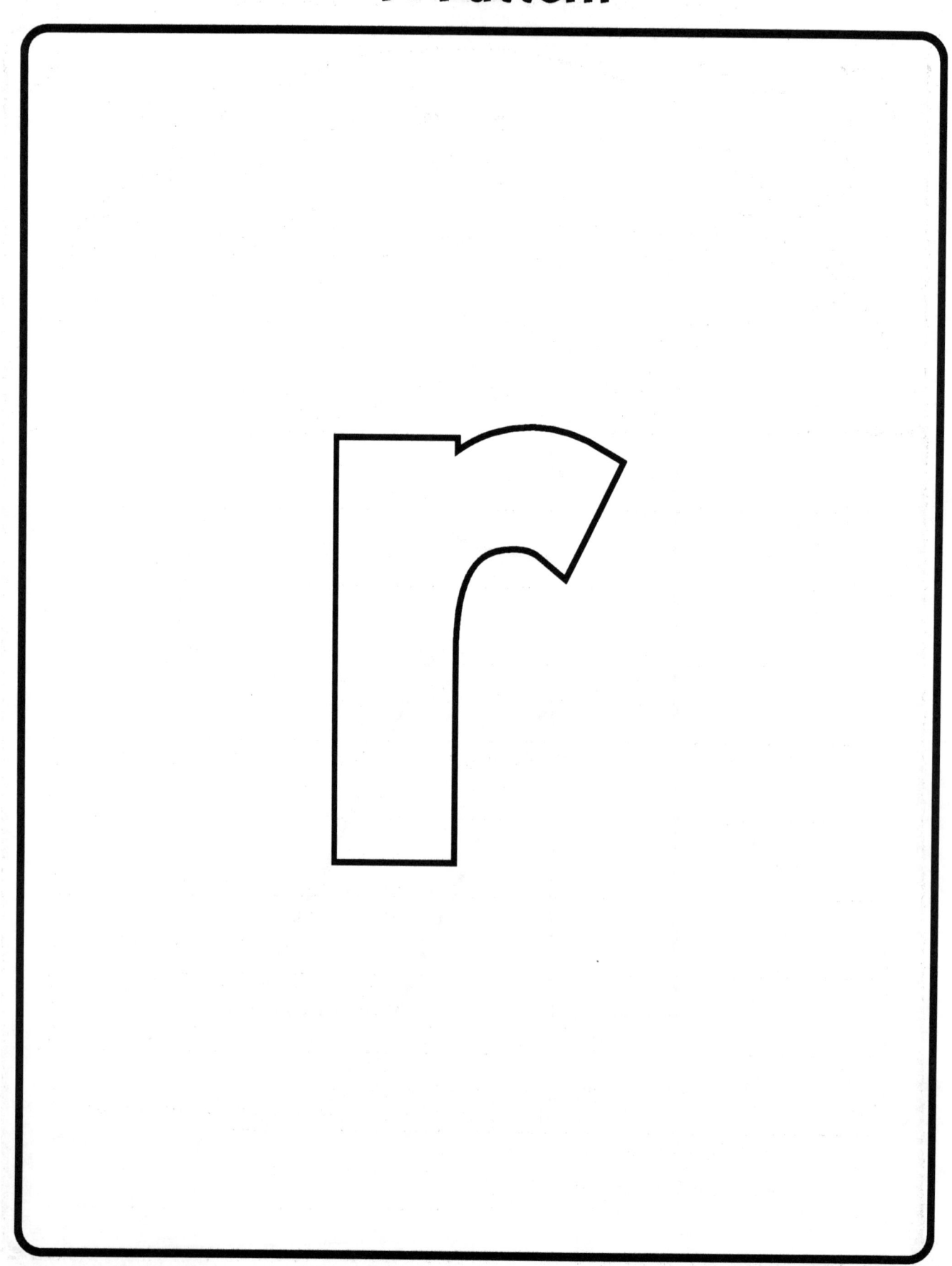

#791 Teaching Basic Skills through Literature: Phonics 194 ©1995 Teacher Created Materials, Inc.

Rr *A Rainbow of My Own*

The End of the Rainbow

by: _____

©1995 Teacher Created Materials, Inc. #791 Teaching Basic Skills through Literature: Phonics

A Rainbow of My Own   *Rr*

Rocking Horse Pattern

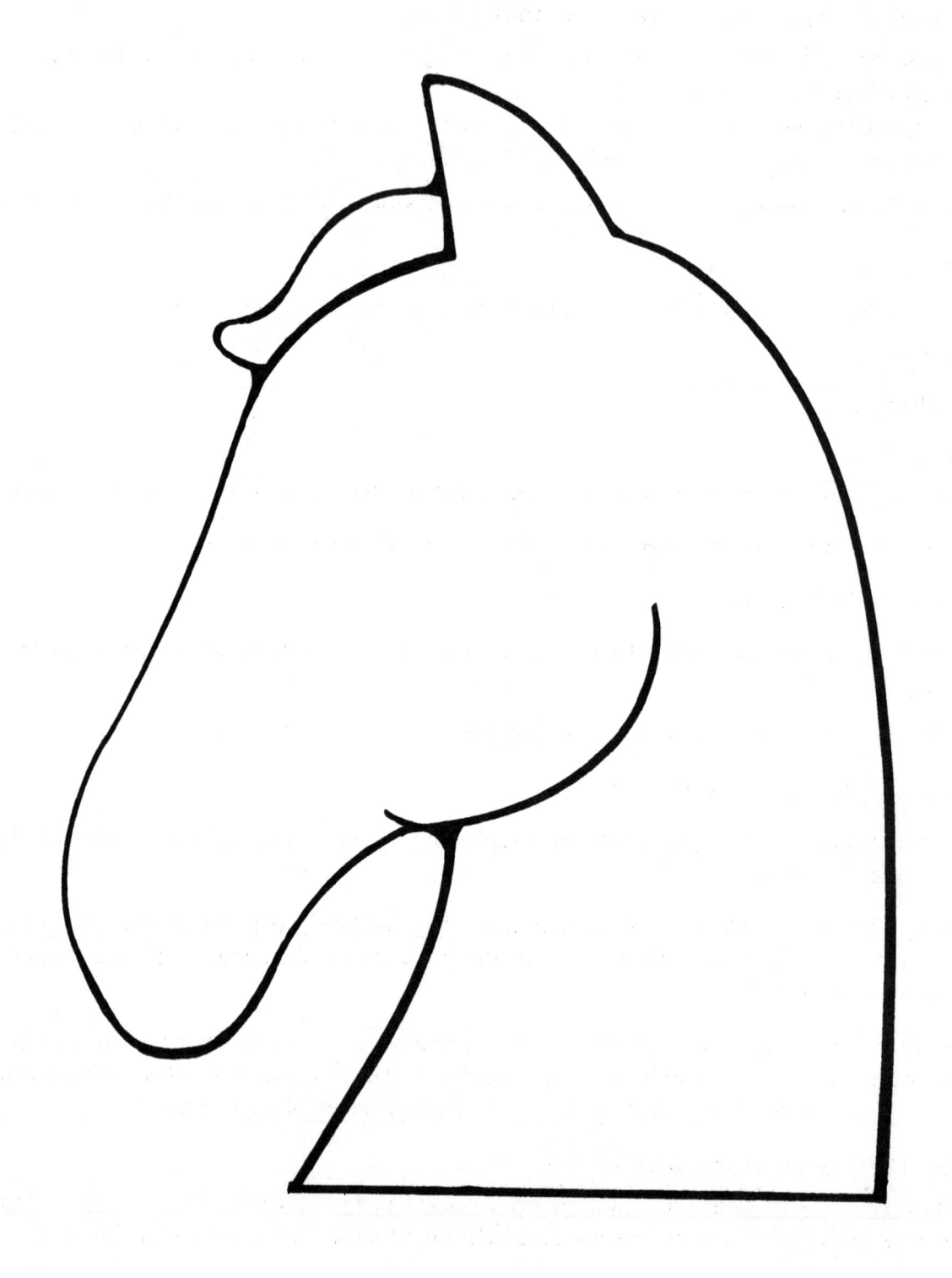

Phonics Skills in Context: Letter "S"

Book: *Six Sleepy Sheep*
Author: Jeffie Ross Gordon
Publisher: Trumpet Club, New York, 1991
Summary: This is a countdown book about six sheep and their attempts to fall asleep.
Recommended Grade Level: K–1
Related Poetry: "Silly Sleep Sheep" by Helen C. Smith, *Poetry Works* (Modern Curriculum Press, New York, 1990). For additional titles see page 386.

Skill Activity

Students identify "s" words by snapping their fingers as they listen to the story.

Materials

- chart paper

Lesson

Introduce the Literature: Show students the cover and ask them to predict what the story is about.

Read the Literature: Read the literature selection. Allow time for discussion.

Introduce the Skill Lesson:

1. Reread the story slowly and have students snap their fingers every time they hear a word that begins with "s."
2. Make a list of the "s" words on the chart paper.
3. Display the list as a word bank.
4. Read another "s" book from the bibliography on page 392. Ask students to snap each time they hear an "s" word.

Learning Center Activity: Provide students with white and black construction paper, crayons, glue, and cotton to make their own individual "Silly Sheep." They can then write an idea to finish the sentence box on page 200.

Cooperative Learning: Have students work in cooperative groups of six. Each member of the group decides which sheep he/she will be in a dramatization of the story. Have students wear sheep masks for the activity. A pattern can be found on page 201. (Enlarge pattern if necessary.)

Across the Curriculum: Math

Use the small sheep patterns (page 202) to create a flannel story in which students record subtraction problems as the story *Six Sleepy Sheep* is read. Or, students can sequence the sheep by size.

Six Sleepy Sheep Ss

Extension Activities

Movement Activities
Stress the letter "s" as students participate in the following movements: playing "Simon Says", skipping, swinging, squeezing, sliding, stretching, splashing, smiling, sneezing, and making shadows.

Multisensory Activity
On 6" x 8" (15 cm x 20 cm) tagboard, have students glue sand onto an upper and lowercase "s." Patterns are provided on pages 203 and 204.

Creative Writing
Have students write a soaring soccer simile by completing this sentence: "I kicked my soccer ball as high as ..." A cover pattern and prompt are located on page 205.

Handwriting
On 12" x 18" (30 cm x 46 cm) lined newsprint, ask children to copy this sentence: "S is for seal, snowman (make a paper snowman), sun, and six slithering snakes."

Cooking

Snowballs

Ingredients
- peach halves
- cottage cheese
- knife
- fork
- plates

Directions
1. Put peach half on plate.
2. Use a knife to spread cottage cheese on peach.
3. Draw your recipe.
4. Clean up.

Interdisciplinary Topics

spider	seasons	sun	soup
snake	solar system	senses	stew
sea life	snow	safety	strawberries
seal	stars	soccer	squash
swamp life	space	sandwich	spinach

Extension Activities (cont.)

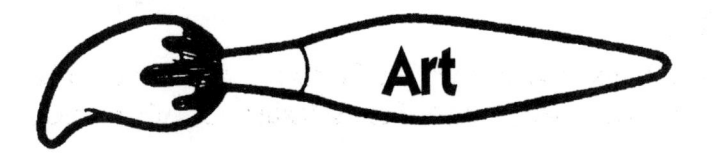

Art

Sailboat
Materials
- Styrofoam meat tray
- toothpicks
- scissors
- markers

Process
1. Cut two triangular shapes from the tray.
2. Use toothpick to attach sail to boat.
3. Decorate if desired.

Spider
Materials
- black paint
- construction paper
- string
- paper bowls
- scissors
- glue

Process
1. Paint two bowls black.
2. When dry, poke a hole into the middle of one bowl and attach string.
3. Curl eight paper strips around pencil and glue to edge of other bowl.
4. Glue bowls together at brims.
5. Cut out and glue eyes.

Spray Scenes
Materials
- many colors of crepe paper
- construction paper
- spray bottle
- water

Process
1. Spray a small amount of water on construction paper.
2. Tear very small pieces of crepe paper.
3. Place crepe paper pieces on construction paper, completely covering it.
4. Spray more water so crepe will bleed into paper.
5. Allow to dry thoroughly.

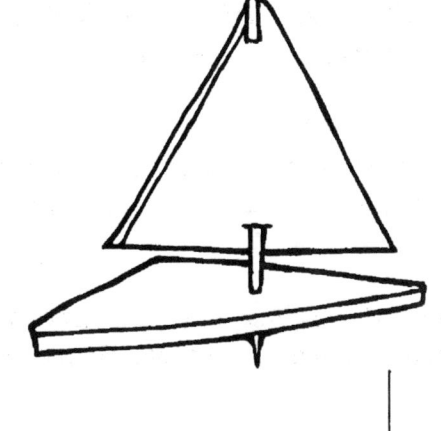

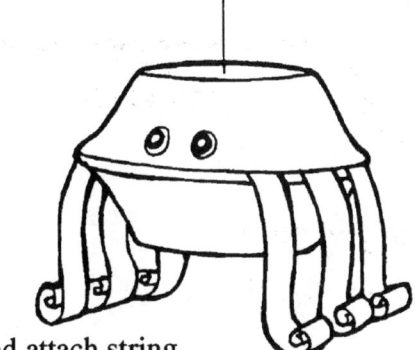

Six Sleepy Sheep Ss

"Silly Sheep" Pattern

My sheep is so silly

#791 Teaching Basic Skills through Literature: Phonics ©1995 Teacher Created Materials, Inc.

Ss *Six Sleepy Sheep*

Mask Pattern

©1995 Teacher Created Materials, Inc. 201 #791 *Teaching Basic Skills through Literature: Phonics*

Six Sleepy Sheep   Ss

Sheep

Ss *Six Sleepy Sheep*

"S" Pattern

©1995 Teacher Created Materials, Inc. 203 #791 *Teaching Basic Skills through Literature: Phonics*

Six Sleepy Sheep   *Ss*

"s" Pattern

#791 Teaching Basic Skills through Literature: Phonics   ©1995 Teacher Created Materials, Inc.

Ss   *Six Sleepy Sheep*

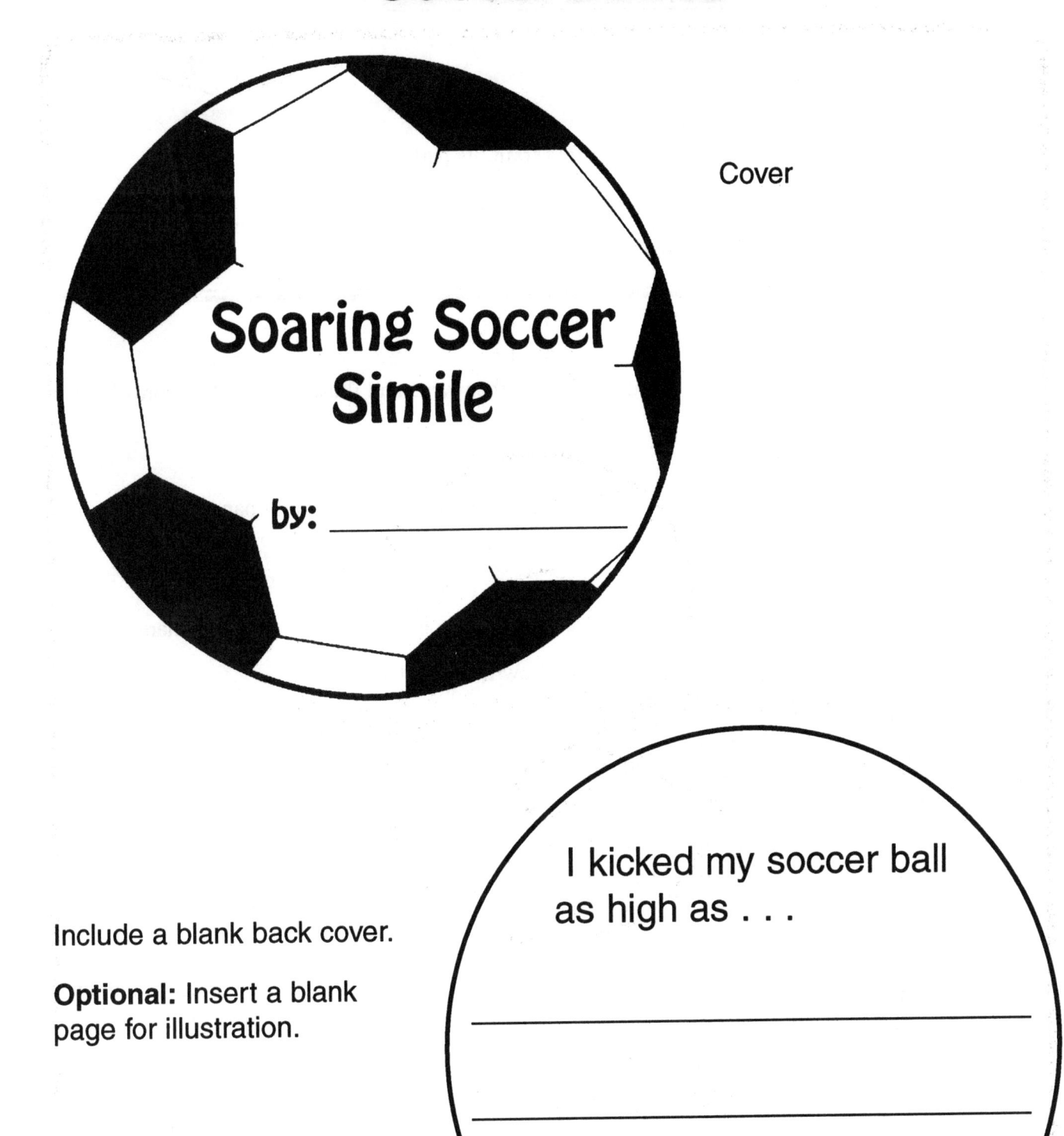

Soccer Simile

Cover

Soaring Soccer Simile

by: _____

Include a blank back cover.

Optional: Insert a blank page for illustration.

I kicked my soccer ball as high as . . .

_____

_____

_____

Phonics Skills in Context: Letter "T"

Book: *Freight Train*
Author: Donald Crews
Publisher: Scholastic, New York, 1989
Summary: This is a simple story of the freight train, its part, and its destination.
Recommended Grade Level: K–1
Related Poetry: "Engine on the Track" by Liz Cromwell, *Finger Frolics* (Partner Press, New York, 1976). For additional titles see page 386.

Skill Activity

Students form a train as they name "t" words. Students then write and illustrate their "t" words in their tent shape books.

Materials

- tent book cover (page 209)
- tent book page (page 210)
- writing paper
- chart paper
- scissors

Lesson

Introduce the Literature: Ask students if they have ever ridden on a train. Allow time to share.

Read the Literature: Read the literature selection. Allow time for discussion.

Introduce the Skill Lesson:

1. Reread the book and ask students to identify the "t" words.
2. Write the "t" words on the chart paper and display for use as a word bank.
3. Have each student name a "t" word and line up to form a train. "Chug" around the room.
4. Have students make their own tent books by writing and illustrating several "t" words on tent book pages. (Reproduce copies of page 210.) A cover pattern can be found on page 209.

Learning Center Activity: Students make a train using patterning. Provide the students with the patterns on pages 211 and 212. Have them cut out patterns and make a number train or color train by adding numbers or colors to each car and gluing the cars in the correct order on a piece of construction paper. Trains can also be used to retell the story.

Cooperative Learning Activity: Have students work together to make milk carton trains. Students decorate the cartons and attach cars together with pipe cleaners. If desired, group stories can be written about the trains.

Across the Curriculum: Social Studies

Develop a unit of study on several modes of transportation. Arrange a field trip for students to actually ride a train, trolley, or other mass transit.

Tt *Freight Train*

Extension Activities

Movement Activities

Stress the letter "t" as students participate in the following movements: turtle walk, tag, walk tall, walk on tiptoes, tie your shoes, touch your toes, and tumble.

Multisensory Activity

On 6" x 8" (15 cm x 20 cm) tagboard, have children paste toothpicks onto an upper and lowercase "t." Patterns are provided on pages 213 and 214.

Creative Writing

Have students write a telephone conversation onto a piece of paper. Use the cover on page 215 to make a telephone book.

Handwriting

On 12" x 18" (30 cm x 46 cm) lined newsprint, ask children to copy this sentence: "T is for tadpoles, tent, turtle, and two tall teepees" (make from toothpicks).

Cooking

Tuna Telescopes

Ingredients
- slices of bread without crust
- tuna
- mayonnaise
- knife
- spoons
- plates
- tablespoons

Directions
1. Mix 1 tablespoon (15 mL) of mayonnaise with 2 tablespoons (30 mL) of tuna.
2. Spread tuna mixture on a slice of bread.
3. Roll bread up like a telescope.
4. Draw your recipe.
5. Clean up.

Interdisciplinary Topics

turtle	tulips	town	time
tiger	teepee	teacher	Thanksgiving
teddy bear	truck	telephone	teeth
turkey	tractor	telescope	tangerine
tarantula	taxicab	television	turnip
tadpoles	train	temperature	tuna
trees	trolley		

©1995 Teacher Created Materials, Inc.

Freight Train   Tt

Extension Activities (cont.)

Art

Team Work Turtle
Materials
- turtle pattern (page 216)
- construction paper scraps
- crayons or markers
- glue
- scissors

Process
1. Children work in teams to tear and glue paper to a turtle pattern. Add facial features and color.

Television
Materials
- cardboard box
- markers
- aluminum foil
- construction paper
- two plastic drinking staws
- tape
- scissors

Process
1. Cut out a small square shape to be the screen and glue onto one side of box.
2. Draw in controls.
3. Roll each straw in aluminum foil. Attach straws at one end to form a "V" shaped antenna. Tape on the back of the television.

Treehouse
Materials
- construction paper
- craft sticks
- crayons or paint
- glue

Process
1. Draw or paint a tree, putting a box-shaped treehouse in branches.
2. Glue craft sticks to two long pieces of construction paper to form a ladder.

Totem Pole
Materials
- 4 Styrofoam cups per student
- glue
- construction paper
- scissors
- crayons or markers

Process
1. Glue cups together as illustrated.
2. Cut out totem pole features from construction paper and glue to cups.

Tt *Freight Train*

Tent Book Cover

My "T" Book

by: _____

©1995 Teacher Created Materials, Inc. 209 #791 *Teaching Basic Skills through Literature: Phonics*

Freight Train   *Tt*

Tent Book Page

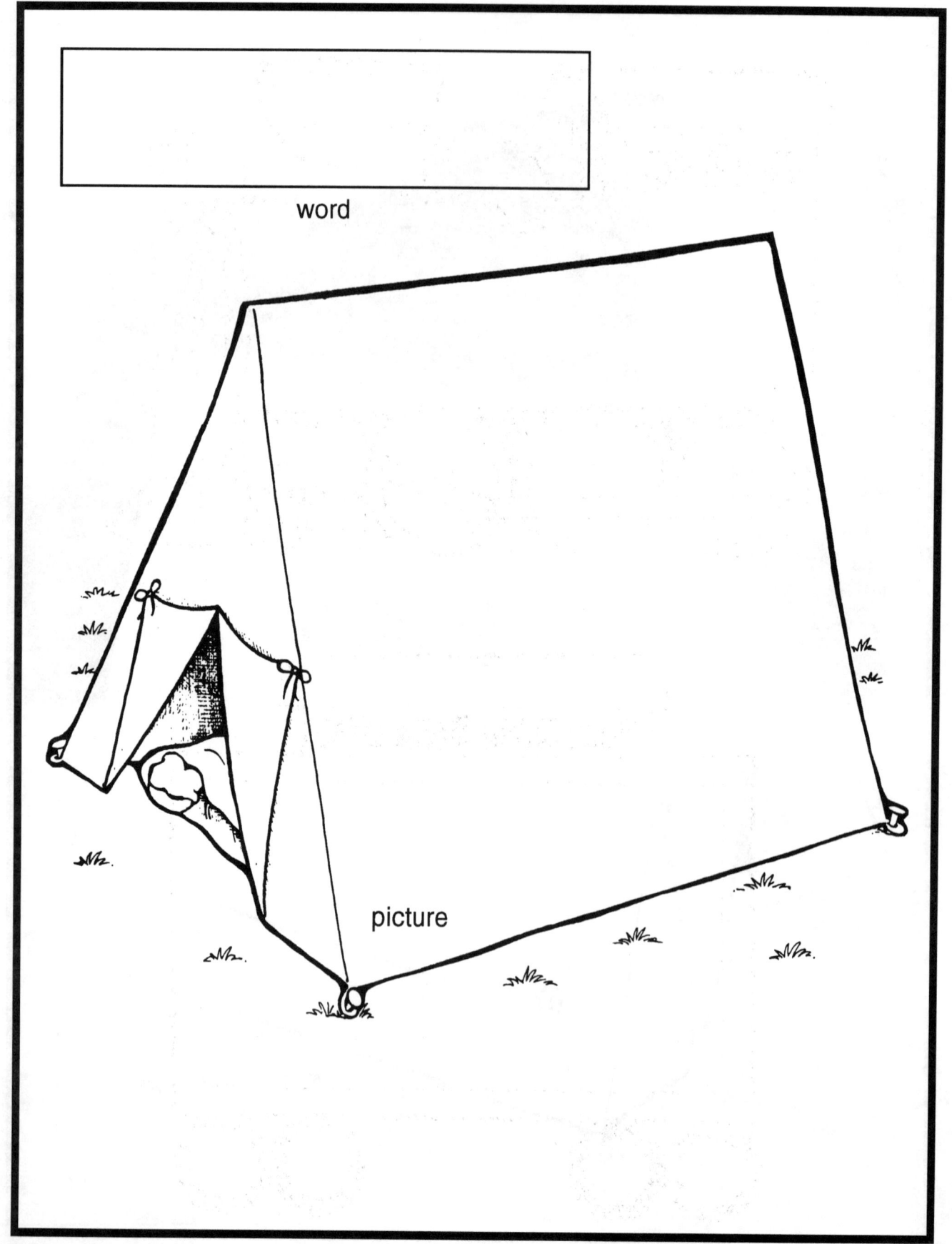

word

picture

#791 *Teaching Basic Skills through Literature: Phonics*   ©1995 Teacher Created Materials, Inc.

Tt

Freight Train

Train Engine and Caboose

Freight Train   Tt

Train Cars

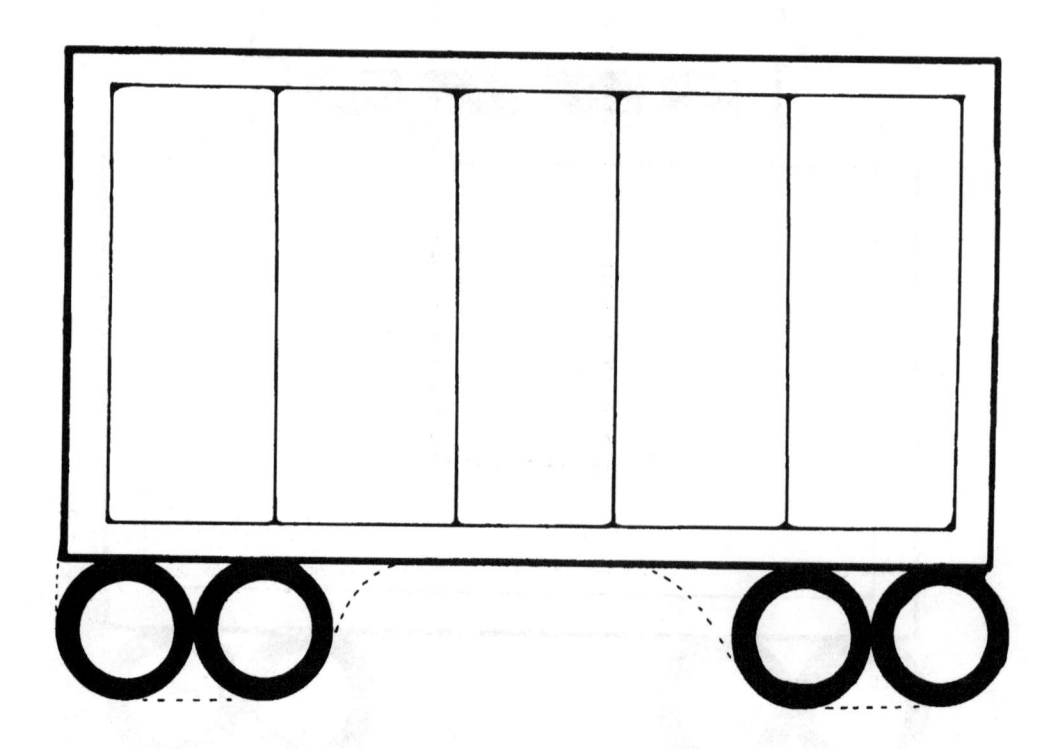

#791 *Teaching Basic Skills through Literature: Phonics*   ©1995 Teacher Created Materials, Inc.

Tt   *Freight Train*

"T" Pattern

©1995 Teacher Created Materials, Inc.   213   #791 Teaching Basic Skills through Literature: Phonics

Freight Train   Tt

"t" Pattern

#791 Teaching Basic Skills through Literature: Phonics   214   ©1995 Teacher Created Materials, Inc.

Tt   *Freight Train*

Telephone Conversation

Cut out telephone and receiver. Attach receiver with yarn. Make shape book from telephone.

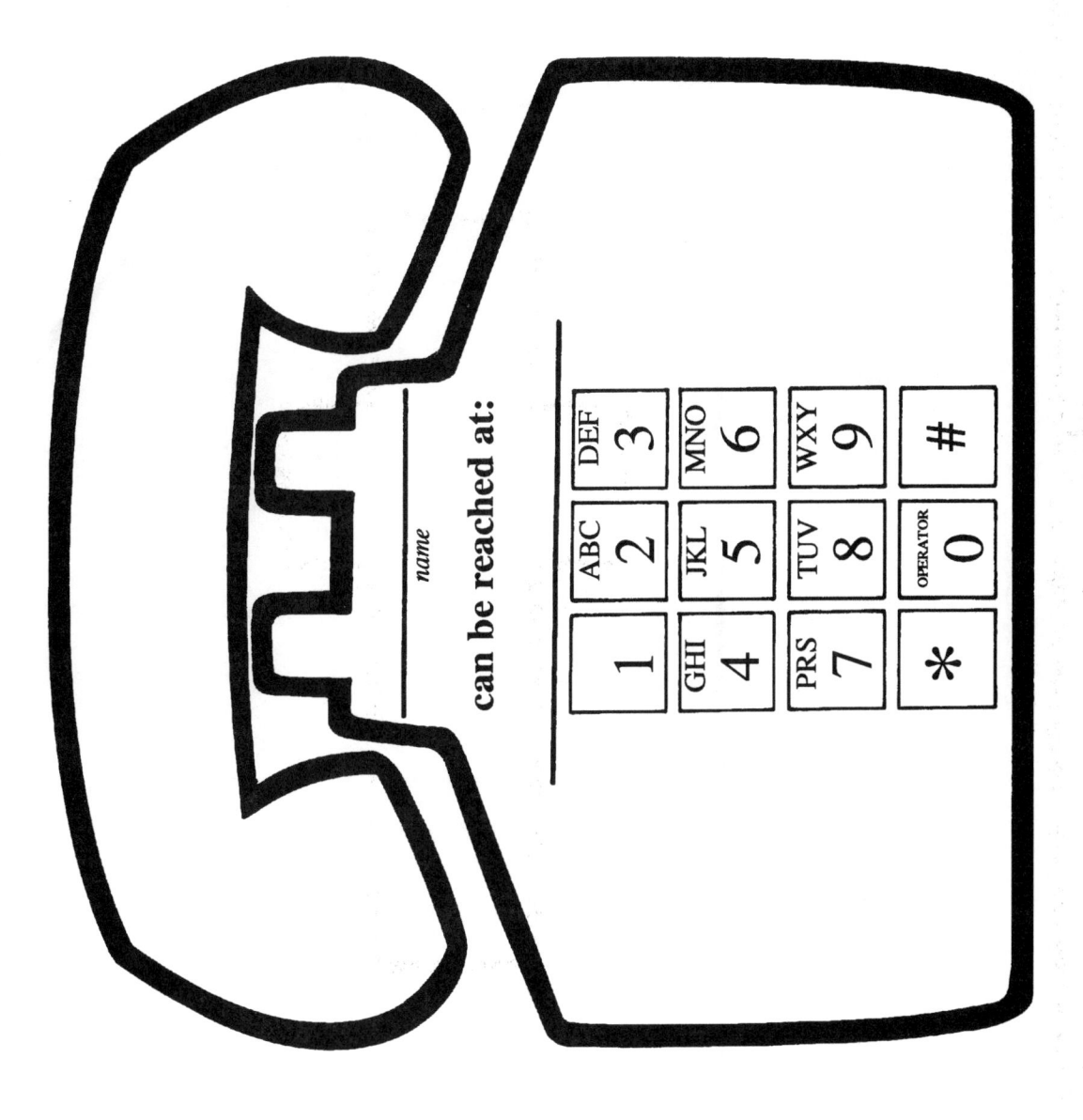

_____
name

can be reached at:

1	ABC 2	DEF 3
GHI 4	JKL 5	MNO 6
PRS 7	TUV 8	WXY 9
*	OPERATOR 0	#

Freight Train *Tt*

Turtle Pattern

#791 Teaching Basic Skills through Literature: Phonics   216   ©1995 Teacher Created Materials, Inc.

Phonics Skills in Context: Letter "V"

Book: *The Very Hungry Caterpillar*
Author: Eric Carle
Publisher: Philomel, New York, 1987
Summary: This is the classic story of a caterpillar's metamorphosis from an egg to butterfly and his adventures along the way.
Recommended Grade Level: K–2
Related Poetry: "The Violet" by William Wordsworth, *A Child's Book of Poems* (Grosset, New York, 1972). For additional titles see page 386.

Skill Activity

Students create their own "very" poems and illustrate them using a collage technique as in the Eric Carle "very" series.

Materials

- crayons or markers
- collage materials such as construction paper or tissue paper
- glue
- chart paper
- scissors
- story pattern (page 220)

Lesson

Introduce the Literature: Ask students what they think caterpillars eat.

Read the Literature: Read the literature selection. Allow time for discussion.

Introduce the Skill Lesson:
1. Write the word "very" on the chart paper and ask students to try to think of other words that start with a "v."
2. Write the words on chart paper. Display the chart paper as a word bank.
3. Have students create their own "very" stories, using the pattern activity sheet on page 220.
4. Allow students to illustrate their "very" stories, using the collage technique Eric Carle uses in his books.
5. Display completed art projects with the stories on a bulletin board entitled "Our Very, Very Best!"

Learning Center Activity: Have students make a viewer, using the patterns on pages 221 and 222. In the rectangular boxes on the wheel, students are to draw pictures of things that begin with "v" on the wheel. Then, attach the wheel to the viewer, using a brad fastener.

Cooperative Learning Activity: Have students work in small groups to create a village out of blocks.

Across the Curriculum: Science

Have students grow vegetables in a garden or planter box.

The Very Hungry Caterpillar   *Vv*

Extension Activities

Movement Activities
Stress the letter "v" as students participate in the following movements: fly like a vulture, play volleyball, act like vehicles, watch a video, play a violin, and make vibrations.

Multisensory Activity
On 6" x 8" (15 cm x 20 cm) tagboard, have children paste velvet onto an upper and lowercase "v." Patterns are provided on pages 223 and 224.

Creative Writing
Have students design vegetable gardens. Have them make a list of the vegetables they will grow, then draw a picture of their garden.

Handwriting
On 12" x 18" (30 cm x 46 cm) lined newsprint, ask children to copy this sentence: "V is for vine, valentine (glue on a heart doily), vase, and violet volcano."

Cooking

Vegetable Bouquets

Ingredients
- assortment of vegetables
- knife
- cups

Directions
1. Cut vegetables into sticks.
2. Arrange in small cup.
3. Draw your recipe.
4. Clean up.

Interdisciplinary Topics

vulture	Venus	vandalism	vitamin
vine	vice president	vibration	vanilla
Valentine's Day	vote	vaccination	vegetables
violets	veterinarian	vein	vinegar
volcano	vehicle		

Vv *The Very Hungry Caterpillar*

Extension Activities (cont.)

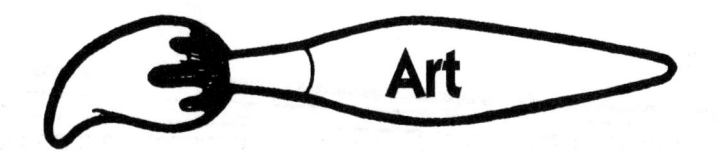

Art

Viper Fish
Materials
- white crayon or chalk
- black, red, and yellow construction paper
- hole punch
- glue

Process
1. Draw viper fish on large black paper with white crayon or chalk.
2. Hole punch red and yellow "lights" and glue onto fish.

Visor
Materials
- visor pattern (page 225)
- strip of paper for headband
- scissors
- construction paper
- crayons or markers
- stapler

Process
1. Reproduce or trace on construction paper. Cut out visor pattern.
2. Draw any type of picture on front of visor.
3. Teacher staples headband to fit child's head.

Volcano
Materials
- volcano pattern (page 226)
- brown construction paper
- crayons or markers
- glue
- scissors

Process
1. Reproduce or trace volcano pattern on the brown construction paper.
2. Color top section of volcano to look like lava.
3. Roll in cone shape and secure with glue.
4. Cut strips into one side of 3" (8 cm) square pieces of yellow and orange tissue paper that have been stapled together at one corner.
5. Roll up and glue to inside of volcano.

The Very Hungry Caterpillar   Vv

"Very" Story Pattern

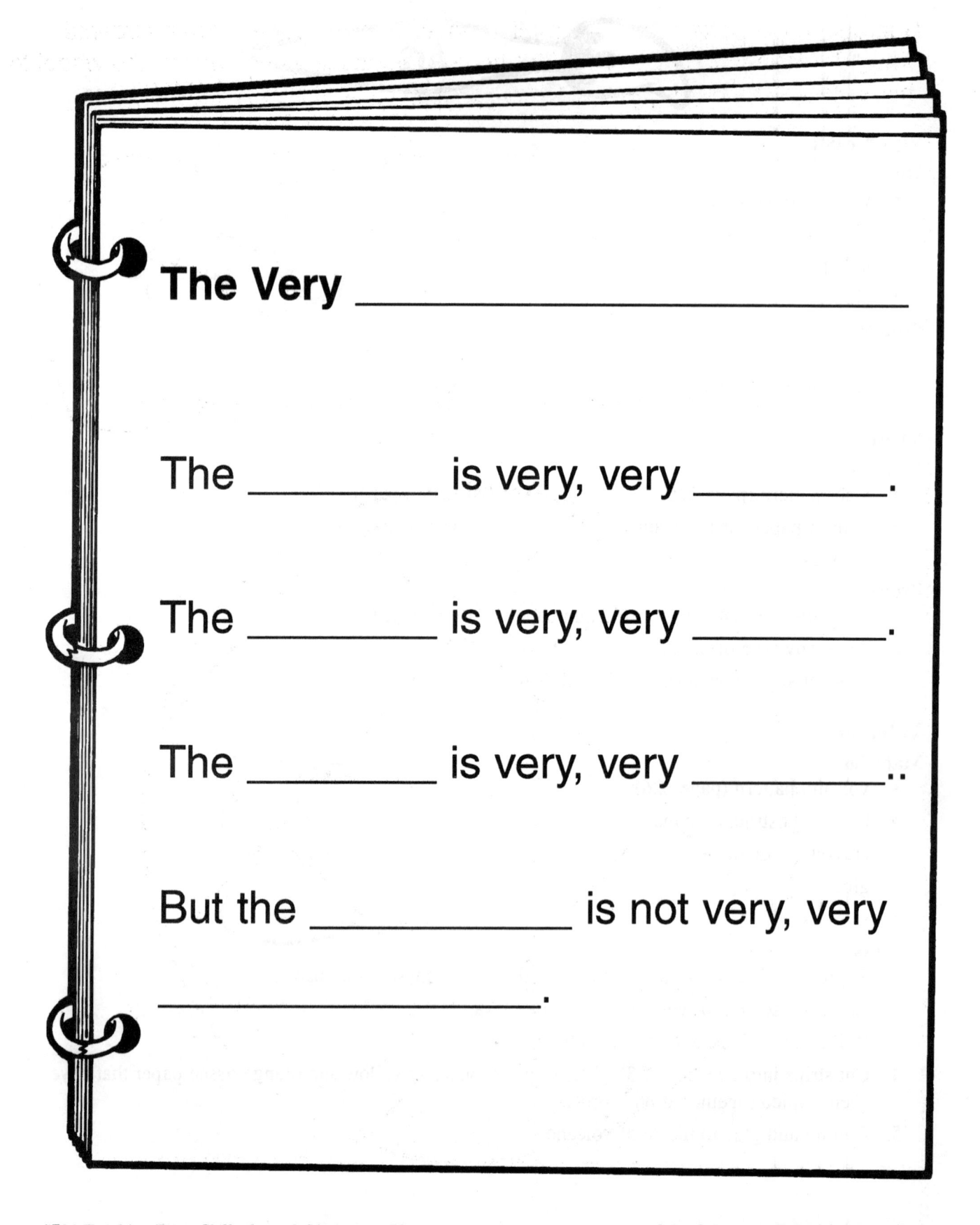

The Very _____

The _____ is very, very _____.

The _____ is very, very _____.

The _____ is very, very _____..

But the _____ is not very, very _____.

Vv   *The Very Hungry Caterpillar*

Picture Wheel

Reproduce the pattern on construction paper or index paper. After students draw "V" pictures in each of the four rectangles on the wheel, attach the wheel to the back of the viewer (page 222) with a brad.

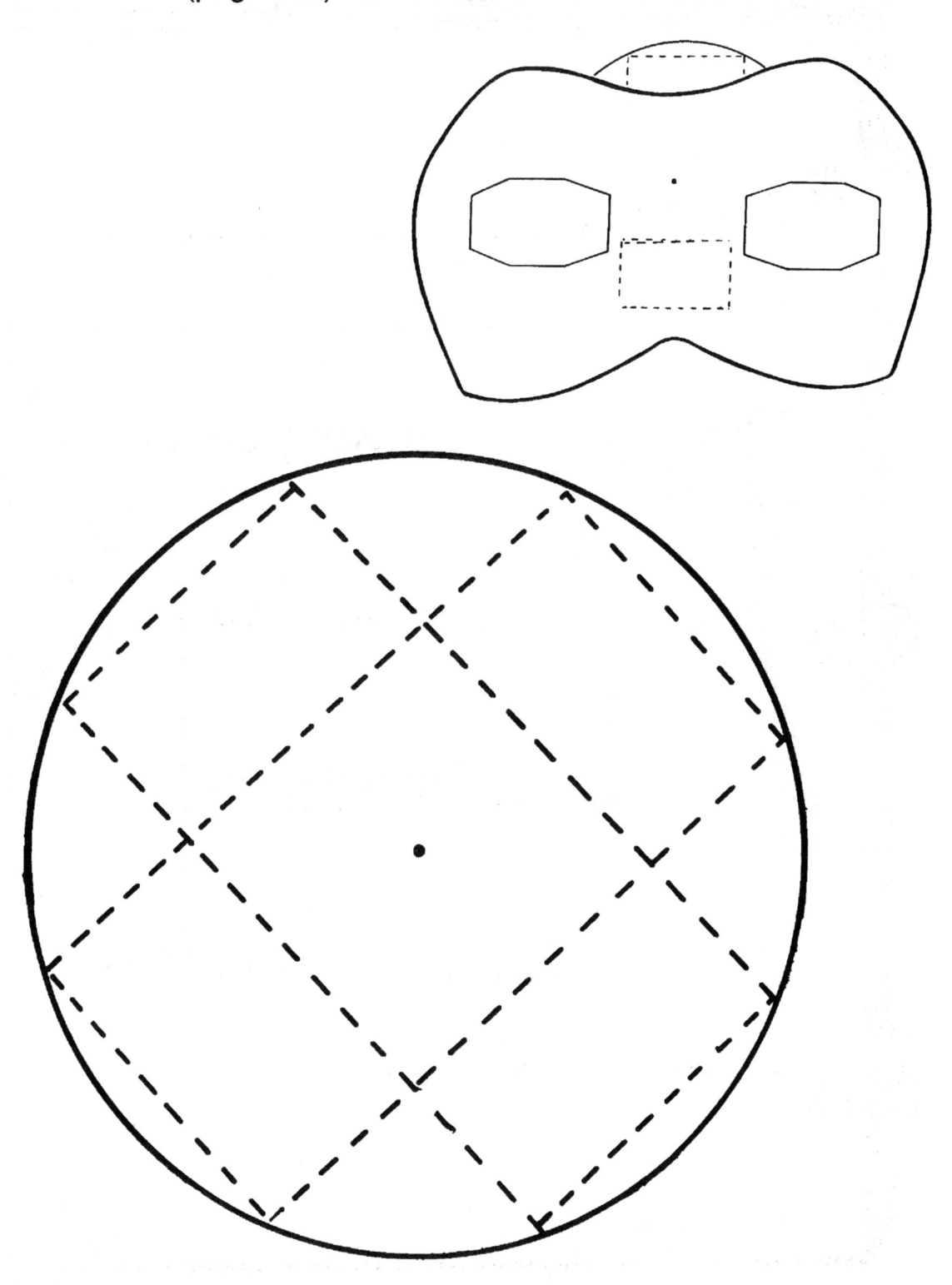

©1995 Teacher Created Materials, Inc.   221   #791 Teaching Basic Skills through Literature: Phonics

The Very Hungry Caterpillar — Vv

Viewer

Cut out.

#791 Teaching Basic Skills through Literature: Phonics ©1995 Teacher Created Materials, Inc.

Vv *The Very Hungry Caterpillar*

"V" Pattern

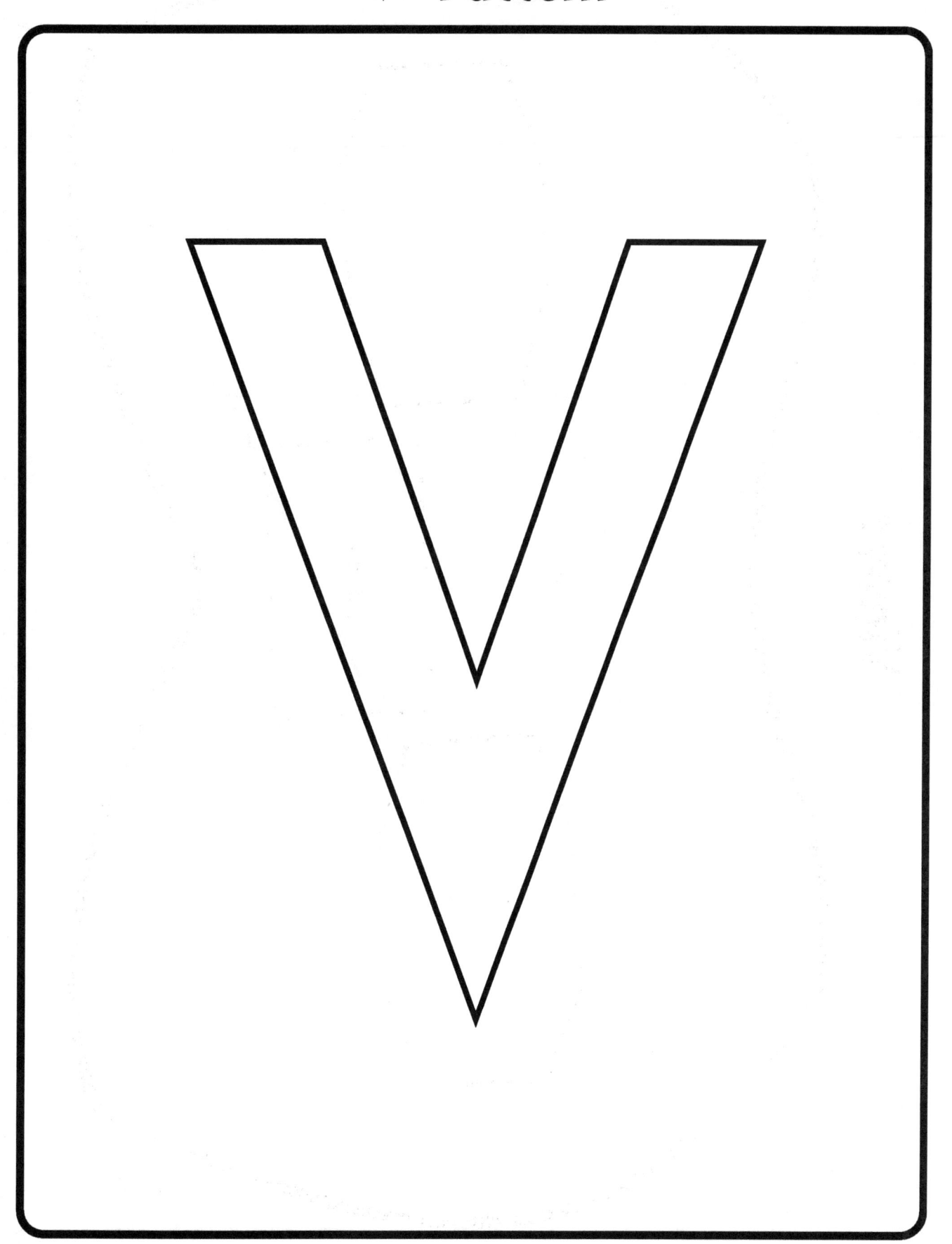

©1995 Teacher Created Materials, Inc. 223 #791 Teaching Basic Skills through Literature: Phonics

The Very Hungry Caterpillar   *Vv*

"v" Pattern

Vv   *The Very Hungry Caterpillar*

Visor Pattern

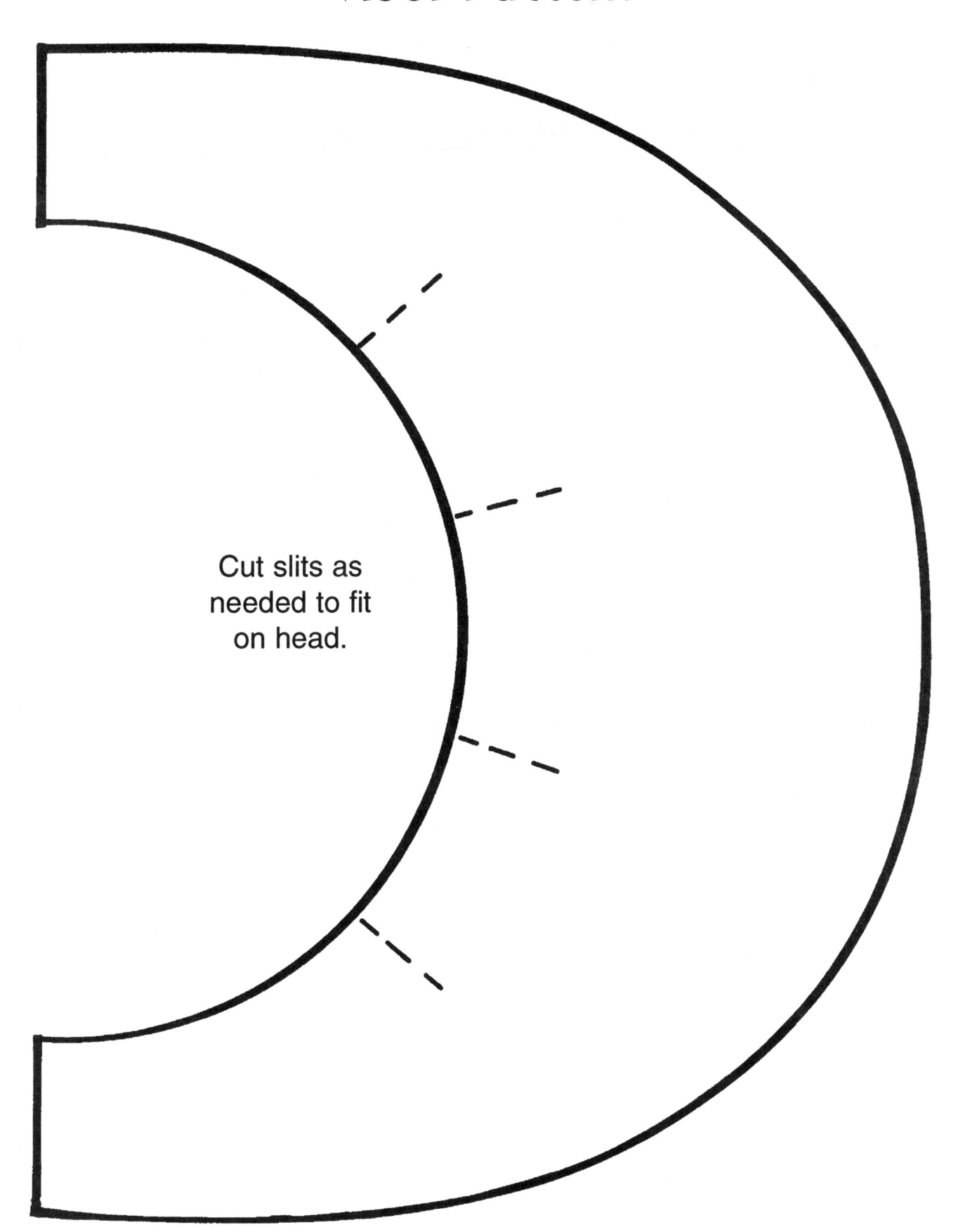

Cut slits as needed to fit on head.

©1995 Teacher Created Materials, Inc.   #791 Teaching Basic Skills through Literature: Phonics

The Very Hungry Caterpillar   Vv

Volcano Pattern

#791 Teaching Basic Skills through Literature: Phonics   226   ©1995 Teacher Created Materials, Inc.

Phonics Skills in Context: Letter "W"

Book: *I Went Walking*
Author: Sue Williams
Publisher: Harcourt, San Diego, 1989
Summary: This is a pattern story about a young child and all the animals he sees.
Recommended Grade Level: K–1
Related Poetry: "Strange Wind" by Shel Silverstein, *A Light in the Attic* (HarperCollins, New York, 1981). For additional titles see page 386.

Skill Activity

Students play an oral language game using "I went walking" and "What did you see?" as they name "w" words.

Materials

- chart paper

Lesson

Introduce the Literature: Ask students "Where is your favorite place to walk?" Show the cover of the book. Ask students where they think the little boy will walk.

Read the Literature: Read the literature selection. Allow time for discussion.

Introduce the Skill Lesson:
1. Reread the book and encourage students to join in wherever they know the story.
2. Ask students to brainstorm "w" words they know or heard in the story. List these on chart paper to display as a word bank.
3. Play an oral language game in which one student says "I went walking." The rest of the group responds "What did you see?" The students must then name a "w" word.
4. Repeat the game so each child has a turn.

Learning Center Activity: Have students make a windsock with "w" pictures on it. Students decorate a 9" x 12" (23 cm x 30 cm) piece of construction paper with "w" pictures from page 230. Then they roll the construction paper into a cylinder shape and secure. Attach long crepe paper streamers to one end and a piece of yarn or string to the other end. Students will enjoy running in the wind with their windsocks.

Cooperative Learning Activity: Have students work in groups of four to complete a class book titled "Look out the Window. What Do You See?" Have each student in the group create a part of the window scene using the art activity on page 229. Each student then writes about his/her own part of the window scene using a frame of the window pattern on page 231.

Across the Curriculum: Science

Have students work on a weather watch for a week. Each day for one week go on a walk and observe the weather. When students return to the classroom, have them record their findings on the activity sheet on page 232. This project can be extended to a home learning activity by asking parents to help their children look at the weather report in the newspaper.

©1995 Teacher Created Materials, Inc.

I Went Walking Ww

Extension Activities

Movement Activities
Stress the letter "w" as students participate in each of the following movements: walk, whisper, wiggle, run like the wind, wink, write, wait, and act wild and woolly.

Multisensory Activity
On 6" x 8" (15 cm x 20 cm) tagboard, have students paste white tissue squares onto an upper and lowercase "w." Patterns are provided on pages 233 and 234.

Creative Writing
Have students complete this story: "A genie has appeared and has given you three wishes. What will those wishes be?" Students can record their responses on page 235.

Handwriting
On 12" x 18" (30 cm x 46 cm) lined newsprint, ask children to copy this sentence: "W is for wall, watch, water (use felt pens to draw water), and wicked witch."

Cooking

Wonderful Wedges of Fruit

Ingredients
- apples
- oranges
- knife
- plates

Directions
1. Cut apples and oranges into wedges.
2. Arrange onto plate.
3. Draw your recipe.
4. Clean up.

Interdisciplinary Topics

worm	wasp	weight	women
walrus	weather	world	windmill
woodpecker	winter	wood	wilderness
wolf	wind	Washington	wool
weasel	water		

Extension Activities (cont.)

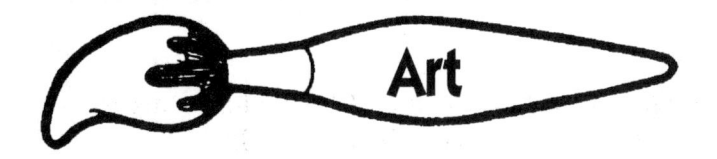

Art

Watercolor Wash
Materials
- construction paper
- crayons
- watercolors

Process
1. Children draw pictures of anything they wish.
2. When finished, apply a watered-down watercolor wash over it.

Weather Wheel
Materials
- paper plates
- crayon or markers
- brad fastener
- construction paper
- scissors

Process
1. Children draw weather symbols onto paper plate.
2. Use a brad fastener to attach an arrow to the plate.
3. Students point arrows to today's weather.

Window Scene
Materials
- 2 colors of construction paper
- crayons or markers
- scissors
- paste
- clear plastic (optional)

Process
1. Draw an outdoor scene.
2. After coloring, paste onto larger piece of construction paper.
3. Take two thin strips of same color as background and paste in a cross form to make a window pane.
4. Clear plastic can be glued over scene before forming window.

I Went Walking   Ww

"W" Pictures

Ww   *I Went Walking*

Window Frame

1.

2.

3.

4.

I Went Walking   *Ww*

Weather Watch Record Sheet

Monday	Tuesday	Wednesday	Thursday	Friday

I recorded the weather for the week of _____.

I predict next week's weather will be _____.

My favorite weather is _____. Here is my picture:

Ww *I Went Walking*

"W" Pattern

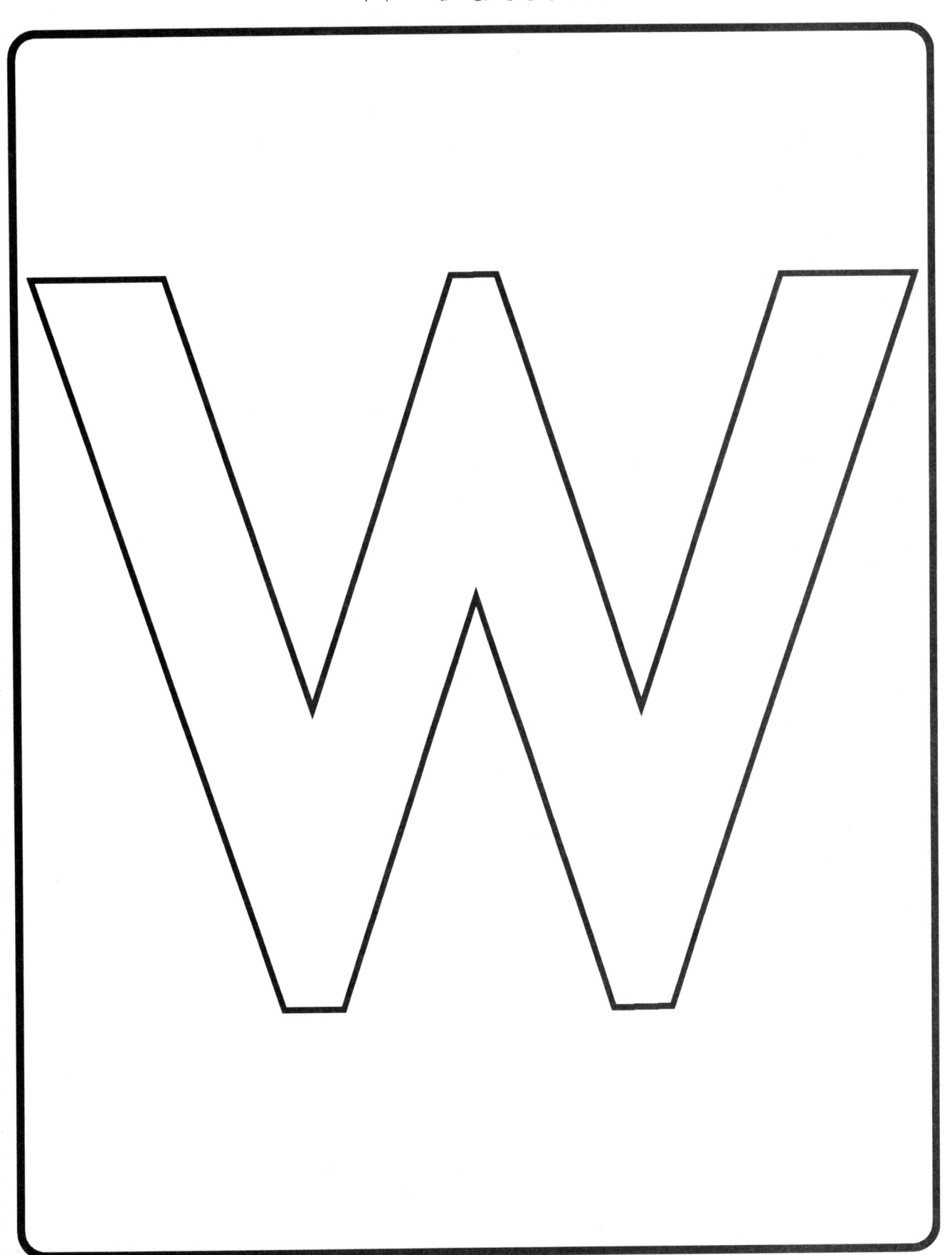

I Went Walking Ww

"w" Pattern

Wishes

My Three Wishes

by: _____

_____

_____

_____

_____

_____

_____

_____

Phonics Skills in Context: Letter "X"

Book: *Baby in the Box*
Author: Frank Asch
Publisher: Holiday House, New York, 1989
Summary: Baby, a fox, and an ox play with blocks in a box.
Recommended Grade Level: K–2
Related Poetry: "Two Boxes" by Shel Silverstein, *Where the Sidewalk Ends* (Harper & Row, New York, 1974). For additional titles see page 387.

Skill Activity

Students make a box and glue "x" word pictures on each side. Students roll the box to practice reading "x" words.

Materials

- two 4" x 16" (10.5 cm x 40 cm) strips of construction paper per student. (Make one strip a little shorter to fit inside the other.)
- "x" pictures (page 239)
- crayons or markers
- chart paper
- scissors
- glue
- tape

Lesson

Introduce the Literature: Read students the title of the story. Encourage them to listen for rhyming words in the story.

Read the Literature: Read the literature selection. Allow time for discussion.

Introduce the Skill Lesson:

1. Reread the story several times, inviting the students to read along with you.
2. Have students brainstorm any words they know that begin with "x." Then, have them brainstorm words that end in "x." Write the words on chart paper and display as a word bank.
3. Have students construct a "box" by folding two 3" x 12" (8 cm x 30 cm) strips of construction paper into fourths to form part of a cube shape. Tape ends of paper together.
4. Repeat the procedure with other strip. Slide the smaller strip into the middle of the longer strip to complete the box. Tape as needed.
5. Have students read the picture words on page 239. Then, color, cut, and paste them onto the sides of the box.
6. Have students roll the box (as if rolling dice) and read the "x" word that lands on top.

Learning Center Activity: Provide students with construction paper and crayons or markers and have students create "Extra Special Love Notes" for their families or friends. Show students how to make X's and O's for hugs and kisses.

Cooperative Learning Activity: Have students make an "X marks the spot" treasure map. In small groups, have children make pretend maps to secret treasures. Be sure that students make an "X" wherever the treasure is.

Across the Curriculum: Science

Discuss how X-rays are used. If possible, ask a doctor or radiologist for some X-rays to show the class.

Xx *Baby in the Box*

Extension Activities

Movement Activities
Stress the letter "x" as students participate in the following movements: make X's on the playground, make X's in the air, and exit the room.

Multisensory Activity
On 6" x 8" (15 cm x 20 cm) tagboard, have students glue cardboard box pieces to an upper and lowercase "x." Patterns are provided on pages 240 and 241.

Creative Writing
Have students choose five or six words from the list of words that end in the letter "x." Then, challenge them to write the words in their "x" book or write a story using the words. The "x" book pattern is located on page 242. Provide six blank x-shaped pages for each student to create the book's interior.

Handwriting
On 12" x 18" (30 cm x 46 cm) lined newsprint, ask children to copy this sentence: "X is for X-ray, exit (make exit sign), ax, and six boxes."

Cooking

"X" Marks the Spot

Ingredients
- English muffins
- mayonnaise
- lettuce
- cheese
- knife
- teaspoon
- plates

Directions
1. Spread 1 teaspoon (5mL) of mayonnaise on muffin.
2. Place lettuce on top.
3. Cut cheese in strips. Make an "X" on top of the lettuce.
4. Draw your recipe.
5. Clean up.

Interdisciplinary Topics

X-rays   exit signs   X-mas   xylophone

Baby in the Box Xx

Extension Activities (cont.)

Art

Exit Sign
Materials
- construction paper
- yarn or glitter
- glue
- scissors
- crayons

Process
1. Cut a large door from construction paper and fold open.
2. Glue on top of another piece of paper.
3. Write "exit" above the door with glue and cover with glitter.
4. Draw a picture of what is inside the door.

X-Ray
Materials
- medium-sized dog biscuits
- white paint
- black construction paper
- paint brush

Process
1. Dip dog biscuits in black paint.
2. Glue onto construction paper to form the bones of the body.
3. Use a paint brush to paint in a skull.

X-traordinary People
Materials
- craft sticks
- glue
- construction paper
- crayons or markers

Process
1. Glue craft sticks into an "X" shape on paper.
2. Create a character using crayons or markers.

#791 Teaching Basic Skills through Literature: Phonics 238 ©1995 Teacher Created Materials, Inc.

Xx   *Baby in the Box*

"X" Pictures

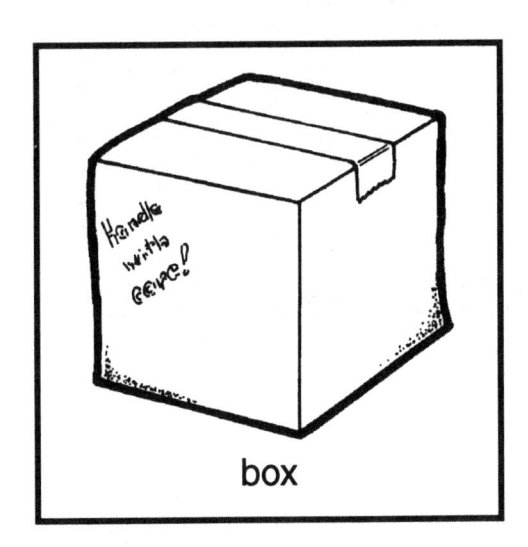

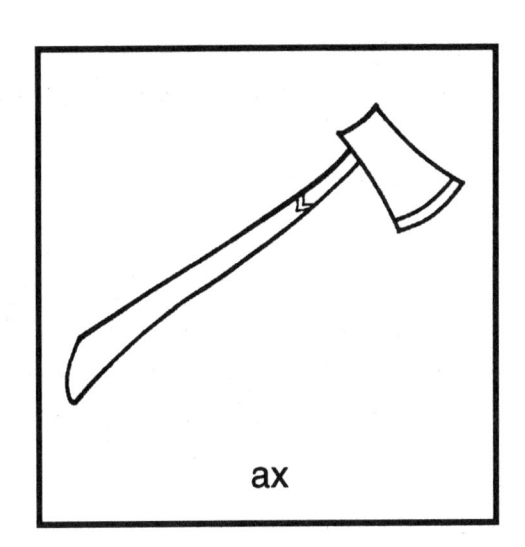

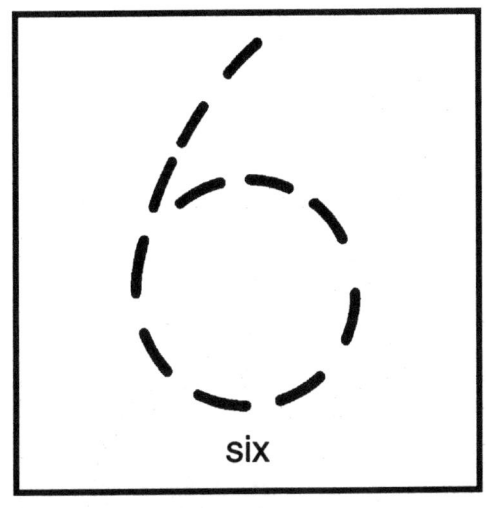

fox

ox

box

ax

six

mix

©1995 Teacher Created Materials, Inc.   239   #791 Teaching Basic Skills through Literature: Phonics

Baby in the Box Xx

"X" Pattern

Xx *Baby in the Box*

"x" Pattern

©1995 Teacher Created Materials, Inc. 241 #791 Teaching Basic Skills through Literature: Phonics

Baby in the Box

"X" Book

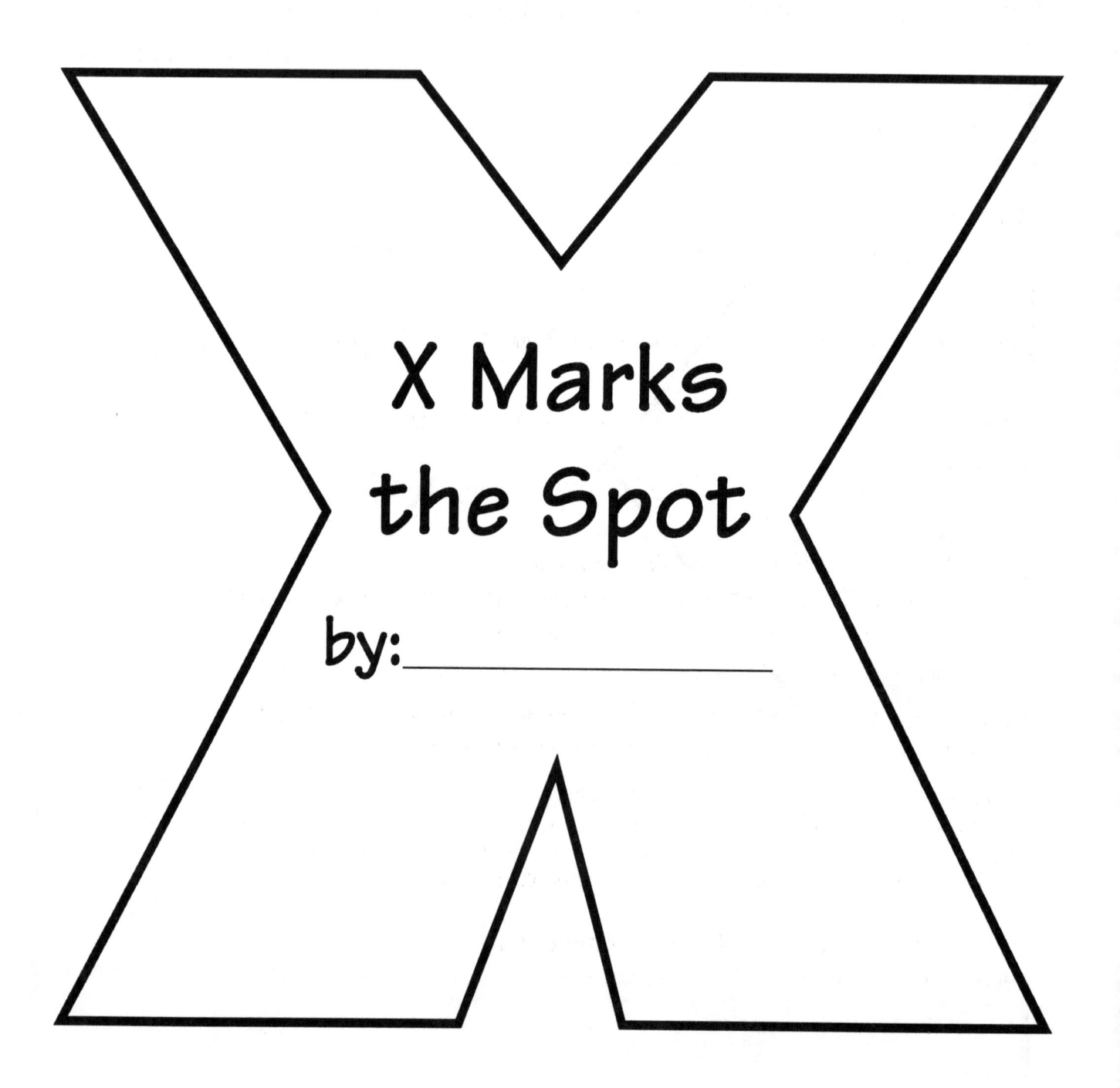

X Marks
the Spot

by:_____

Phonics Skills in Context: Letter "Y"

Book: *Yo! Yes?*
Author: Chris Raschka
Publisher: Orchard, New York, 1993
Summary: Two ethnically different boys find out they can be good friends.
Recommended Grade Level: K–2
Related Poetry: "Yellow Butter" by Mary Ann Hoberman, *Yellow Butter, Purple Jelly, Red Jam, Black Bread* (Viking, New York, 1981). For additional titles see page 387.

Skill Activity
Students dramatize the story by using expression as they read.

Materials
- chart paper

Lesson
Introduce the Literature: Show students the cover and read the title. Have them predict what the book might be about.

Read the Literature: Read the literature selection. Allow time for discussion.

Introduce the Skill Lesson:
1. Reread the story and ask students to listen for words that begin with "y" or have a "y" in them.
2. List words that begin with "y" on chart paper to be used as a word bank.
3. Have students divide into two lines and face each other.
4. The teacher shows the book to one line and students read the page as if talking to the other line.
5. The second line responds by reading the next page.
6. Encourage students to use expression when reading.

Learning Center Activity: Have students answer the questions on page 246. Older students could also create their own questions to ask other students or their families.

Cooperative Learning Activity: Have students work cooperatively to create a "Yard of Y Words." Provide each team with yellow index cards, markers, and a yardstick. As students think of a "y" word, they write it on the index card and line it up along the yardstick. The goal is to reach the end of the yardstick. Older students may enjoy racing with other teams.

Across the Curriculum: Physical Education
Have students listen to quiet music and learn the beginning techniques of yoga.

©1995 Teacher Created Materials, Inc.

Yo! Yes?   Yy

Extension Activities

Movement Activities
Stress the letter "y" as students participate in the following movements: yawning, doing yoga exercises, yelling, and playing with a yo-yo.

Multisensory Activity
On 6" x 8" (15 cm x 20 cm) tagboard, have students paste yellow yarn onto an upper and lowercase "y." Patterns are provided on pages 247 and 248.

Creative Writing
Have students write the directions for how to play with a yo-yo in a how-to book. A cover pattern is located on page 249. Add blank writing sheets and a book cover using the same shape. Attach pages with yarn.

Handwriting
On 12" x 18" (30 cm x 46 cm) lined newsprint, ask children to copy this sentence: "Y is for you, yak, yam, and yellow yarn (glue on yarn)."

Cooking

Yolanda Yak's Yogurt Sundae

Ingredients
- yogurt
- fruit
- wheat germ
- bowls
- spoons

Directions
1. Add fruit to yogurt in bowl.
2. Sprinkle wheat germ on top.
3. Draw your recipe.
4. Clean up.

Interdisciplinary Topics

yellow jackets	youth	yarn	yogurt
yaks	Yankee Doodle	yeast	
you	yachts	yams	

#791 Teaching Basic Skills through Literature: Phonics   ©1995 Teacher Created Materials, Inc.

Yy   Yo! Yes?

Extention Activities (cont.)

Art

Yacht
Materials
- yacht pattern (page 250)
- scissors
- thread spools
- glue
- construction paper
- yarn
- paint
- crayons or markers

Process
1. Reproduce or trace pattern.
2. Cut out pattern and glue to construction paper.
3. Decorate with crayons, markers, yarn, and flag.
4. Portholes can be either traced from thread spools or dipped in paint and stamped on yacht.

Yellow Jacket
Materials
- yellow jacket patterns (page 251)
- yellow and black construction paper
- wax paper
- glue
- scissors

Process
1. Trace and cut out body.
2. Glue alternating 1" (3 cm) yellow and black strips onto yellow jacket body. Trim excess strips.
3. Trace wings onto wax paper.
4. Cut out and attach black paper strips for antennae.

Yearbook
Materials
- construction paper
- materials may vary

Process
1. Design a cover for the yearbook using school pictures, self portraits, or handprints.
2. Fill the book with mementos from special events during the school year.

You
Materials
- large tagboard
- crayons or markers

Process
1. Give each child a piece of large tagboard with a face-sized hole cut near the top.
2. They make pictures of themselves or any character and put their faces through the hole to dramatize.

©1995 Teacher Created Materials, Inc.

Yo! Yes?
Name _____

Yy

Yes or No?

		Yes	No
Can you ride a  [bicycle] ?	_____	_____
Can you jump a  [rope] ?	_____	_____
Can you tie a 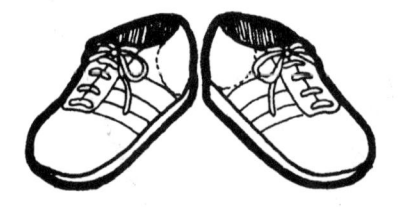 [shoes] ?	_____	_____
Can you bounce a  [ball] ?	_____	_____
Can you [write] your name?	_____	_____
Can you button your  [jacket] ?	_____	_____

#791 Teaching Basic Skills through Literature: Phonics   ©1995 Teacher Created Materials, Inc.

Yy   *Yo! Yes?*

"Y" Pattern

"y" Pattern

Yy   *Yo! Yes?*

How to Yo-Yo Book

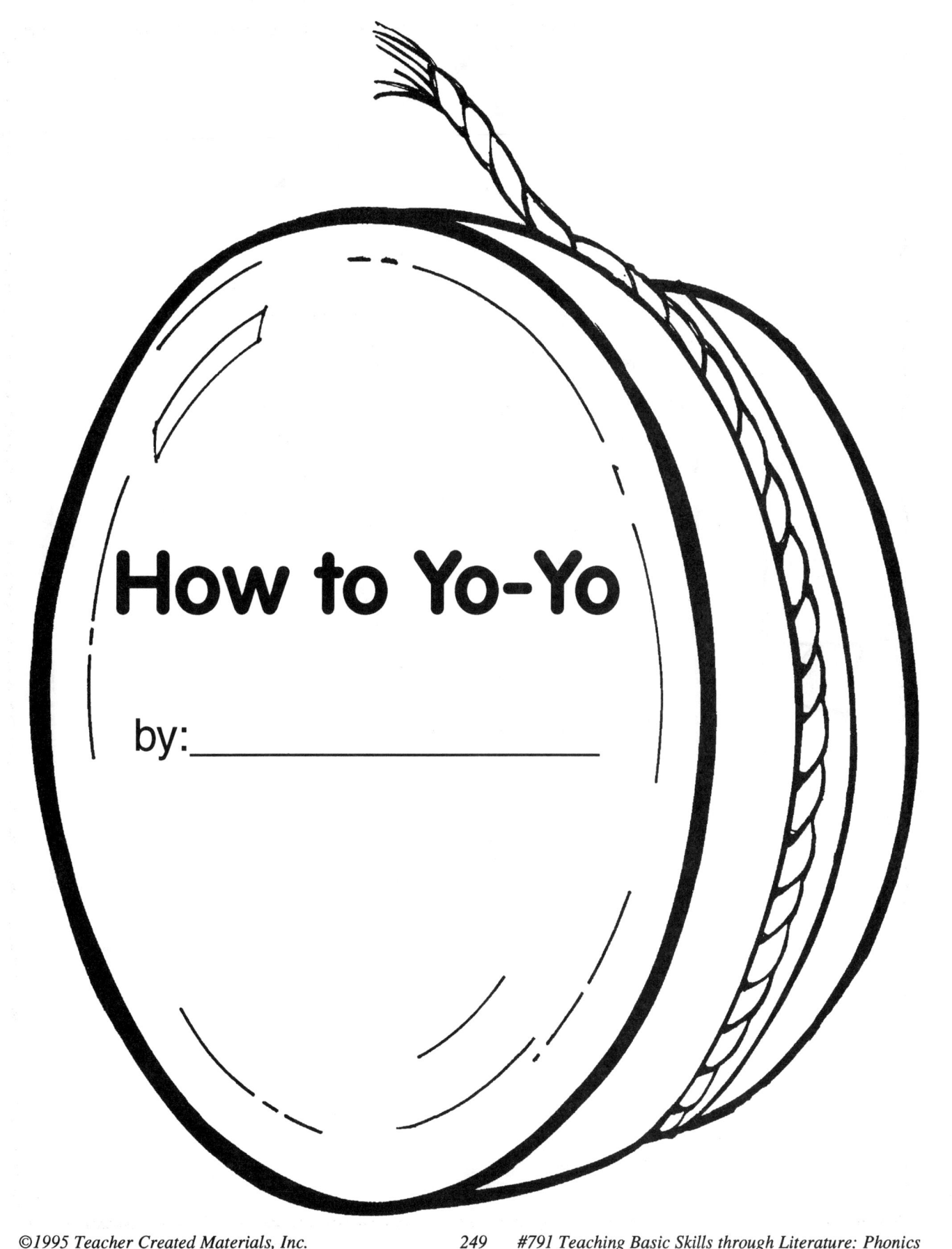

How to Yo-Yo

by: _____

Yo! Yes?   *Yy*

Yacht Pattern

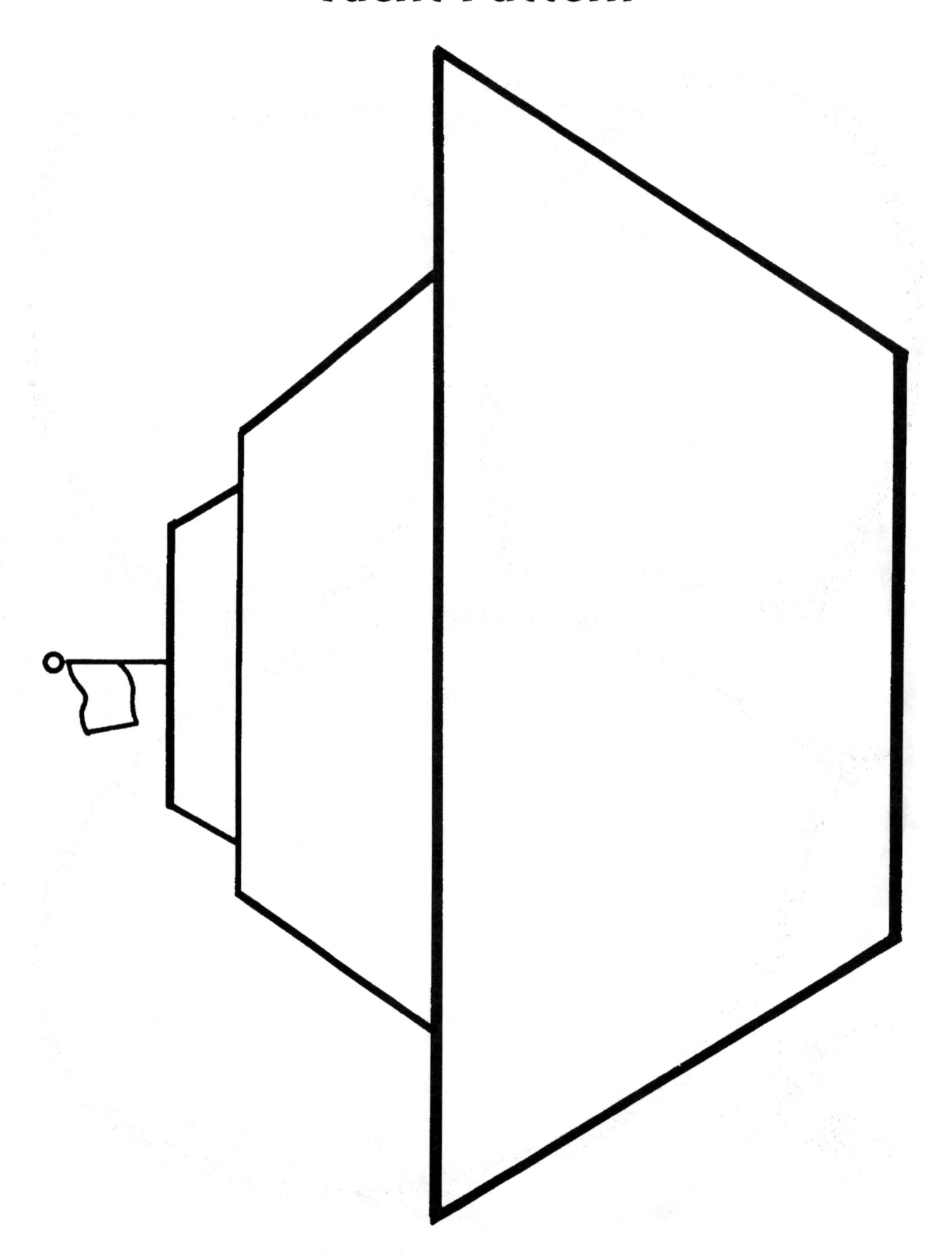

#791 Teaching Basic Skills through Literature: Phonics   250   ©1995 Teacher Created Materials, Inc.

Yy   *Yo! Yes?*

Yellow Jacket Patterns

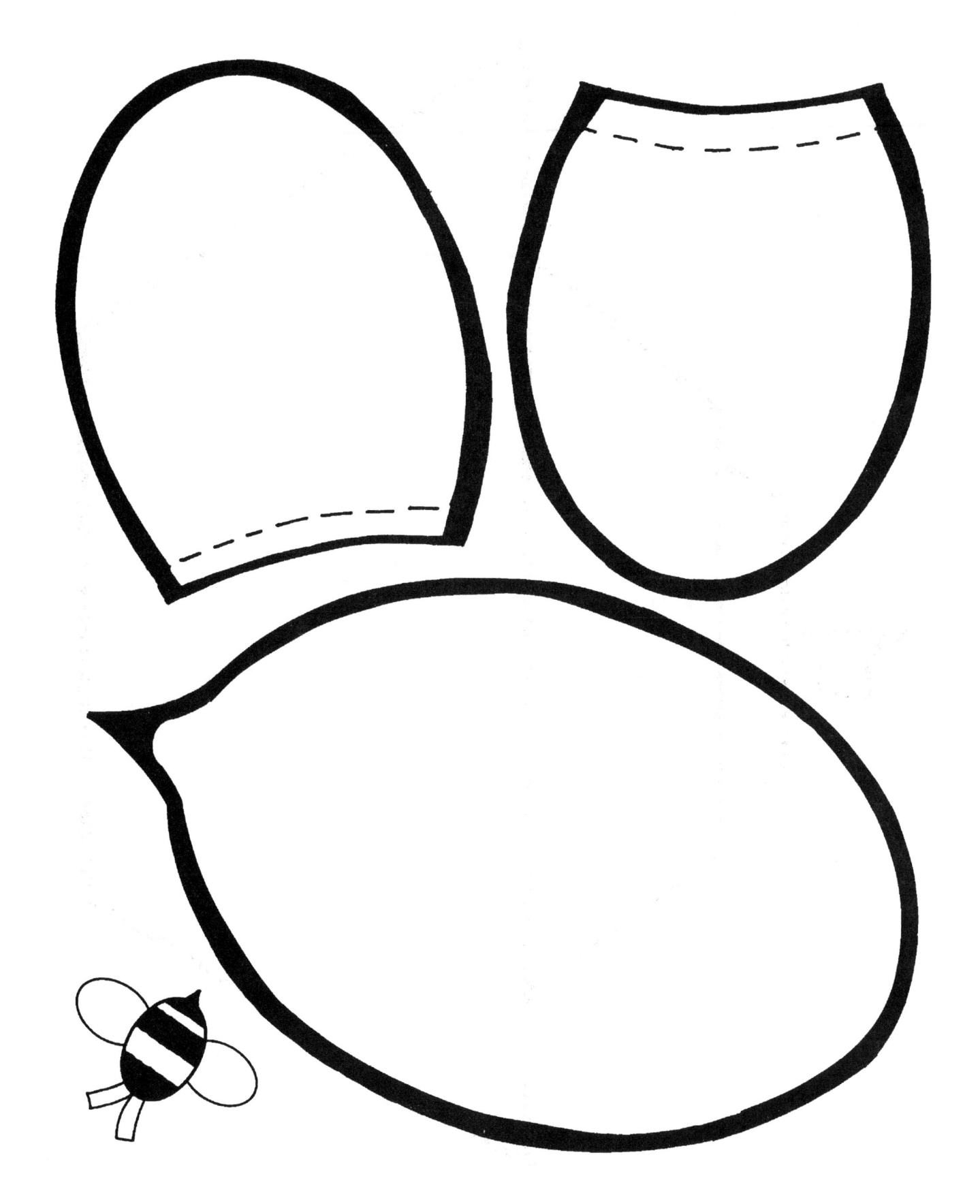

©1995 Teacher Created Materials, Inc.   251   #791 Teaching Basic Skills through Literature: Phonics

Phonics Skills in Context: Letter "Z"

Book: *50 Below Zero*
Author: Robert Munsch
Publisher: Annick Press, New York, 1986
Summary: This is the humorous story of Jason who tries to keep his sleepwalking father from freezing in the 50 below zero weather outside.
Recommended Grade Level: K–2
Related Poetry: "Zeppelin" by Sylvia Casey, *Zoomerimes, Poems About Things that Go* (HarperCollins, New York, 1993). For additional titles see page 387.

Skill Activity
Students create a zipper shape book with "z" words inside.

Materials
- zipper book pattern (page 255)
- crayons or markers
- chart paper
- drawing or writing paper to fit in book
- scissors
- thermometer

Lesson
Introduce the Literature: Discuss the meaning of the title, using a thermometer to explain.

Read the Literature: Read the literature selection. Allow time for discussion.

Introduce the Skill Lesson:

1. Point out the "z" sound in the story and have students imitate the sound as if they are sleeping.
2. Brainstorm words that start with the "z" sound. List these on chart paper to use as a word bank.
3. Have students make a zipper shape book by folding the pattern on page 255 along dashed lines so that zipper meets in the middle.
4. Students decorate the inside of their books and add pages to write on.
5. On each page students write and illustrate a "z" word.

Learning Center Activity: Have students draw a picture of someone or something sleeping in an unusual place. Have students write and complete this sentence, "In the middle of the night, ____ was asleep: zzzzz-zzzzz-zzzzz-zzzzz-zzzzz." Students can write or dictate how the person fell asleep. This prompt is printed for students on page 256.

Cooperative Learning Activity: Have students work cooperatively to write several different math problems using the number zero. Groups can share their problems with each other.

Across the Curriculum: Science
Discuss and compare the two types of measurement: Celsius and Fahrenheit. Also, talk about places in the world that might have temperatures below zero.

Zz   *50 Below Zero*

Extension Activities

Movement Activities
Stress the letter "z" as students participate in the following movements: act like a zoo animal, zoom around the playground, walk in a zig-zag, and zip up a jacket.

Multisensory Activity
On 6" x 8" (15 cm x 20 cm) tagboard, have students glue zig-zags (rickrack from fabric stores) onto an upper and lowercase 40 "z." Patterns are provided on pages 257 and 258.

Creative Writing
Have students write stories about visiting a zoo.

Handwriting
On 12" x 18" (30 cm x 46 cm) lined newsprint, ask children to copy this sentence: "Z is for zero (paste on Cheerios®), zebra, zipper, and zany zoo."

Cooking

Zoo Cages

Ingredients
- 1/4 banana per child
- shredded carrots
- peanut butter
- raisins
- orange slices
- toothpicks
- knife
- plates

Directions
1. Spread peanut butter on banana.
2. Roll banana in shredded carrots.
3. Decorate with raisins for eyes, nose, and mouth.
4. Put banana on orange slice.
5. Stick toothpicks around orange slice like the cages at the zoo.
6. Add another orange slice on top of toothpicks.
7. Draw your recipe.
8. Clean up.

Interdisciplinary Topics

zoo animals	Zuni Indian	zucchini	zwieback crackers
zebra	zoo keeper		

Extension Activities (cont.)

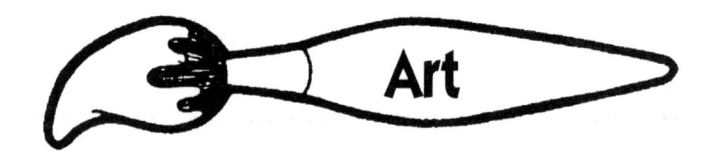

Art

Zebra
Materials
- black yarn
- white construction paper
- hole punch
- scissors
- tape
- crayons or markers

Process
1. Cut out large white rectangle. Punch holes on top and bottom and string yarn to form zebra stripes.
2. Cut strands of black yarn and glue to end of rectangle for tail.
3. Smaller rectangles are used for head and neck.
4. Cut out triangle for ear and glue.
5. Glue small strands of black yarn on head for mane.
6. Draw facial features on head.
7. Attach head and neck to body.
8. Legs are two long strips folded to form a V and glued to body.
9. Hole punch and tie a piece of yarn for hooves.

Zipper People
Materials
- 8" (20 cm), or longer, zipper
- felt pieces
- scissors
- wiggle eyes
- buttons
- yarn

Process
1. Unzip zipper to form legs.
2. Glue felt arms and shoes to zipper.
3. For head, cut a circle from felt and glue on eyes, hair, etc.
4. Glue head to top of zipper.

Zoo Animal Collage
Materials
- animal pictures
- glue
- construction paper

Process
1. Cut out several zoo animal pictures.
2. Glue into a collage.

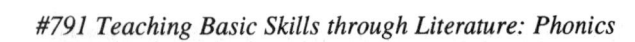

Zz 50 Below Zero

Zipper Shape Book

50 Below Zero

"ZZZZZZZ" Story

In the middle of the night,
_____ was asleep.

_____

_____

_____

_____

_____

_____

_____

by: _____

Zz *50 Below Zero*

"Z" Pattern

50 Below Zero Zz

"z" Pattern

Phonics Skills in Context: Short "A"

Book: *The Cat in the Hat*
Author: Dr. Seuss
Publisher: Random House, New York, 1967
Summary: The classic, rhyming story of the cat in the hat who entertains two small children for the day.
Recommended Grade Level: K–2
Related Poetry: "Anteater" by Shel Silverstein, *A Light in the Attic* (HarperCollins, New York, 1981). For additional titles see page 387.

Skill Activity

Students listen for short "a" words in the story. Then they create their own "Cat in the Hat" paper bag hats and decorate them with short "a" pictures.

Materials

- grocery-size paper bags
- word cards (pages 262 and 263)
- picture cards (pages 264 and 265)
- crayons or markers
- glue
- chart paper
- scissors

Lesson

Introduce the Literature: Show students the cover and ask how many of them have heard the story before.

Read the Literature: Read the literature selection. Allow time for discussion.

Introduce the Skill Lesson:
1. Have students listen for the short "a" sound as you read the title of the book. Then, ask students for other short "a" words and add to chart paper to use as a word bank.
2. Hold up the word cards on pages 262 and 263 one at a time for children to read. Pass out cards to students or small groups. As you read the story ask them to hold up the cards when the word is read.
3. Allow students to make their own hats by rolling up the bottom of a paper bag (to form the brim) and turning the bag upside down.
4. Have students color and cut out the short "a" picture cards on pages 264–265. Glue them to the hat.

Learning Center Activity: Have students make cats by cutting out the pattern on page 266. Students can use crayons to decorate their cats. Have students paint over their cats with a wash of diluted paint or food coloring.

Cooperative Learning Activity: Have students brainstorm and write short "a" words on the hat pattern located on page 267.

Across the Curriculum: Physical Education

Have students do an aerobic workout or some acrobatics.

©1995 Teacher Created Materials, Inc.

The Cat in the Hat Short "A"

Extension Activities

Movement Activities
Stress the short "a" sound as students participate in the following movements: ant crawl, alligator crawl, swing an ax, follow after, breathe air, and run like an antelope.

Multisensory Activity
On 6" x 8" (15 cm x 20 cm) tagboard, have children paste capital and lowercase "a's" from magazines onto an upper and lowercase "a." Patterns are provided on pages 268 and 269.

Creative Writing
Have students complete this story starter: "I planted an apple seed in my garden, but instead of an apple tree, up came ..." A book cover and this prompt are located on page 270. Provide blank apple shape patterns for students to complete. Attach student pages to the cover and the first page.

Handwriting
On 12" by 18" (30 cm x 46 cm) lined newsprint, ask children to copy this sentence: "A is for apple, ant (make thumbprints), alphabet, and antler."

Cooking

Applesauce Ants

Ingredients
- applesauce
- raisins
- spoons
- bowls

Directions
1. Serve each child two scoops of applesauce.
2. Decorate with raisins (ants).
3. Draw your recipe.
4. Clean up.

Interdisciplinary Topics

ants	airplanes	apple	antonym
animals	Africa	antelope	adverb
amphibian	Alaska	Aztec Indians	adjective
Arbor Day	air	Antarctic	Alabama
astronauts	address	alligator	acid rain

Extension Activities *(cont.)*

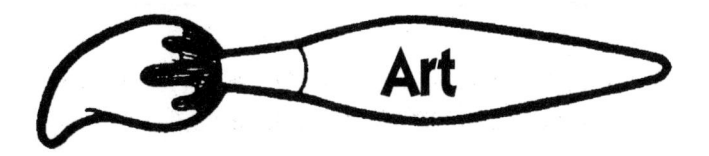

Art

Acrobats
Materials
- construction-paper strips
- crayons or markers
- glue
- scissors

Process
1. Form two large capital A's with strips.
2. Cut out two circles for heads. Glue to tops of A's.
3. Place one acrobat on top of the other.
4. Draw facial and body characteristics, allowing hands to touch.

Air Blowing
Materials
- watered-down paint
- straws
- construction paper

Process
1. Drop small splats of paint onto paper.
2. Use straw to blow paint across paper to make creative designs

Alligator
Materials
- alligator pattern (page 271)
- construction paper
- crayons or markers
- sandpaper
- wiggle eyes (optional)
- glue
- scissors

Process
1. Precut alligator from sandpaper.
2. Color it green and glue onto construction paper.
3. Glue on wiggle eye.
4. Draw in teeth and environment.

Short "A" Word Cards

sat	that
mat	at
and	Sally
sad	have
cat	hat

Short "A" Word Cards (cont.)

can	man
has	fan
another	fast
back	ran
bad	pack

The Cat in the Hat   Short "A"

Short "A" Picture Cards

Name each picture. Listen for the short "a" sound. Paste the short "a" pictures on your hat.

#791 Teaching Basic Skills through Literature: Phonics   ©1995 Teacher Created Materials, Inc.

Short "A"   *The Cat in the Hat*

Short "A" Picture Cards (cont.)

©1995 Teacher Created Materials, Inc.   265   #791 *Teaching Basic Skills through Literature: Phonics*

The Cat in the Hat   Short "A"

Cat Pattern

#791 Teaching Basic Skills through Literature: Phonics   266   ©1995 Teacher Created Materials, Inc.

Short "A" | The Cat in the Hat

Hat Pattern

The Cat in the Hat   Short "A"

"A" Pattern

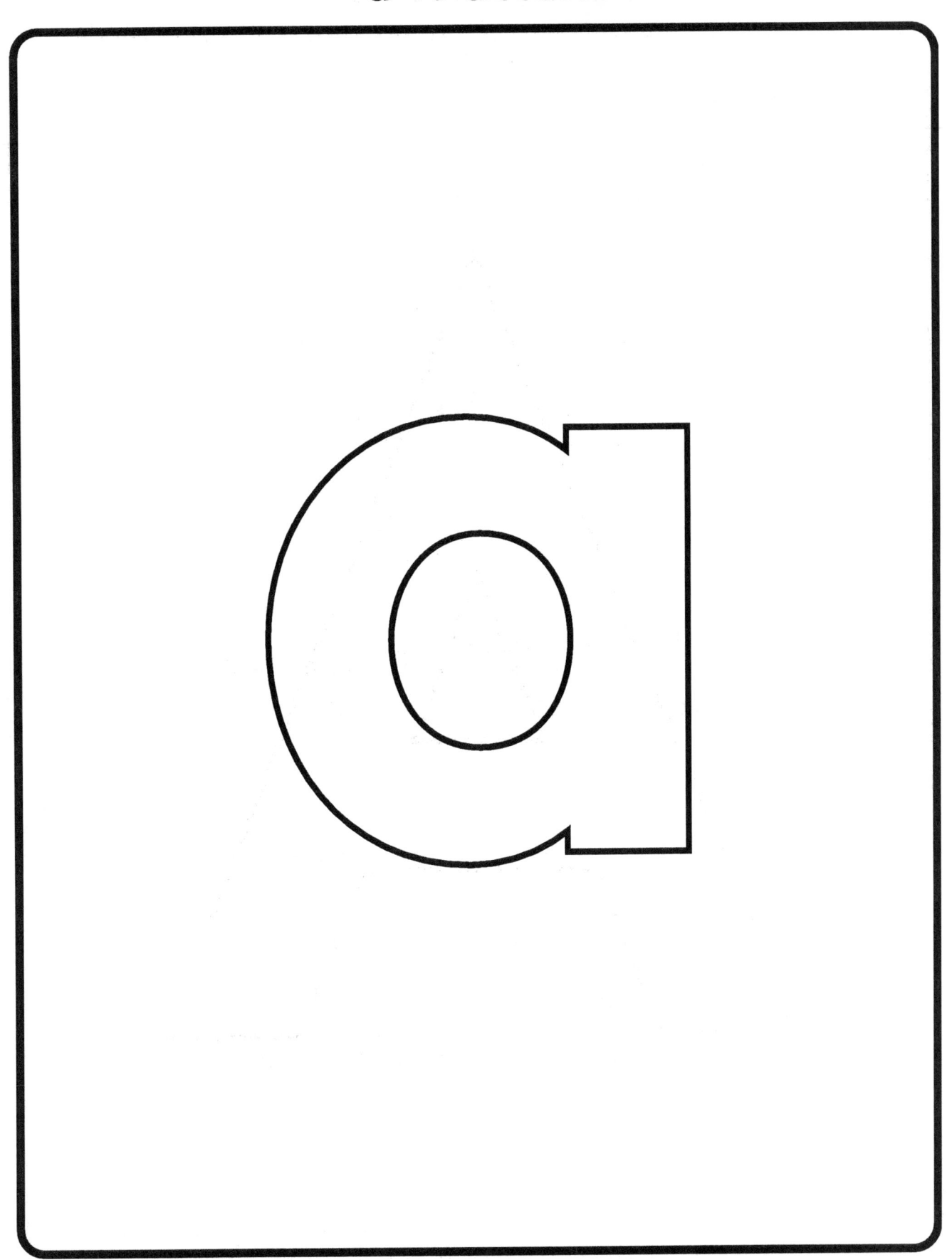

Short "A" | "a" Pattern | The Cat in the Hat

The Cat in the Hat

Short "A"

Apple Seed Story

The Apple Seed Story Mix-Up

by:_____

I planted an apple seed in my garden, but instead of an apple tree, up came . . .

Short "A" | The Cat in the Hat

Alligator Pattern

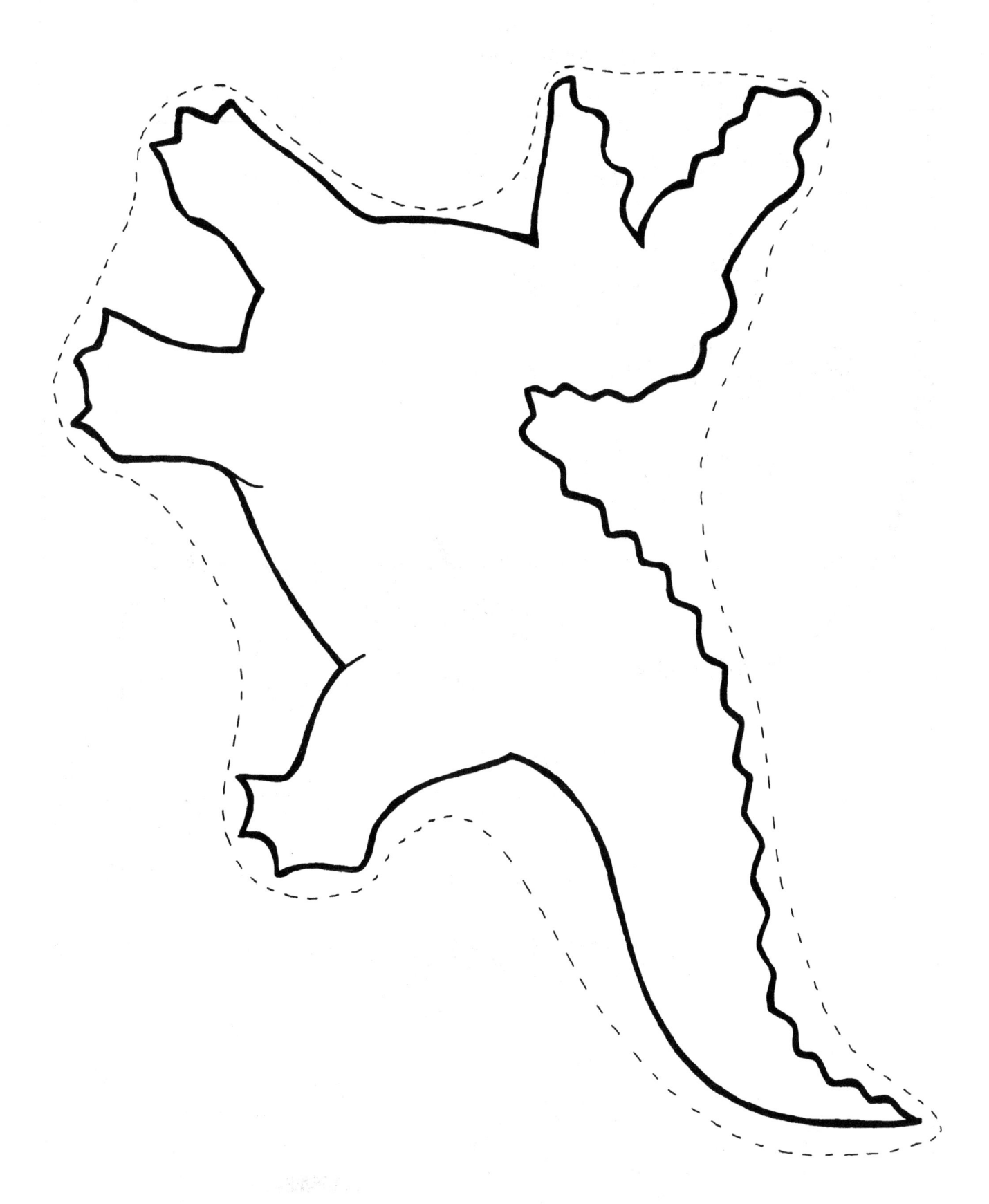

Phonics Skills in Context: Long "A"

Book: *Bringing the Rain to Kapiti Plain*
Author: Verna Aardema
Publisher: Scholastic, New York, 1981
Summary: This is a cumulative story about Kapiti, who helped to end the drought on the African plain of Kapiti.
Recommended Grade Level: K–2
Related Poetry: "Rain" by Robert Louis Stevenson, *A Child's Book of Poems* (Grosset & Dunlap, 1972). For additional titles see page 387.

Skill Activity
Students create an accordion-fold book titled "My Long 'A' Book" in which three lists of different long "a" words are written and illustrated.

Materials
- long "a" word cards (pages 275 and 276)
- pocket chart
- chart paper
- construction paper
- crayons or markers

Lesson
Introduce the Literature: Show students the globe and locate Africa. Tell students that this is a Nandi tale from Africa.

Read the Literature: Read the literature selection. Allow time for discussion.

Introduce the Skill Lesson:

1. Read the story again and invite students to join in the reading of the repeating phrases. Also, encourage them to listen for long "a" words. List all long "a" words on chart paper to display as a word bank.
2. Pass out the long "a" word cards (pages 275 and 276) to the class (one per student).
3. Have students walk around and read all the words to discover all the ways the long "a" sound is spelled. Tell students to form a line with those who have the same long "a" pattern as they do.
4. When the lines are formed, students can read their cards and place them in three columns on the pocket chart.
5. Provide each student with construction paper and models for how to fold their accordion books. Students select three to five words from each list to write and illustrate in their booklets.

Learning Center Activity: Allow students to make dioramas of their favorite scenes in the story. Students will need a shoebox, construction paper, crayons or markers, glue, and scissors. Students may write about their favorite parts and glue writings to the tops of the boxes.

Cooperative Learning Activity: Divide the class into eight cooperative groups and give each a part of the story: Kapiti Plain, the cloud, the grass, the cows, Ki-pat, the eagle, the arrow and bow, and the other animals. When all parts are complete, have the students sequence the scenes and read the story.

Across the Curriculum: Science
Talk about what a drought is and the effect it can have on our environment. Discuss ways we can conserve water.

Long "A" *Bringing the Rain to Kapiti Plain*

Extension Activities

Movement Activities
Stress the long "a" sound as students participate in the following movements: swing like an ape, fly like an angel, and practice your aim by tossing beans into a can.

Multisensory Activity
On 6" x 8" (15 cm x 20 cm) tagboard, have students paste acorns to an upper and lowercase "a." Patterns are provided on pages 268 and 269.

Creative Writing
Have students write stories about an alien visiting their school.

Handwriting
On 12" x 18" (30 cm x 46 cm) lined newsprint, ask children to copy this sentence: "A is for April, anchor (draw one), apron, and Abraham Lincoln."

Cooking

Abe Lincoln Faces

Ingredients
- crackers
- raisins
- shredded carrots
- plates

Directions
1. Have student place raisins on the cracker as eyes, nose, and mouth.
2. Add shredded carrots as a beard.
3. Draw your recipe.
4. Clean up.

Interdisciplinary Topics

ape	ache	April	Asia
acorn	Abraham Lincoln	angel	aviary
acre	ancient	angle	atrium

©1995 Teacher Created Materials, Inc. 273 #791 Teaching Basic Skills through Literature: Phonics

Bringing the Rain to Kapiti Plain Long "A"

Extension Activities (cont.)

Art

Aviary
Materials
- construction paper strips thinly cut
- crayons or markers
- large sheets of construction paper
- glue

Process
1. Draw birds on the construction paper.
2. Glue construction paper strips over picture to look like a cage.

Angel
Materials
- angel pattern (page 277)
- construction paper
- glue
- scissors
- crayons or markers
- glitter (optional)

Process
1. Cut out angel pattern.
2. Fold ends so they overlap and glue together.
3. Paint on a face and robe decorations. Use glitter if desired.
4. Angel will stand on its own.

Abe Lincoln Face
Materials
- black paint
- Styrofoam cups
- crayons or markers
- black construction paper
- scissors

Process
1. Turn the paper cup upside down. Paint the top half with black paint.
2. Draw a face on the lower half of the cup.
3. From a 6" (15 cm) square of black paper, cut out a doughnut shape for a hat brim.
4. Slip the doughnut on the cup so it sits just above the face.
5. Curl small strips of black construction paper.
6. Glue them on the bottom of the cup as a beard.

Long "A" — *Bringing the Rain to Kapiti Plain*

Long "A" Word Cards

hay	may
cake	way
same	make
care	lake
late	made

Bringing the Rain to Kapiti Plain — Long "A"

Long "A" Word Cards *(cont.)*

paint	rain
pair	train
plain	mail
play	day
clay	say

Long "A" *Bringing the Rain to Kapiti Plain*

Angel Pattern

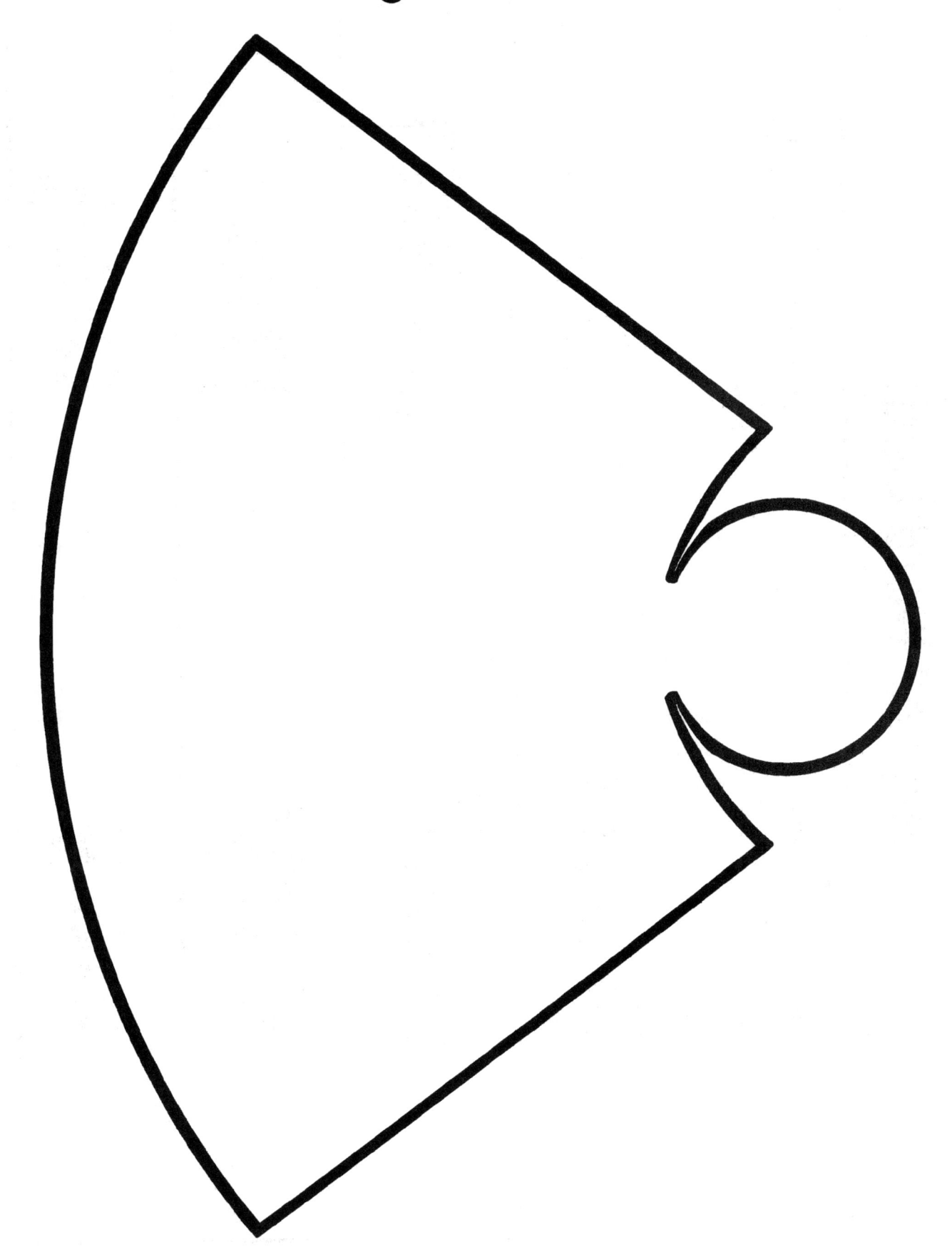

©1995 Teacher Created Materials, Inc. #791 Teaching Basic Skills through Literature: Phonics

Phonics Skills in Context: Short "E"

Book: *Red is Best*
Author: Kathy Swinson
Publisher: Annick Press, New York, 1983
Summary: A little girl insists on all the ways that red is best, much to her mother's dismay.
Recommended Grade Level: K–2
Related Poetry: "The Elephant" by Arnold Sundgaard, *Eric Carle's Animals, Animals* (Philomel Books, New York, 1989). For additional titles see page 388.

Skill Activity

Students work in teams to discriminate between short "e" sounds.

Materials

- short "e" word cards (pages 281 and 282)
- bag or other container for students to draw cards from
- chart paper

Lesson

Introduce the Literature: Ask students what colors they like best. Encourage students to give reasons why certain colors are best.

Read the Literature: Read the literature selection. Allow time for discussion.

Introduce the Skill Lesson:

1. Have students brainstorm short "e" words. List these on chart paper and display as a word bank.
2. Divide the group into two teams and have them stand several feet apart facing each other.
3. Draw a line or use a rope down the middle of the two teams.
4. Have one member of a team pull a word card from pages 281 or 282 out of a bag and read it to the class. That student must be able to identify whether the word is a short "e" word.
5. If the student answers correctly, he/she may step forward toward the other team. The first team to step all the way to the line is the winner.

Learning Center Activity: Have students make individual books entitled "What I Like Best." Patterns are located on pages 283 through 286. Students fill in the pages of the book by writing and drawing things they like.

Cooperative Learning Activity: Give each small group an envelope along with several blank index cards and crayons or markers. Have students brainstorm words that have the short "e." Each student will write and illustrate a short "e" word on a card and put it in the envelope. Each student can then take turns reading all the cards.

Across the Curriculum: Science

Have students experiment with red paint by mixing it with other colors of paint. Students may use the Science Experiment Sheet on page 287 to record their findings.

Short "E" • Red is Best

Extension Activities

Movement Activities
Stress the short "e" sound as students participate in the following movements: egg roll, exercise, explore the school environment, exit the room, and sway like an elephant.

Multisensory Activity
On 6" x 8" (15 cm x 20 cm) tagboard, have students paste upper and lowercase "e's" from magazines on an upper and lowercase "e." Patterns are provided on pages 288 and 289.

Creative Writing
Have students write the story of an envelope's adventure. Provide envelopes for students to work with.

Handwriting
On 12" x 18" (30 cm x 46 cm) lined newsprint, ask students to copy this sentence: "E is for elephant, elf, eggs (draw eggs), and Eskimos."

Cooking

Egg Sandwich

Ingredients
- hard-boiled eggs
- mayonnaise
- bread
- tablespoon
- knife
- fork
- plates or bowls

Directions
1. Peel eggs.
2. Mash eggs with fork on plate.
3. Add 1 tablespoon (15 mL) of mayonnaise.
4. Spread egg mixture on bread.
5. Draw your recipe.
6. Clean up.

Interdisciplinary Topics

Earth	Eskimo	endangered	elderberry
energy	education	extinction	environment
egg	empty	editor	elementary school
elephant	exercise		

©1995 Teacher Created Materials, Inc.   279   #791 Teaching Basic Skills through Literature: Phonics

Red is Best   **Short "E"**

Extension Activities (cont.)

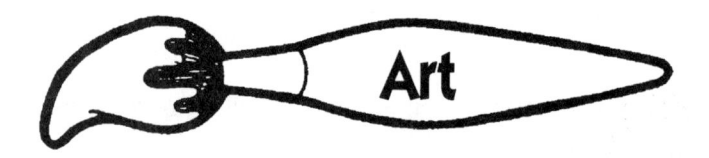

Art

Eggshell Mosaics
Materials
- egg pattern (page 290)
- eggshells
- food coloring
- plastic containers
- tagboard
- yarn (optional)
- glue

Process
1. Crush eggshells and place them in various containers to mix with food coloring. Spread out to dry.
2. Spread glue in areas on pattern and sprinkle eggshells on. Outline in yarn.

Elephant
Materials
- elephant pattern (page 291)
- real peanuts
- gray and white construction paper
- crayons or markers
- scissors
- glue

Process
1. Reproduce or trace elephant pattern on gray paper.
2. Cut white construction paper for eyes.
3. Cut 12" (30 cm) of gray strip for accordion-folded nose.
4. Outline all pieces and add wrinkle features. Peanut goes on tip of nose.

Elf
Materials
- elf patterns (page 292)
- construction paper
- paste
- scissors

Process
1. Fold 9" x 12" (23 cm x 30 cm) construction paper in half in both directions.
2. Fold in half again lengthwise. Open paper and lay it flat vertically.
3. Cut off the two bottom, outside boxes. Save for arms.
4. Cut on bottom center-fold line until you reach the middle-fold line (this makes the legs).
5. Fold in the two upper outside boxes to make a jacket. Fold down the corners to make collar.
6. Attach the arms in back.
7. Cut out patterns on page 292 and assemble head. Draw in facial features. Add ears and hat. Attach head to body.

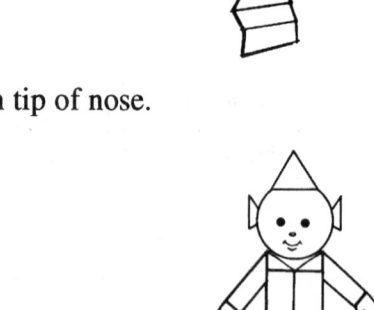

Short "E" Word Cards

red	them
best	better
dress	yellow
jacket	when
weather	blankets
steps	barrettes

Red is Best Short "E"

Short "E" Word Cards (cont.)

left	juice
instead	hair
mitts	paint
snowballs	jump
kick	stockings
cup	feet

Short "E" — Red is Best

What I Like Best

What I Like Best

by: _____

I like _____ the best.
(color)

Red is Best Short "E"

What I Like Best (cont.)

I like _____ the best.
(animal)

I like _____ the best.
(sport)

Short "E"   *Red is Best*

What I Like Best (cont.)

I like _____ the best.
                 (food)

I like _____ the best.
                (clothing)

Red is Best   Short "E"

What I Like Best (cont.)

I like _____ the best.
                   (friend)

I like _____ the best.
                 (your choice)

Short "E"   Red is Best

Science Experiment Sheet

Name _____

This is what happened when I mixed:

red and yellow

_____

red and blue

_____

red and green

_____

red and white

_____

red and purple

_____

red and _____

_____

Red is Best **Short "E"**

"E" Pattern

Short "E" *Red is Best*

"e" Pattern

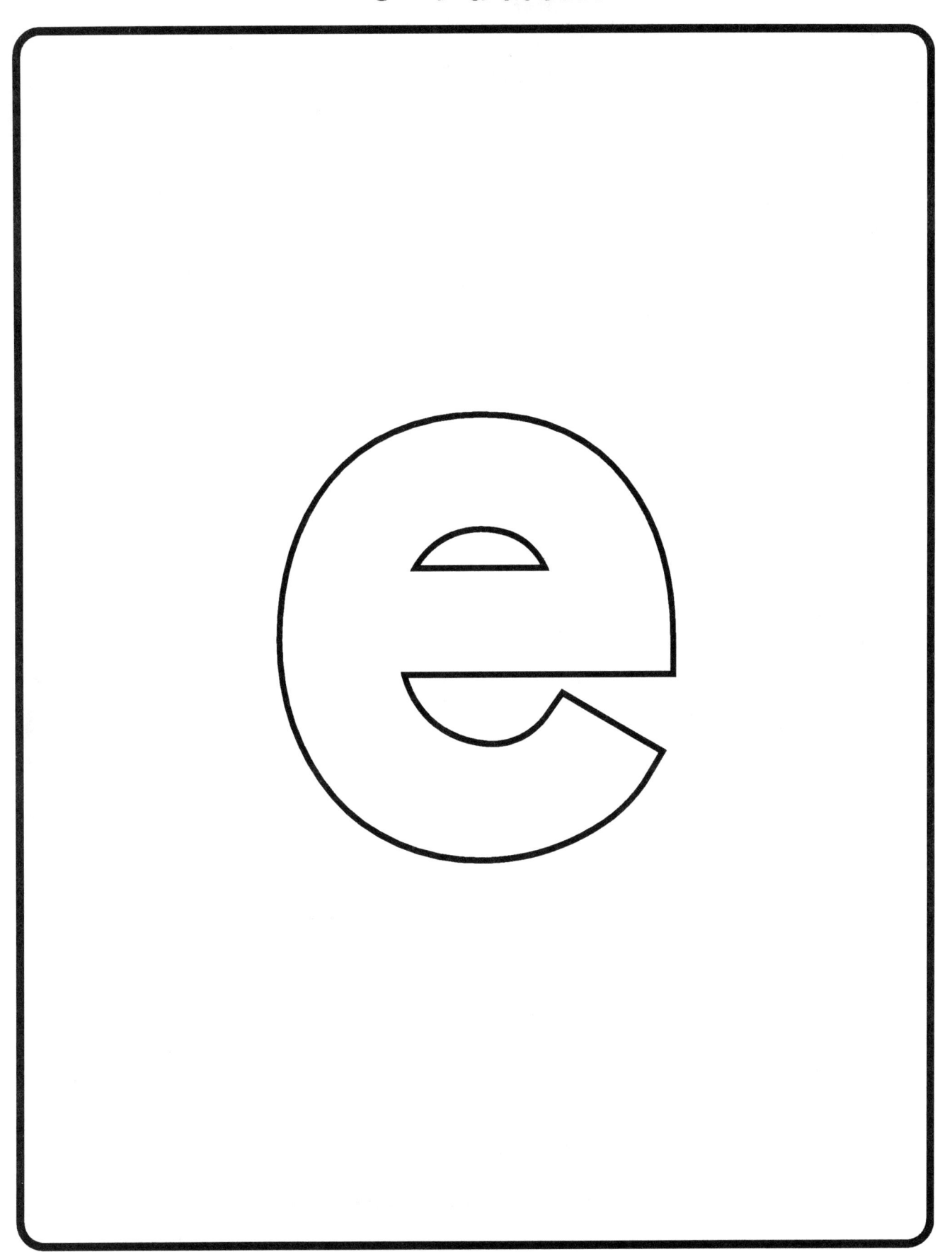

Red is Best   **Short "E"**

Egg Pattern

#791 Teaching Basic Skills through Literature: Phonics   ©1995 Teacher Created Materials, Inc.

Short "E" *Red is Best*

Elephant Pattern

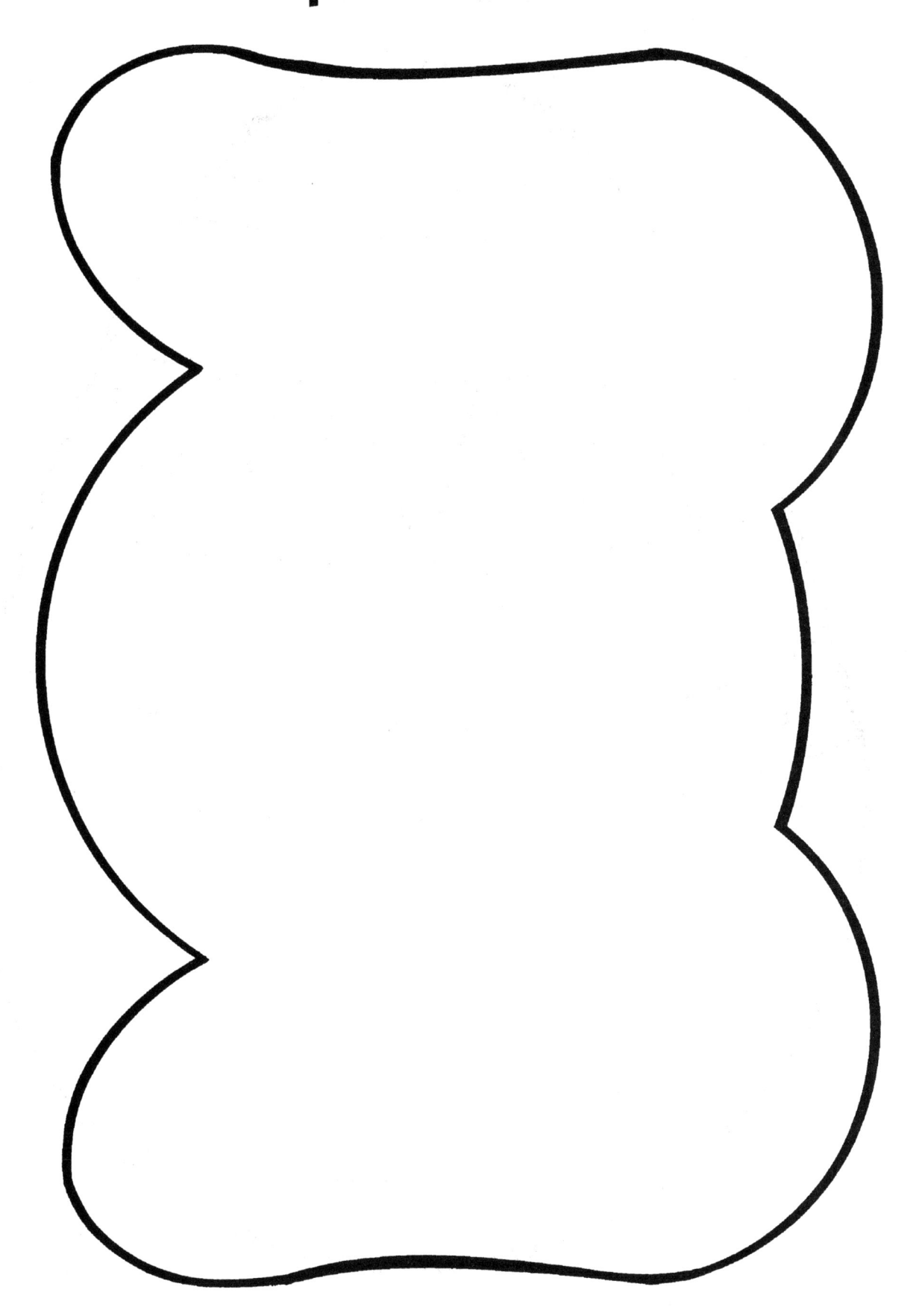

©1995 Teacher Created Materials, Inc. 291 #791 *Teaching Basic Skills through Literature: Phonics*

Red is Best   Short "E"

Elf Head and Hat

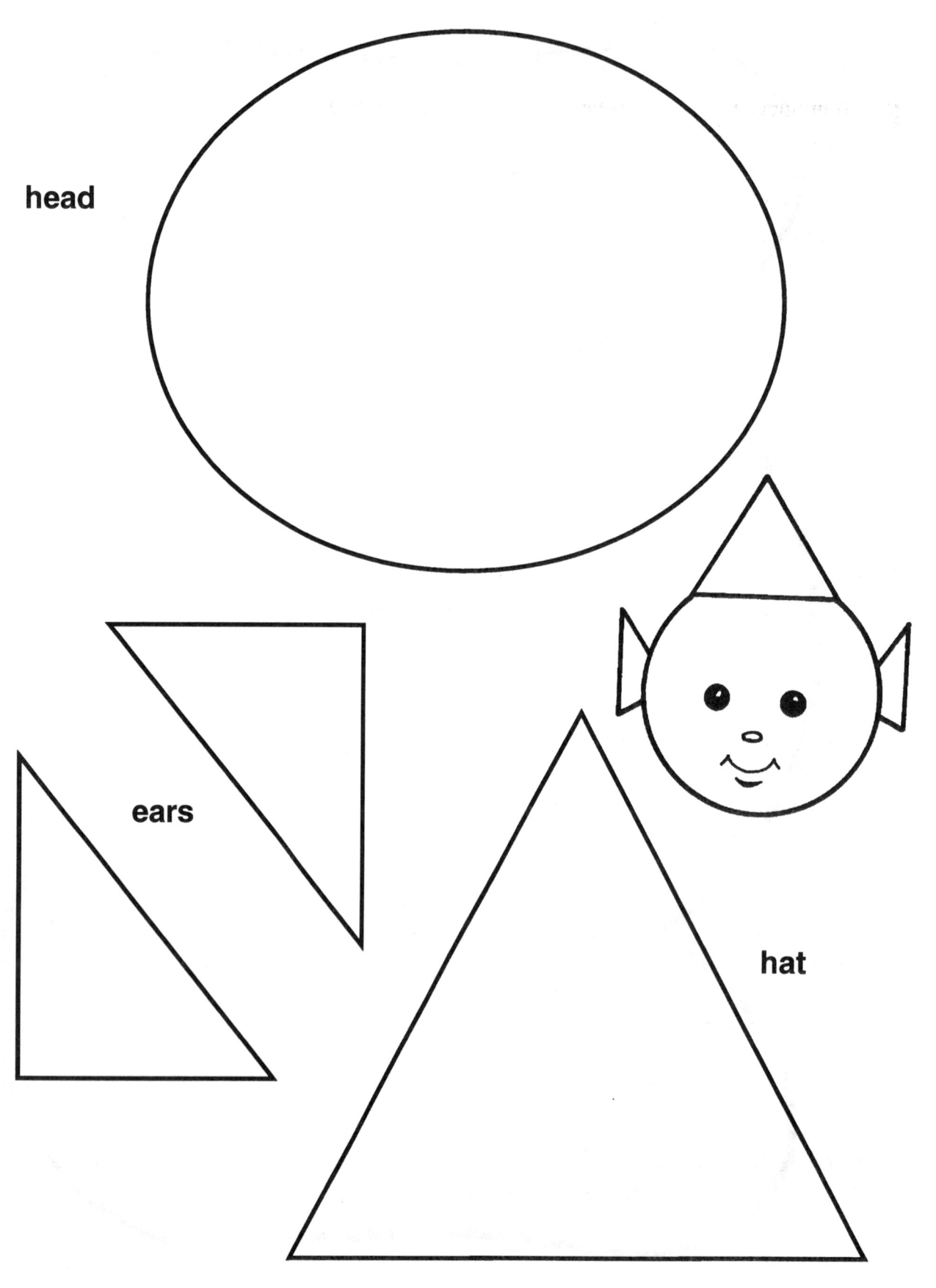

head

ears

hat

#791 Teaching Basic Skills through Literature: Phonics   292   ©1995 Teacher Created Materials, Inc.

Phonics Skills in Context: Long "E"

Book: *Sheep in a Jeep*
Author: Nancy Shaw
Publisher: Houghton Mifflin, Boston, 1986
Summary: This is the adventurous story of a group of sheep who go riding in a jeep.
Recommended Grade Level: K–2
Related Poetry: "Sheep" by Jack Prelutsky, *Zoo Doings* (Greenwillow, New York, 1983). For additional titles see page 388.

Skill Activity

Students will create a "Where's the Sheep?" class book emphasizing long "e" words.

Materials

- chart paper
- drawing paper
- crayons or markers
- yarn

Lesson

Introduce the Literature: Ask students if they have ever been in a jeep. Talk about the experiences.

Read the Literature: Read the literature selection. Allow time for discussion.

Introduce the Skill Lesson:

1. Ask students to identify the long "e" words in the story. Write them on chart paper to use as a word bank.
2. Have students use long "e" words to create pictures of scenes that represent where the sheep may be going. For example: The sheep is in a jeep. The sheep is at the beach. The sheep is going to sleep.

Learning Center Activity: Provide students with long "e" picture word cards from pages 296 through 298. Ask them to illustrate the words. Then, have the students sort the cards into the various categories such as food and drink, animals, and things to do. They can record their responses on page 299. Encourage students to sort the cards in other ways.

Cooperative Learning Activity: Have students work in groups to play "Sneak a Peek." Provide students with small chalkboards and a list of long "e" words. One student copies a word onto the chalkboard and shows it to the others. Then, the student erases one letter and the others have to try to guess what letter is missing after looking at the word.

Across the Curriculum: Science

Have students read books about sheep and their characteristics.

©1995 Teacher Created Materials, Inc.

Sheep in a Jeep   Long "E"

Extension Activities

Movement Activities
Stress the long "e" sound as students participate in the following movements: erase the chalkboard, point to the east, slither like an eel, and pretend to eat.

Multisensory Activity
On 6" x 8" (15 cm x 20 cm) tagboard, have children paste "e's" from magazines to an upper and lowercase "e." Patterns are provided on pages 288 and 289.

Creative Writing
Have students write stories about what an eagle saw as he flew across the country.

Handwriting
On 12" x 18" (30 cm x 46 cm) lined newsprint, ask children to copy this sentence "E is for ecology, Easter, eclipse (draw one), and an enormous eel."

Cooking

Eels

Ingredients
- string cheese
- raisins
- plates

Directions
1. Arrange the cheese to look like an eel.
2. Add raisins for eyes.
3. Draw your recipe.
4. Clean up.

Interdisciplinary Topics

eagle	emergency	ecosystem	eel
ecology	east	Egypt	erosion
Easter	easel	election	eruption
eclipse	economy		

Long "E" — Sheep in a Jeep

Extension Activities (cont.)

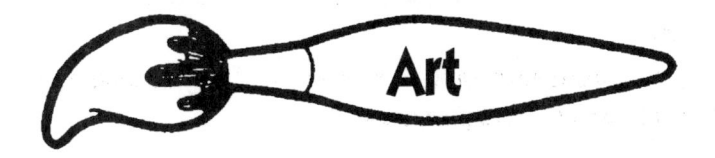

Art

Eraser Printing
Materials
- paint
- construction paper
- gum erasers

Process
1. Cut designs into erasers.
2. Using different colors of paint, dip erasers and use as stamps.
3. Decorate the construction paper.

Easel Art
Materials
- large piece of cardboard for easel (A refrigerator box works well.)
- paints (and paint brushes), markers, or crayons
- clothesline rope or heavy twine
- newspaper to cover work surface
- scissors

Process
1. Create easel by folding large piece of cardboard in half to form upside down "v" shape.
2. Poke a hole at each of the four corners at the bottom of the easel. (Be sure to poke the holes in the same place at each corner.)
3. Secure easel by pulling a length of rope through opposing holes at one end of the easel. Knot the ends. Do the same for the other end.
4. Have students paint or draw pictures of things that begin with long "e."

Elaborate "E's"
Materials
- pattern (page 288)
- crayons, markers, paints (and paint brushes), or fabric scraps
- scissors
- large piece of construction paper, or butcher paper

Process
1. Have students decorate "E" patterns, using crayons, markers, paints, or scraps of fabric.
2. Cut out the decorated letters.
3. Glue onto construction paper to create a collage effect.

Sheep in a Jeep   Long "E"

Picture Word Cards

peach	peas	tea
peanut	beets	cheese
meat	green beans	seeds

Long "E" — Sheep in a Jeep

Picture Word Cards (cont.)

flea	seal	eagle
beaver	peacock	eel
sheep	weasel	cheetah

©1995 Teacher Created Materials, Inc.

Sheep in a Jeep — Long "E"

Picture Word Cards (cont.)

leap	read	sneak
weave	squeak	scream
sneeze	peel	reach

Long "E" *Sheep in a Jeep*

Category Activity Sheet

Name _____

Food and Drink	Things to Do	Animals

Phonics Skills in Context: Short "I"

Book: *It Looked Like Spilt Milk*
Author: Charles Shaw
Publisher: Scholastic, New York, 1947
Summary: This is a classic pattern book about imagining pictures from the clouds in the sky.
Recommended Grade Level: K–2
Related Poetry: "Ickel Me, Pickle Me, Tickle Me Too" by Shel Silverstein, *Where the Sidewalk Ends* (Harper & Row, New York 1969). For additional titles see page 388.

Skill Activity

Students make letter wheels which they manipulate to make short "i" words. Words are then copied and illustrated in their "Milk Shape Book."

Materials

- Milk Shape Book (page 303)
- wheel patterns (pages 304 and 305)
- small piece of straw (optional)
- brad fasteners
- scissors
- crayons
- chart paper

Lesson

Introduce the Literature: Take the class outside to look at the clouds. Have students discuss what shapes they see. Show students the cover of the book and tell them the author observed clouds just like they did.

Read the Literature: Read the literature selection. Allow time for discussion.

Introduce the Skill Lesson:

1. Have students identify the short "i" words in the title of the story. Write those words on chart paper.
2. Ask students for more short "i" words. Continue to list them on the chart paper and display as a word bank.
3. Have students assemble the wheel patterns on pages 304 and 305, using the directions on each page.
4. Students can turn their wheels to form short "i" words. Words can then be written and illustrated in the Milk Shape Book. A pattern can be found on page 303.
5. A straw can be added to the top of the book if desired.

Learning Center Activity: Allow students to experiment with white paint that is carefully dripped onto blue construction paper. Students then complete the sentences: "Sometimes it looked like ___. But it wasn't ___. It was just a cloud in the sky." These sentences are written for children on page 306.

Cooperative Learning Activity: Have students work in small groups to make ink-print pictures. Provide students with an inked stamp pad, paper, and thin felt pens. Students make prints with their fingers and then make characters out of them.

Across the Curriculum: Social Studies

Have students conduct interviews with someone in their families. An interview form is located on page 307.

Short "I" — It Looked Like Spilt Milk

Extension Activities

Movement Activities
Stress the short "i" sound as students participate in the following movements: crawl like an inchworm, fly like an insect, move in and out a door, and imitate their favorite animal.

Multisensory Activity
On 6" x 8" (15 cm x 20 cm) tagboard, have students write their initials on an upper and lowercase "i." Patterns are provided on pages 308 and 309.

Creative Writing
Have students create "I Am" books to increase their self-esteem. A cover and page to complete can be found on pages 310 and 311.

Handwriting
On 12" x 18" (30 cm x 46 cm) lined newsprint, ask children to copy this sentence: "I is for Indian, igloo (add a paper igloo), inchworm, and iguana."

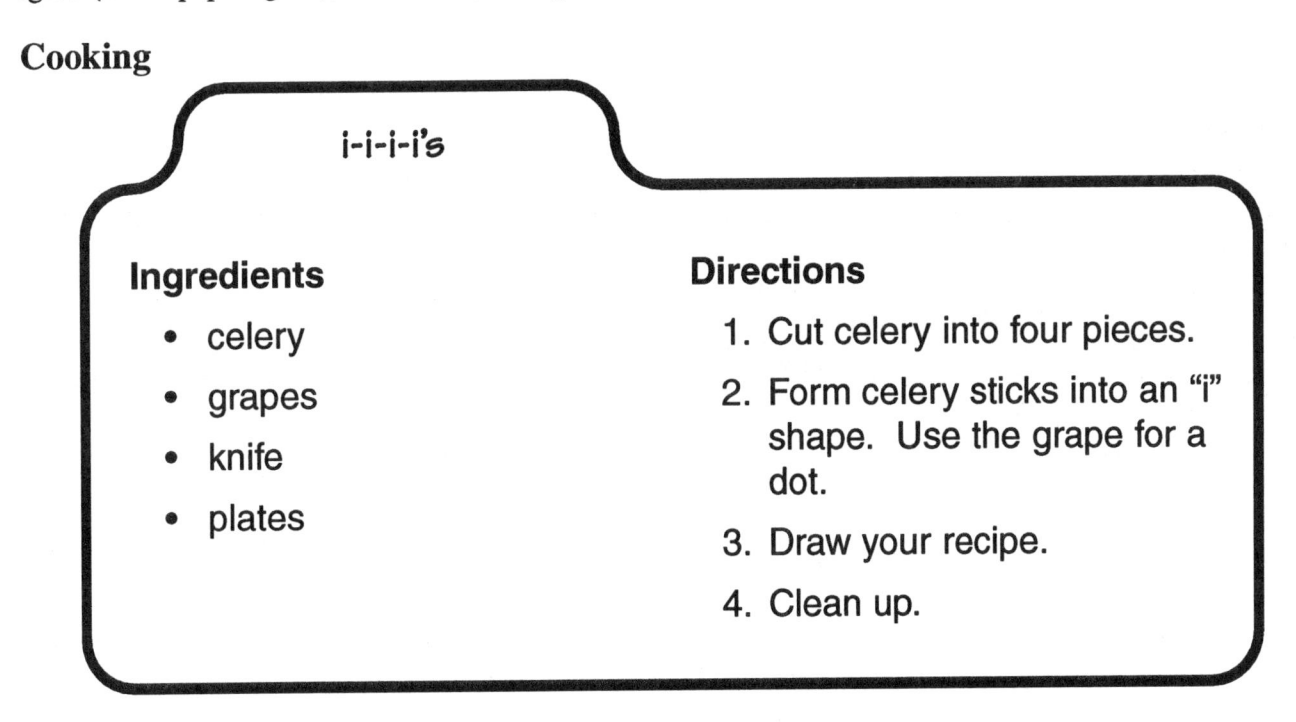

Cooking

i-i-i-i's

Ingredients
- celery
- grapes
- knife
- plates

Directions
1. Cut celery into four pieces.
2. Form celery sticks into an "i" shape. Use the grape for a dot.
3. Draw your recipe.
4. Clean up.

Interdisciplinary Topics

insects	inch	illustrate	international
instruments	incubator	imagination	invention
Independence Day	iguana	immigrant	Israel
industry	illegal	inauguration	Italy
individual	Illinois	initials	

©1995 Teacher Created Materials, Inc.

It Looked Like Spilt Milk   Short "I"

Extension Activities

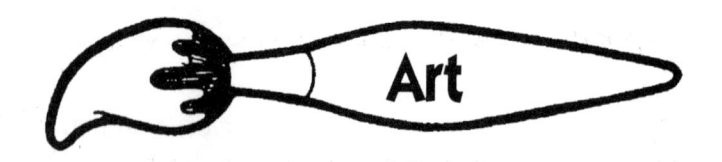

Art

Igloo
Materials
- igloo pattern (page 312)
- white construction paper
- scissors
- Styrofoam meat tray
- 3" x 3" (8 cm x 8 cm) black squares

Process
1. Reproduce and cut out pattern on white construction paper.
2. Paste black square behind hole.
3. Break Styrofoam into small chunks to resemble igloo "blocks."
4. Glue Styrofoam in rows.

Inchworm
Materials
- worm pattern (page 313)
- measuring tape cut into one-inch sections
- construction paper
- crayons
- glue
- scissors

Process
1. Have children color and cut out the worm pattern.
2. Glue front and back of worm.
3. Glue worm to construction paper.
4. Have children add an environment with crayons or construction paper.
5. Place objects against inchworm picture to measure them.

Indian Teepee
Materials
- scissors
- construction paper
- crayons or markers

Process
1. Fold down the two top corners of construction paper.
2. Decorate the flaps with Indian designs.
3. Color the space inside to look like the inside of a teepee.
4. Fold back the bottom strip so the teepee will stand up.

Indian Mural
Materials
- a large piece of butcher paper
- crayons or markers

Process
1. Allow children to work as a class to design a mural.

Short "I"   *It Looked Like Spilt Milk*

Milk Shape Book

It Looked Like Spilt Milk **Short "I"**

Wheel Pattern

Cut out the wheels on this page.

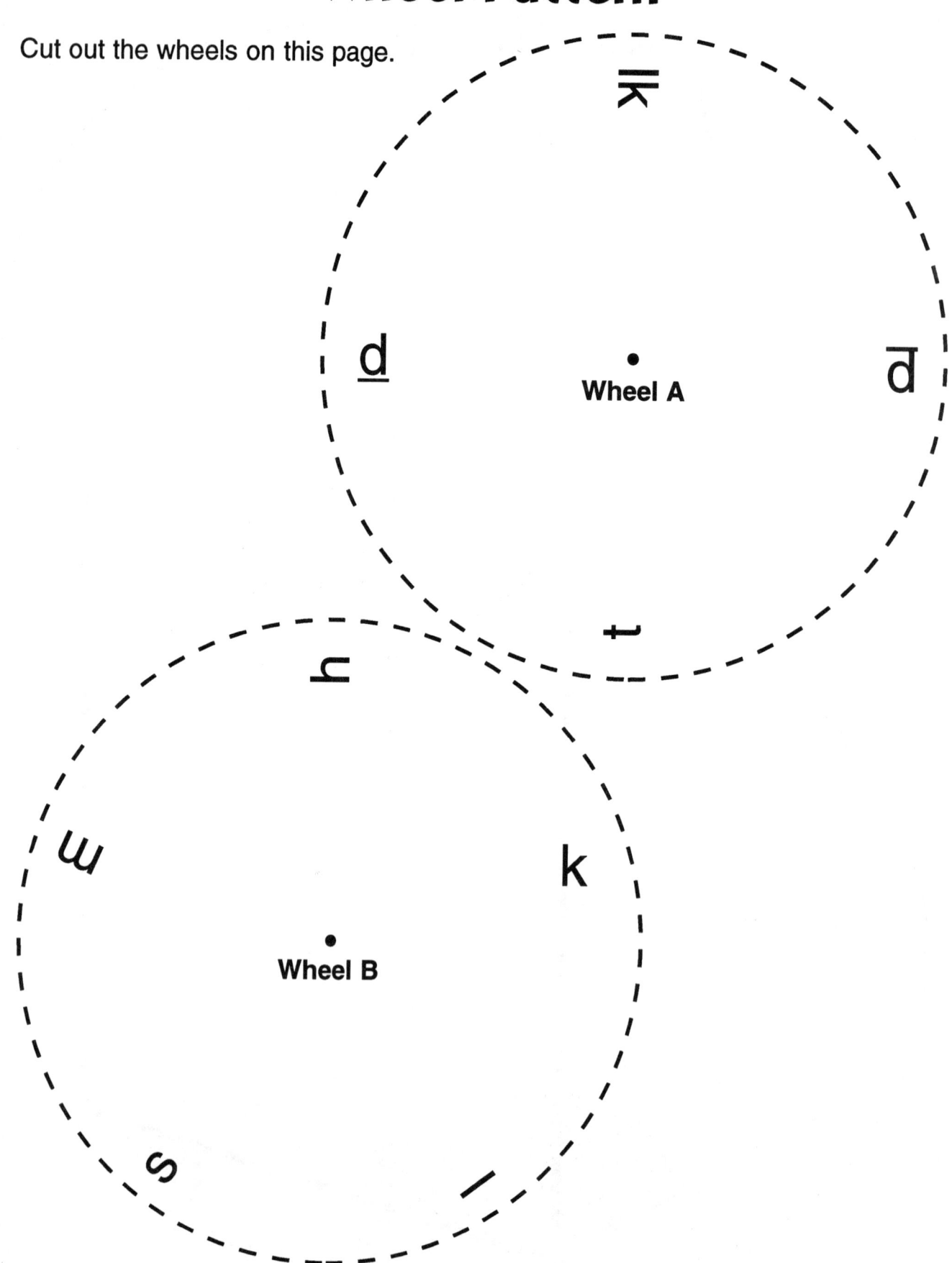

Wheel A — letters around: k, d, d, t

Wheel B — letters around: n, m, k, s, l

#791 Teaching Basic Skills through Literature: Phonics ©1995 Teacher Created Materials, Inc.

Short "I"   *It Looked Like Spilt Milk*

Wheel Pattern (cont.)

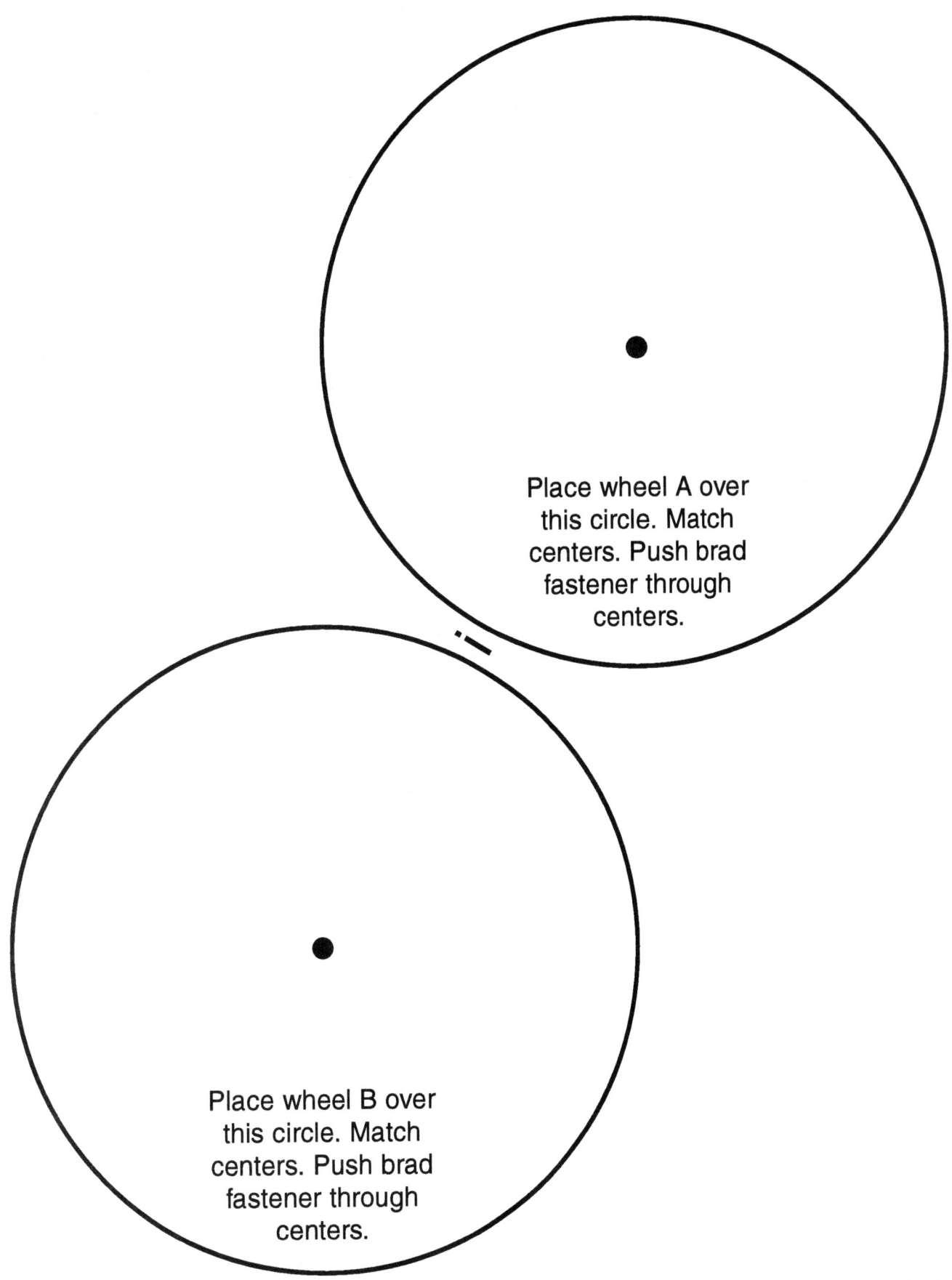

Place wheel A over this circle. Match centers. Push brad fastener through centers.

Place wheel B over this circle. Match centers. Push brad fastener through centers.

It Looked Like Spilt Milk   **Short "I"**

It Looked Like...

Sometimes it looked like _____

_____.

But it wasn't _____

_____.

It was just a cloud in the sky.

Short "I" It Looked Like Spilt Milk

Interview Questions

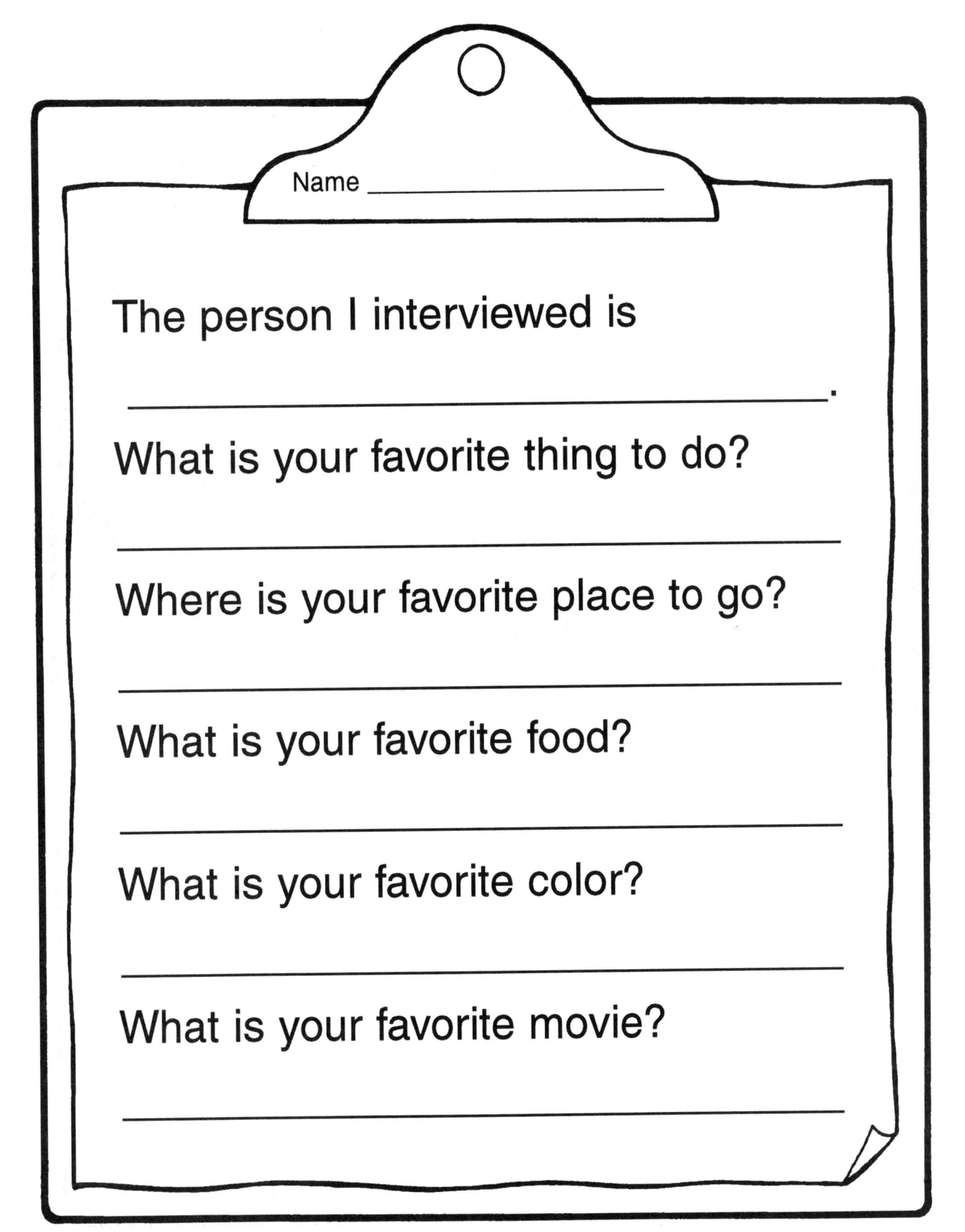

Name _____

The person I interviewed is

_____.

What is your favorite thing to do?

_____

Where is your favorite place to go?

_____

What is your favorite food?

_____

What is your favorite color?

_____

What is your favorite movie?

_____

©1995 Teacher Created Materials, Inc. #791 Teaching Basic Skills through Literature: Phonics

It Looked Like Spilt Milk   **Short "I"**

"I" Pattern

Short "I"   *It Looked Like Spilt Milk*

"i" Pattern

It Looked Like Spilt Milk · Short "I"

"I Am" Book

I Am

_____ _____
Name   Date

#791 Teaching Basic Skills through Literature: Phonics · · · · · · · ©1995 Teacher Created Materials, Inc.

Short "I" | It Looked Like Spilt Milk

"I Am" Book (cont.)

When I was a baby, I was _____ years old.

I liked to _____

_____.

I did not like _____

_____.

When I am old, I will be _____ years old.

I will like to _____

_____.

I will not like to _____

_____.

by: _____

It Looked Like Spilt Milk **Short "I"**

Igloo Pattern

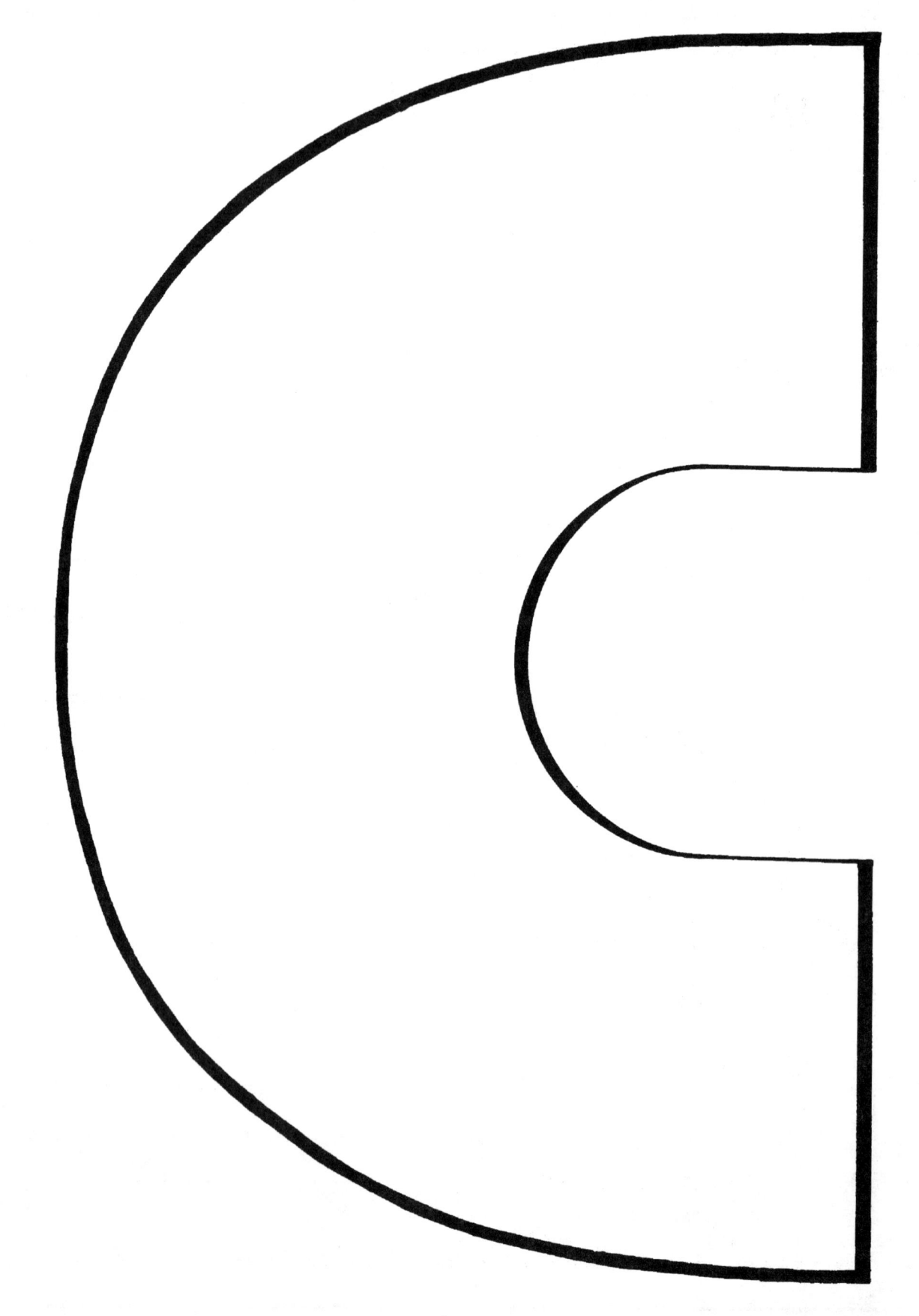

Short "I"　　　　　　　　　　　　　　　　　　　　　　It Looked Like Spilt Milk

Worm Pattern

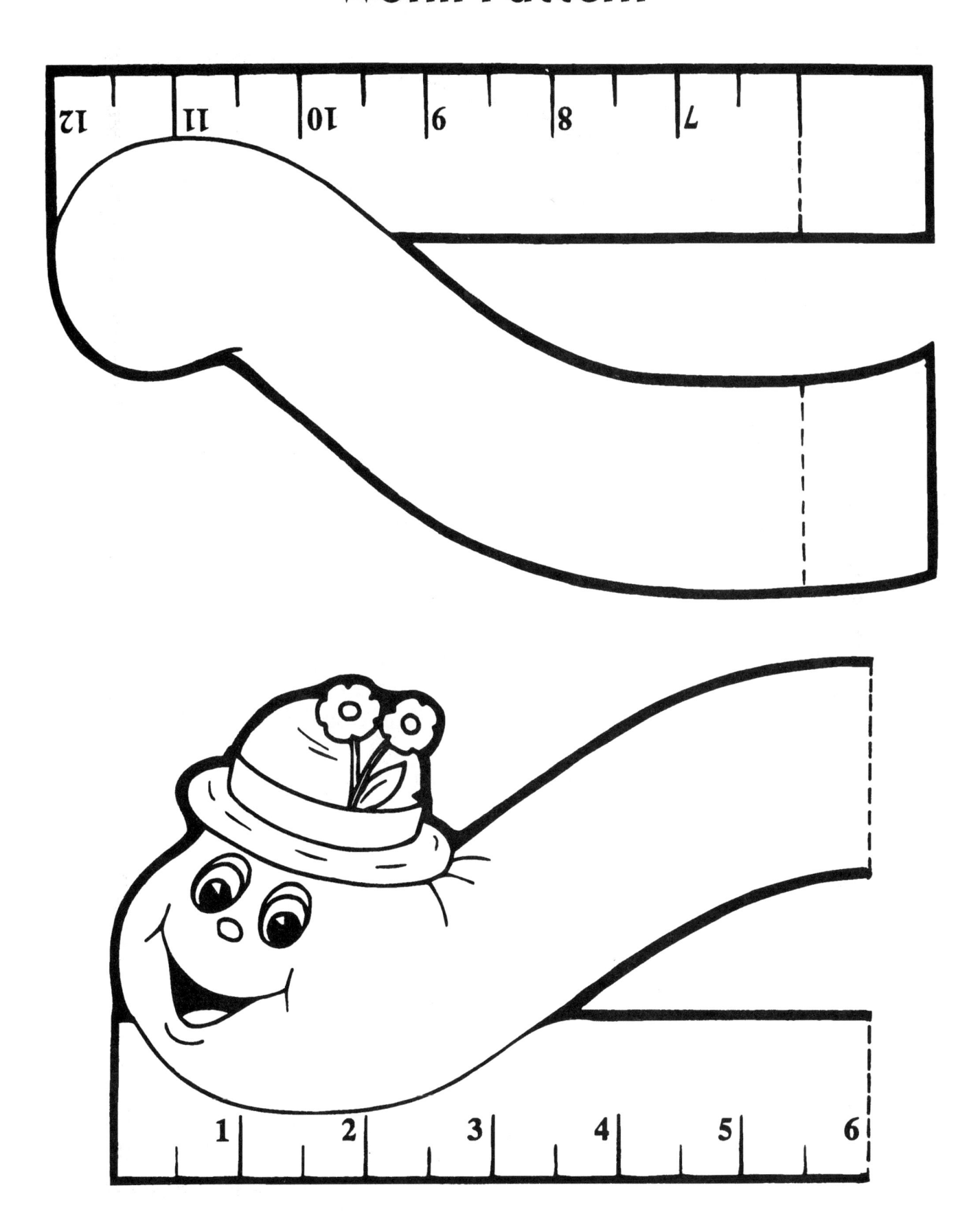

©1995 Teacher Created Materials, Inc.　　　313　　　#791 Teaching Basic Skills through Literature: Phonics

Phonics Skills in Context: Long "I"

Book: *I Like to be Little*
Author: Charlotte Zolotow
Publisher: Thomas Y. Crowell, New York, 1987
Summary: A young girl gives her mother all the reasons she likes to be little.
Recommended Grade Level: K–2
Related Poetry: "I Like Flies" by Margaret Wise Brown, *See Saw* (Merrill Books, New York, 1966). For additional titles see page 388.

Skill Activity
Students create sentences using long "i" words and a story starter.

Materials
- long "i" picture and words cards (pages 317 through 319)
- story starter (page 320)
- chart paper
- pocket chart
- crayons or markers

Lesson
Introduce the Literature: Show students the cover of the book.

Read the Literature: Read the literature selection. Allow time for discussion.

Introduce the Skill Lesson:
1. Have students brainstorm long "i" words for you to list on chart paper as a word bank.
2. Pass out the long "i" picture cards from pages 317 through 319. Have them walk around the room to match all pictures and words.
3. Put all pictures and cards in a pocket chart.
4. Have students select one of the ideas from the pocket chart and complete the story starter on page 320. Invite students to illustrate their sentences.

Learning Center Activity: Ask students to make lists of five things they like. Have them write their ideas in the box on page 321. Then, have them write the five things on the wheel pattern on page 321. Then, have them attach the wheel, using a brad fastener, to the bike pattern on page 322. The wheel turns to show all the things the child likes.

Cooperative Learning Activity: Have students work in small groups to make kites using a large piece of butcher paper and some streamers. Allow them to experiment with their kites outside.

Across the Curriculum: Math
Have students complete an "I Like" graph by writing two statements at the top of the graph such as "I like red," or "I like blue." Students ask others to write their names under their preferences. They can record the data on page 323.

Long "I" | I Like to be Little

Extension Activities

Movement Activities
Stress the long "i" sound as students participate in the following movements: pretend to ice skate, walk on ice, and conceal their identity.

Multisensory Activity
On 6" x 8" (15 cm x 20 cm) tagboard, have children paste white icicles onto an upper and lowercase "i." Patterns are provided on pages 308 and 309.

Creative Writing
Students write stories about spending the day with their idols. They can use the activity sheet on page 324.

Handwriting
On 12" x 18" (30 cm x 46 cm) lined newsprint, ask children to copy this sentence: "I is for Irish, ice cream (paste on little cones), and icy icicle."

Cooking

Ice Treats

Ingredients
- fruit punch
- ice-cube trays

Directions
1. Pour fruit punch into ice-cube trays.
2. Put in freezer.
3. Later, enjoy the frozen treat.
4. Draw your recipe.
5. Clean up.

Interdisciplinary Topics

island	ice age	idol	Iraq
icicle	icing	Irish	iron
ice	ID card	Iran	ivory
ice cream	identical		

©1995 Teacher Created Materials, Inc.

I Like to be Little   Long "I"

Extension Activities *(cont.)*

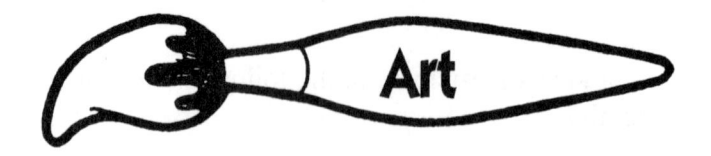

Art

Identification
Materials
- ID card pattern (page 325)
- crayons or markers

Process
1. Have students write in the information on the ID card on page 325.
2. Have them draw a picture of themselves.

Ice Cream Cone
Materials
- cone pattern (page 326)
- tan construction paper
- glue
- variety of tissue
- stapler
- scissors

Process
1. Reproduce cone pattern onto construction paper.
2. Roll into cone shape and staple.
3. Wad up tissue into cone to resemble scoops of ice cream.
4. Glue together.

Ice Painting
Materials
- water
- food coloring
- small cups
- craft sticks
- paper

Process
1. Freeze water colored with food coloring in small cups.
2. Craft sticks can be placed in cups to use as handles.
3. When water is frozen, children paint with the colored ice.

Iron Prints
Materials
- crayon shavings
- wax paper
- warm iron
- construction paper (optional)

Process
1. Sprinkle crayon shavings on wax paper.
2. Cover with another piece of wax paper.
3. Have an adult iron top to melt crayons.
4. Finished product can be framed if desired.

Long "I" — I Like to be Little

Picture and Word Cards

ice	
bike	
kite	
hike	
mice	

I Like to be Little   Long "I"

Picture and Word Cards (cont.)

lion	
slide	
line	
pine cone	
rice	

#791 Teaching Basic Skills through Literature: Phonics   318   ©1995 Teacher Created Materials, Inc.

Long "I" — I Like to be Little

Picture and Word Cards (cont.)

time	
pipe	
light	
pie	
icicle	

©1995 Teacher Created Materials, Inc. 319 #791 Teaching Basic Skills through Literature: Phonics

I Like to be Little Long "I"

"I Like ..."

I like _____

because _____

_____

_____

_____

_____

_____

_____ .

Long "I" I Like to be Little

Bike Wheel

Five Things I Like

1. _____

2. _____

3. _____

4. _____

5. _____

Cut out the wheel. Then use a brad fastener to attach the dot at the center of the wheel to the dot at the center of the front wheel on page 322.

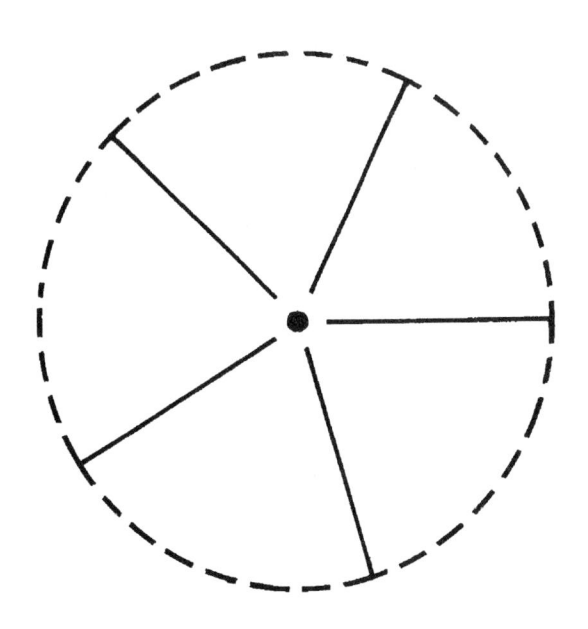

©1995 Teacher Created Materials, Inc.   321   #791 Teaching Basic Skills through Literature: Phonics

I Like to be Little   Long "I"

Bike Pattern

I like

Long "I" I Like to be Little

"I Like" Graph

Name _____

I like _____.	I like _____.
_____ people liked _____.	_____ people liked _____.

©1995 Teacher Created Materials, Inc.   #791 Teaching Basic Skills through Literature: Phonics

I Like to be Little   Long "I"

My Idol

A Day with My Idol

(picture)

_____

_____

_____

_____

Long "I" *I Like to be Little*

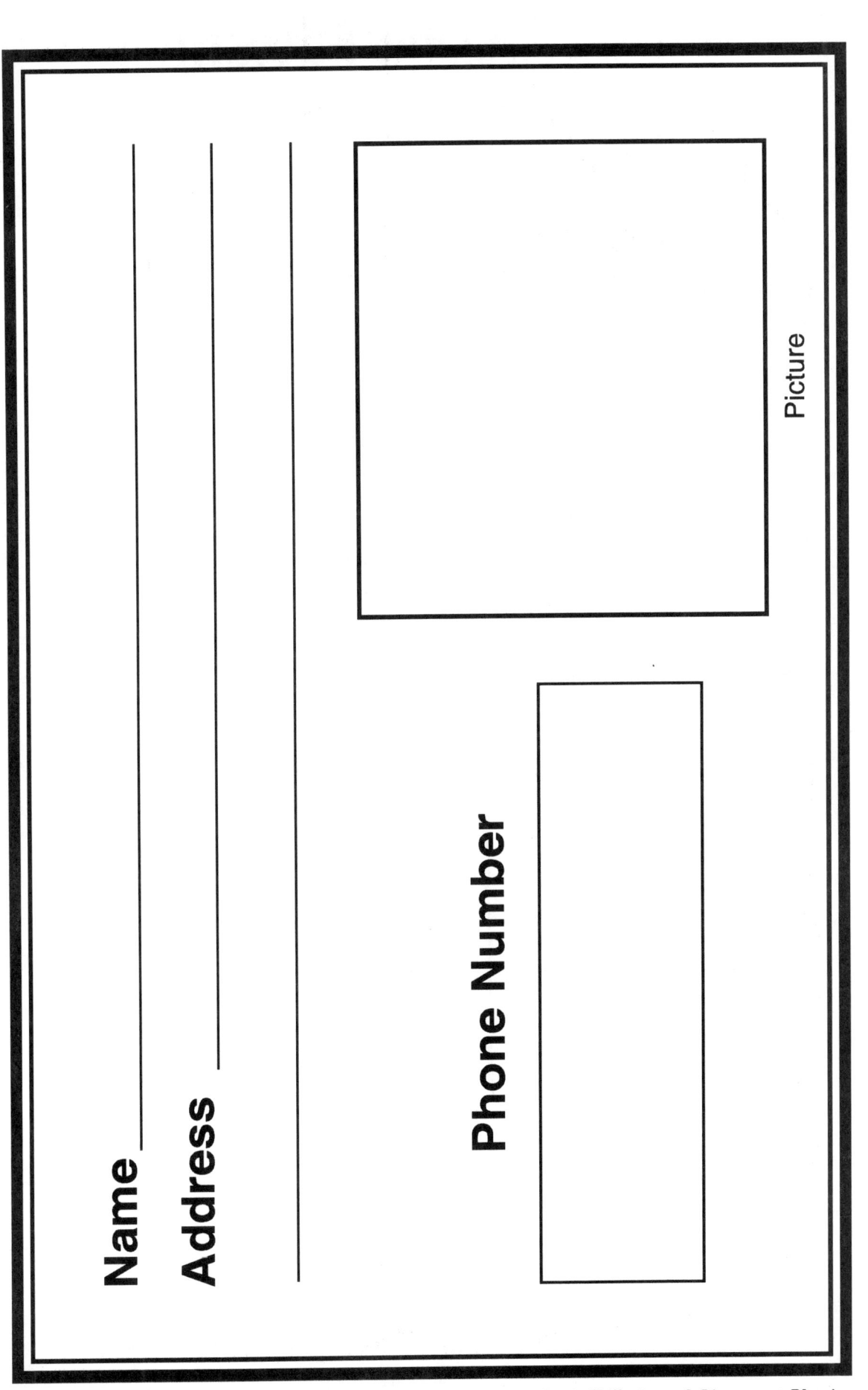

ID Card Pattern

Name _____
Address _____

Picture

Phone Number

©1995 Teacher Created Materials, Inc. 325 #791 *Teaching Basic Skills through Literature: Phonics*

I Like to be Little   Long "I"

Cone Pattern

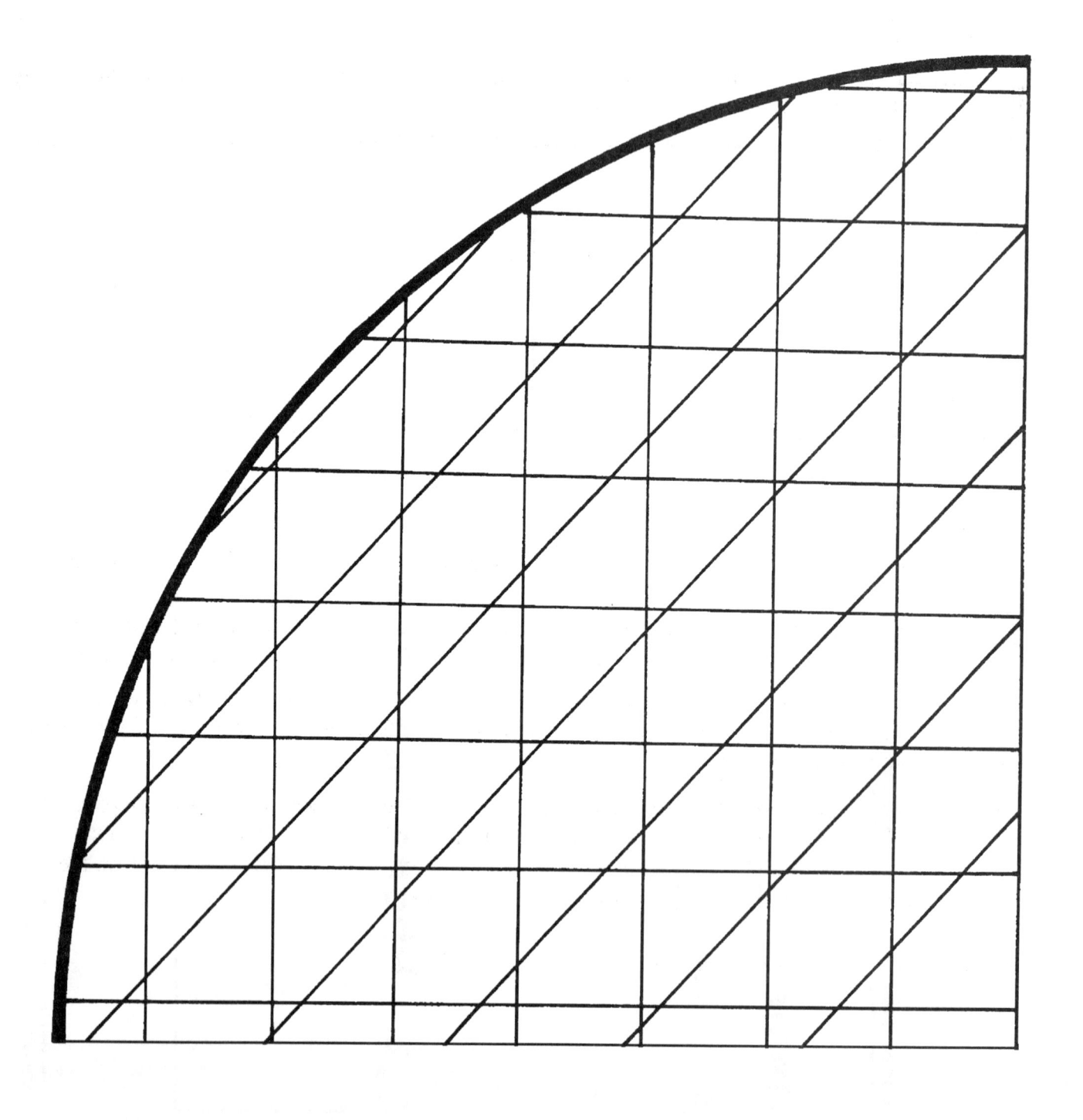

Phonics Skills in Context: Short "O"

Book: *Mop Top*
Author: Don Freeman
Publisher: Puffin, New York, 1955
Summary: This book tell the adventures of Moppy as he makes his way to the barbershop for a long overdue haircut.
Recommended Grade Level: K–2
Related Poetry: "Poemsicle" by Shel Silverstein, *A Light in the Attic* (HarperCollins, New York, 1981). For additional titles see page 388.

Skill Activity

Students will stop and hop as they hear words with the short "o" sound.

Materials

- chart paper

Lesson

Introduce the Literature: Ask students to describe what it is like to get a haircut.

Read the Literature: Read the literature selection. Allow time for discussion.

Introduce the Skill Lesson:

1. Ask students to brainstorm short "o" words. Write them on chart paper to display as a word bank.
2. Explain the stop and hop game to students. While you read the story students will walk slowly around the room. When they hear a word with a short "o" sound, they should stop and hop.

Learning Center Activity: Students will make an "o" shape book. Students select five short "o" words from the word bank and illustrate them on circles. These pages are put together for an "o" book. The cover pattern is on page 330.

Cooperative Learning Activity: Have students play an "opposites" concentration game. Prepare a set of concentration cards (page 331) for each group. Students put all cards face down in a row. One student draws two cards and names the pictures. If the two cards are the opposite of each other, the player can keep the cards. The game continues until all cards are claimed.

Across the Curriculum: Music

Have students listen to opera music.

Mop Top   Short "O"

Extension Activities

Movement Activities
Stress the short "o" sound as students participate in the following movements: jump off a step, swim like an octopus, do the opposite, and hoot like an owl.

Multisensory Activity
On 6" x 8" (15 cm x 20 cm) tagboard, have students paste "o's" from magazines onto an upper and lowercase "o." Patterns are provided on pages 332 and 333.

Creative Writing
Have students write a story about an octopus and otter who meet and become friends.

Handwriting
On 12" x 18" (30 cm x 46 cm) lined newsprint, ask children to copy the following sentence: "O is for octopus, owl, olives (draw them), and oxen."

Cooking

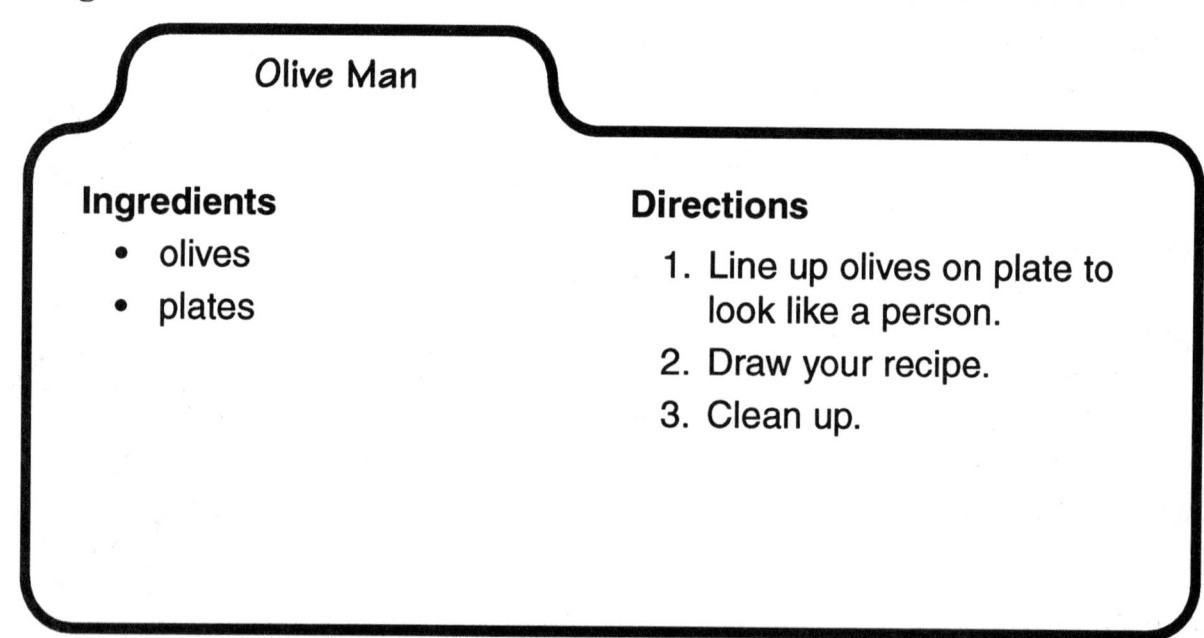

Olive Man

Ingredients
- olives
- plates

Directions
1. Line up olives on plate to look like a person.
2. Draw your recipe.
3. Clean up.

Interdisciplinary Topics

otter	oxygen	ostrich	operation
oxen	omelet	octagon	opera
October	olives	obstacle	optical illusion
opposite	octopus	odd number	on and off

#791 Teaching Basic Skills through Literature: Phonics   328   ©1995 Teacher Created Materials, Inc.

Short "O"   Mop Top

Extension Activities (cont.)

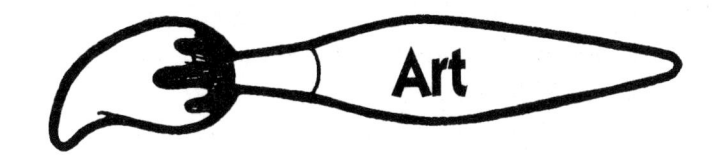

Art

Octopus

Materials
- two paper plates per child
- octopus pattern (page 334)
- scissors
- paint
- Cheerios®

Process
1. Paint two paper plates.
2. Cut out octopus body and two tentacles from one plate.
3. Cut six more tentacles from another plate.
4. Draw and paint eyes.
5. Attach tentacles to body and glue Cheerios® on as tentacles.

Opposites

Materials
- black and white construction paper
- paste
- scissors

Process
1. Cut paper so one color is half the size of the other.
2. Make a design from the top to the bottom of the same side of the paper.
3. Cut on the line and flip the small section over to give the opposite effect.
4. Paste into place.

Ostrich

Materials
- ostrich pattern (pages 335 and 336)
- 7" (18 cm) circle
- small paper plate (for body)
- white and yellow construction paper
- paste
- scissors

Process
1. Trace and cut out ostrich patterns from construction paper.
2. Attach neck and leg pieces to paper plate.
3. Clip across straight edge of half circle (wings) and curl with a pencil to form feathers.
4. Glue on sides of paper plate.
5. Fold a small piece of yellow paper in half and cut triangle to make a beak that opens. Glue on.
6. Cut and paste small circles for eyes.

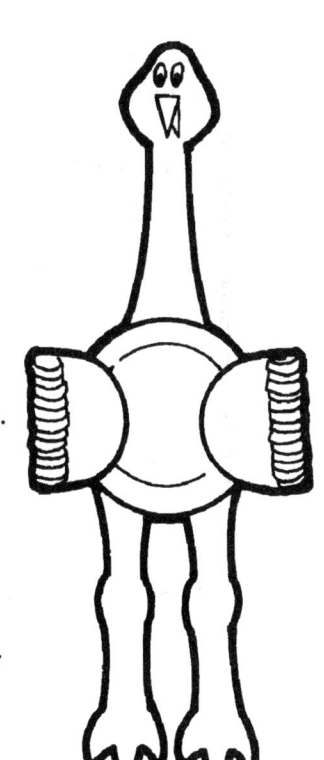

©1995 Teacher Created Materials, Inc.   329   #791 *Teaching Basic Skills through Literature: Phonics*

Mop Top Short "O"

"O" Shape Book

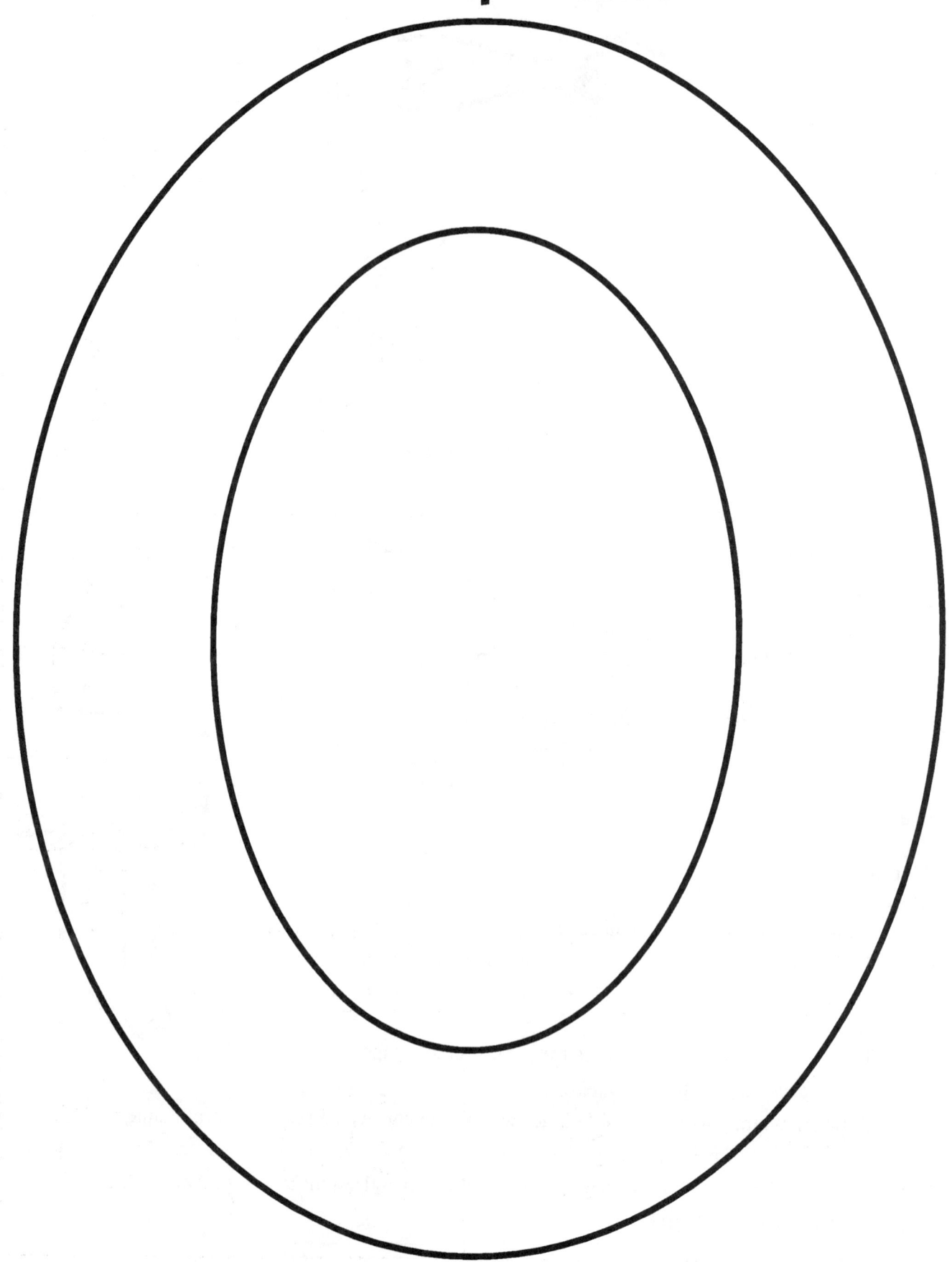

Short "O" Mop Top

Opposite Cards

Mop Top   Short "O"

"O" Pattern

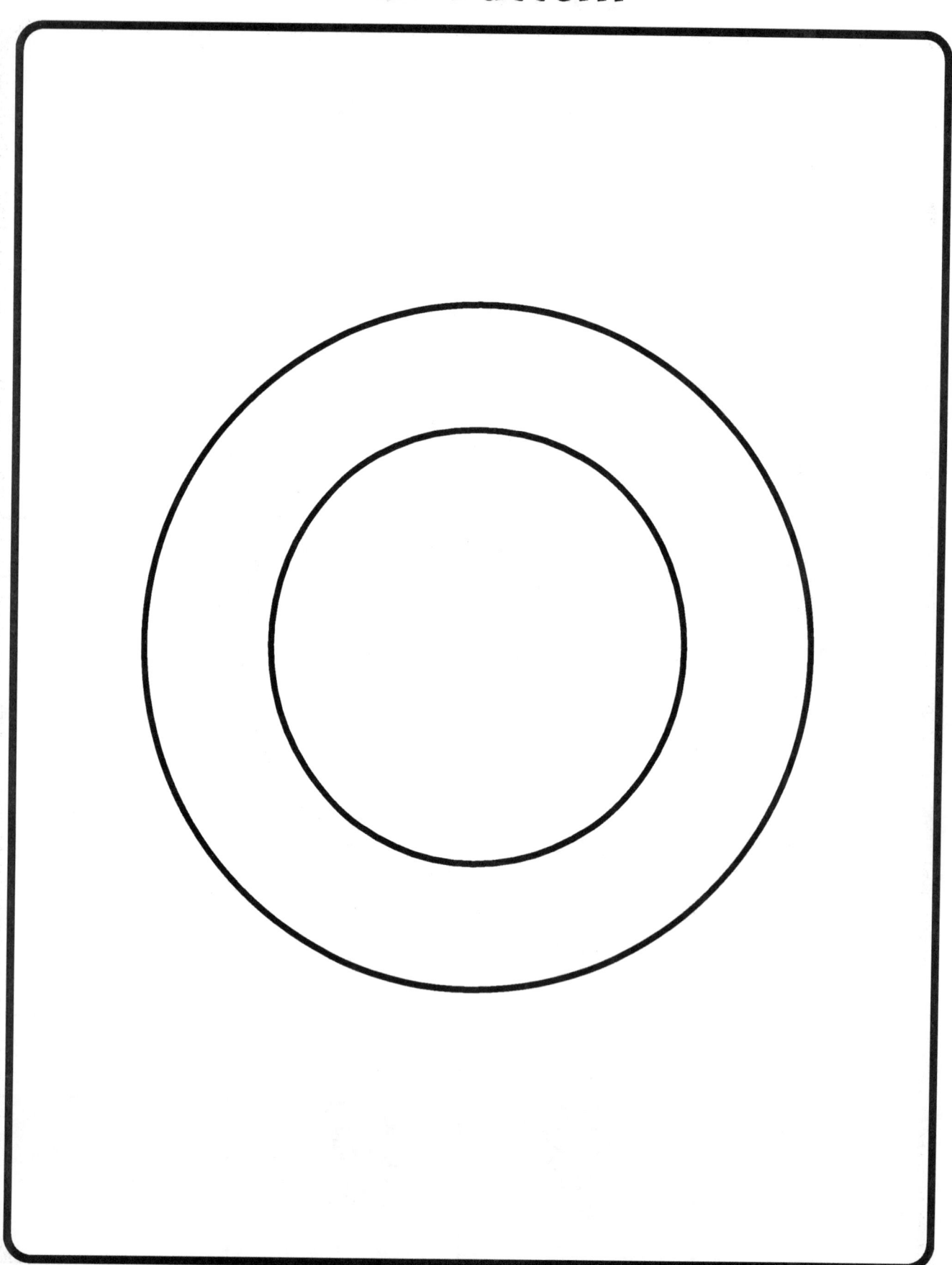

#791 Teaching Basic Skills through Literature: Phonics   332   ©1995 Teacher Created Materials, Inc.

Short "O"   Mop Top

"o" Pattern

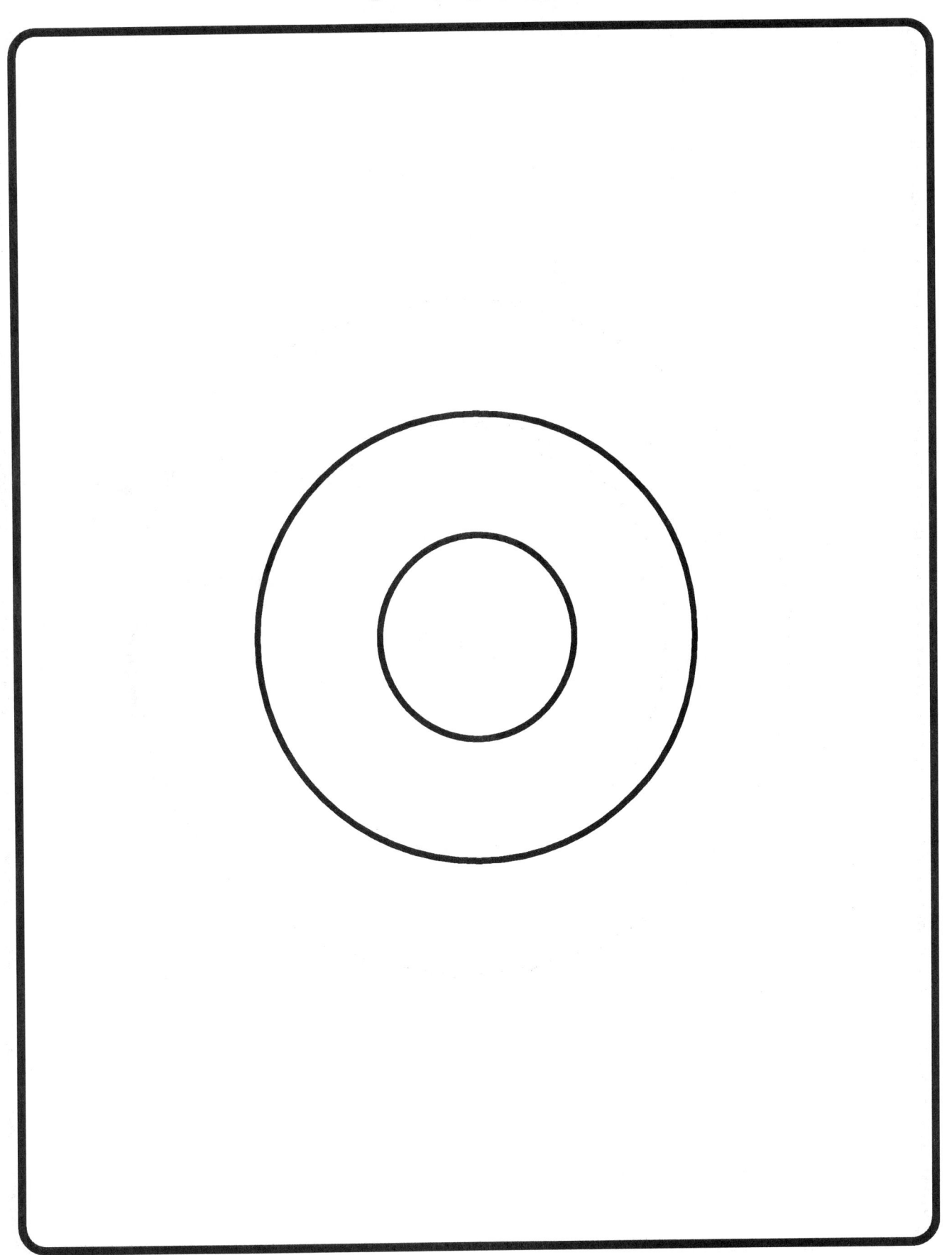

©1995 Teacher Created Materials, Inc.   333   #791 Teaching Basic Skills through Literature: Phonics

Mop Top

Short "O"

Octopus Pattern

Make six tentacles from this pattern.

Short "O"   *Mop Top*

Ostrich Pattern

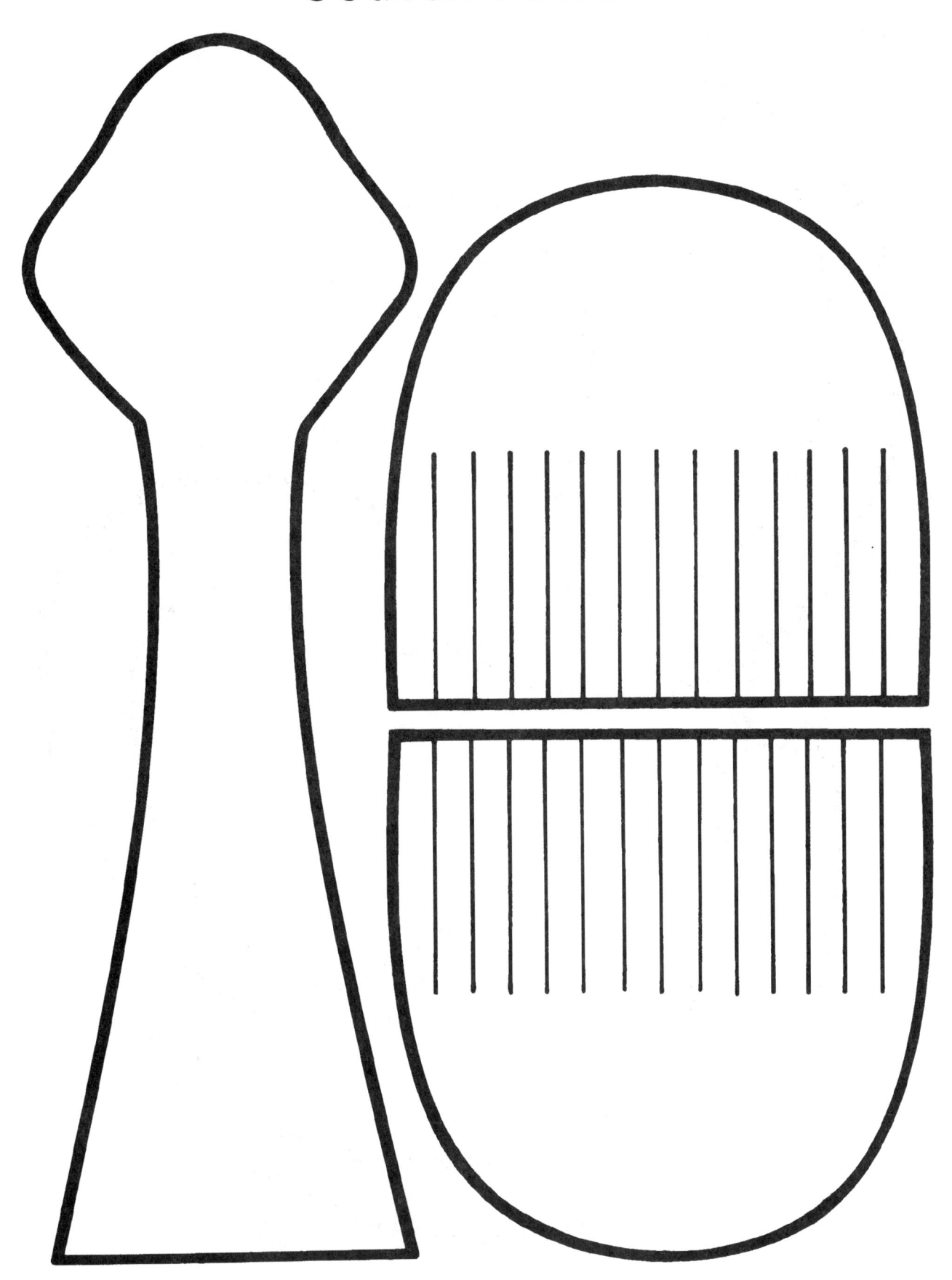

Mop Top **Short "O"**

Ostrich Pattern (cont.)

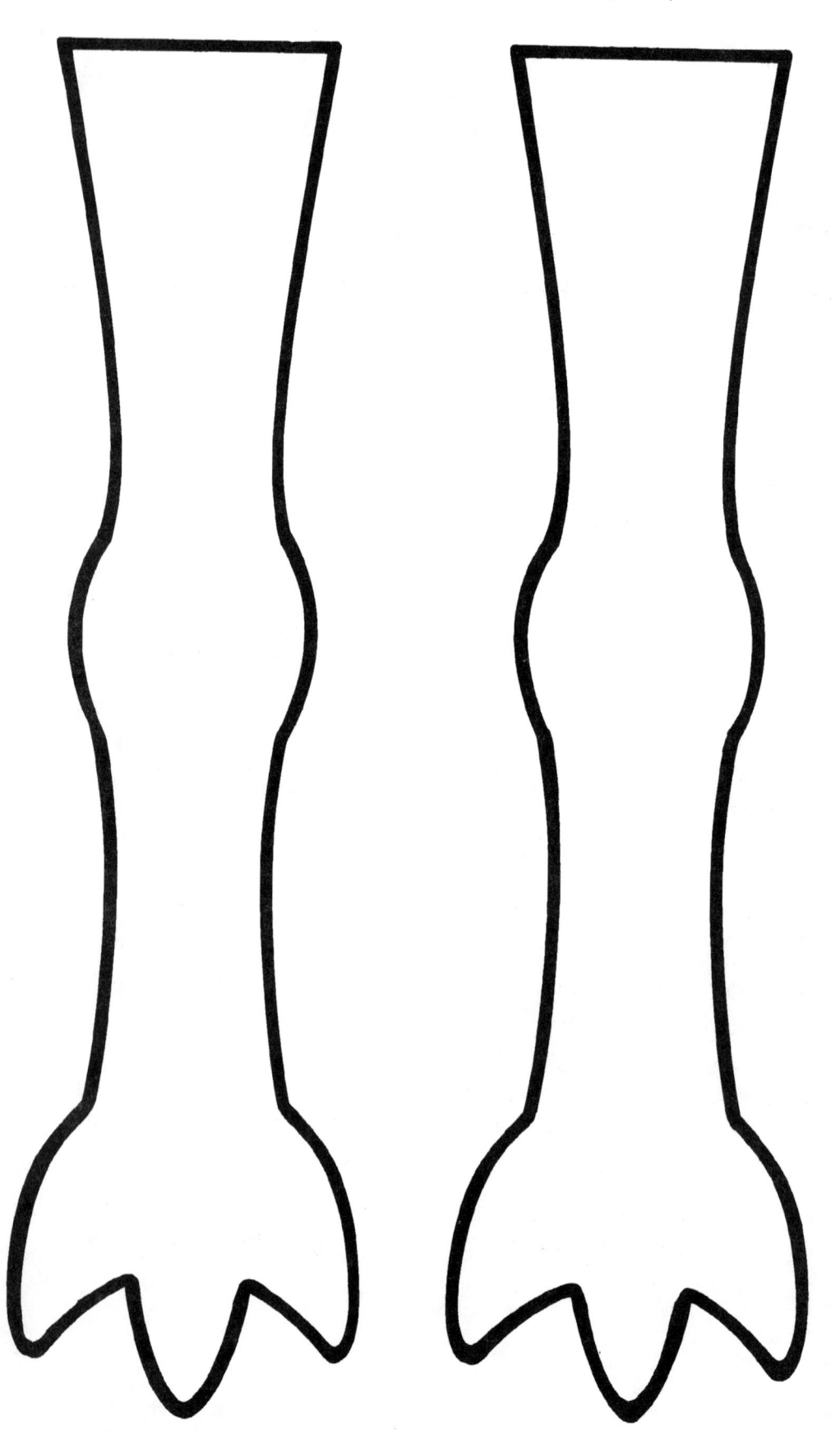

#791 Teaching Basic Skills through Literature: Phonics   336   ©1995 Teacher Created Materials, Inc.

Phonics Skills in Context: Long "O"

Book: *Over in the Meadow*
Author: Erza Jack Keats
Publisher: Scholastic, New York, 1971
Summary: This counting rhyme is about ten mother animals and their young.
Recommended Grade Level: 1–2
Related Poetry: "Open, Shut Them" by Liz Cromwell, *Finger Frolics* (Partner Press, New York, 1976). For additional titles see page 388 and 389.

Skill Activity
Students learn words that can be made with the prefix "over."

Materials
- chart paper
- "over" word list (pages 340 and 341)
- crayons or markers

Lesson
Introduce the Literature: Ask if anyone has ever heard a version of this story before.

Read the Literature: Read the literature selection. Allow time for discussion.

Introduce the Skill Lesson:
1. Brainstorm words that begin with the long "o" sound. Write the list on chart paper to display as a word bank.
2. Ask students if they can think of any words that start with "over."
3. Give students the word list from pages 340 and 341. Ask them to select, cut out, and illustrate any five of the words.

Learning Center Activity: Have students write nonsense long "o" rhymes. Leave these two examples at the center: "goat in a boat" and "toe in the snow."

Cooperative Learning Activity: Give each group several index cards, a marker, a hole punch, and a long piece of yarn. Tell each group to make a row of long "o" words. They write the word on the index card and then punch a hole in it. The cards are strung on the yarn to make a row.

Across the Curriculum: Math
Have the class draw a mural of all the animals in the story. Use the mural to create word problems such as "How many animals are there altogether" and "How many mother animals are there?"

Over in the Meadow Long "O"

Extension Activities

Movement Activities
Stress the long "o" sound as students participate in the following movements: open your mouth, hands, and eyes, jump over a line, walk like an old person, and pretend to smell an odor.

Multisensory Activity
On 6" x 8" (15 cm x 20 cm) tagboard, have students paste Cheerios® onto an upper and lowercase "o." Patterns are provided on pages 332 and 333.

Creative Writing
Have students imagine that they are old oak trees that are going to be cut down. Write a letter from the tree to convince the tree cutter not to cut it down. A tree pattern for the letter is located on page 342.

Handwriting
On 12" x 18" (30 cm x 46 cm) lined newsprint, ask children to copy this sentence: "O is for ocean, oatmeal, Olympics, and orange ovals."

Cooking

Oh Boy Bagels

Ingredients
- bagels
- jam
- knife
- plates

Directions
1. Cut bagels in half. See the O?
2. Spread jam on the bagel.
3. Draw your recipe.
4. Clean up.

Interdisciplinary Topics

ocean life	ozone	Olympics	opal
oats	oboe	Omaha	oval
oasis	o'clock	oak tree	

#791 Teaching Basic Skills through Literature: Phonics   338   ©1995 Teacher Created Materials, Inc.

Long "O" Over in the Meadow

Extension Activities (cont.)

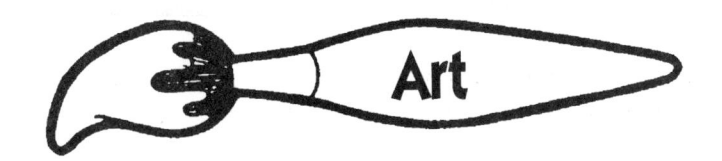

Art

Ocean Life
Materials
- Styrofoam trays
- plastic wrap
- small shells and pebbles
- glue
- construction paper
- tape
- scissors
- magazines with pictures of sea life

Process
1. Cut out various sea life creatures.
2. Glue to a meat tray.
3. Add pebbles and shells.
4. Tape plastic wrap to tray for ocean effect.

Oval Creations
Materials
- drawing paper
- crayons or markers

Process
1. Draw an oval anywhere on the page.
2. Create an object from the oval.

Ocean Drawing
Materials
- crayons
- white construction paper
- watered-down blue watercolor paint

Process
1. Draw an ocean scene on the construction paper.
2. Be sure to press hard when drawing.
3. Paint over the picture with watered-down blue paint.
4. Allow to dry thoroughly. The crayon will resist the paint.

©1995 Teacher Created Materials, Inc.   339   #791 Teaching Basic Skills through Literature: Phonics

"Over" Word List

overalls	overdose
overboard	overdue
overcast	overeat
overcharge	overflow
overcoat	overgrown
overcooked	overhand

"Over" Word List (cont.)

overjoy	oversleep
overlap	overthrow
overlook	overtime
overnight	overweight
overpass	overcrowded
overseas	overheat

Over in the Meadow   Long "O"

Tree Pattern

_____

_____

_____

_____

_____

_____

_____

Phonics Skills in Context: Short "U"

Book: *The Ugly Duckling*
Author: Hans Christian Andersen
Publisher: Troll, New York, 1979 (or other versions)
Summary: This is the classic story of an "ugly" duckling who discovers his true beauty.
Recommended Grade Level: K–2
Related Poetry: "The King of Umpalazzo" by Mary Ann Hoberman, *Yellow Butter, Purple Jelly, Red Jam, Black Bread* (Viking, New York, 1981). For additional titles see page 389.

Skill Activity

When students hear a short "u" sound, they will stand up. Then, they will create a "This Way Up!" book.

Materials

- chart paper
- crayons or markers
- writing paper
- shape book pattern (page 347)
- "u" word list (page 346)
- scissors

Lesson

Introduce the Literature: Ask students if they have ever heard this story before.

Read the Literature: Read the literature selection. Allow time for discussion.

Introduce the Skill Lesson:
1. Have students brainstorm short "u" words. List them on chart paper to use as a word bank.
2. Read the "u" word list (page 346) for students. Ask them to stand up each time a word begins with a short "u."
3. Give students the "This Way Up!" book cover from page 347. Ask them to write and illustrate on blank paper five short "u" words from the word bank.
4. Put the pages together as a book.

Learning Center Activity: Give students the flip book instructions from page 348. Have students make books of short "u" words. Have students write their words and draw pictures on the pages of the flip book, using the prompt from page 348.

Cooperative Learning Activity: In small groups students make a large sun. Have them cut a large circle from yellow construction paper. Then, cut strips to use as the sun's rays. On the sun rays students can write short "u" words.

Across the Curriculum: Physical Education

Have students form teams to participate in run and jump events.

©1995 Teacher Created Materials, Inc. 343 #791 Teaching Basic Skills through Literature: Phonics

The Ugly Duckling   **Short "U"**

Extension Activities

Movement Activities
Stress the short "u" sound as students participate in the following movements: jump up, go under, untie your shoes, unbutton a button, stand under an umbrella, and unsnap something.

Multisensory Activity
On 6" x 8" (15 cm x 20 cm) tagboard, have students put rubber stamped "u's" on an upper and lowercase "u." Patterns are provided on pages 350 and 351.

Creative Writing
Have students write stories about ugly puppies on the dog pattern on page 352.

Handwriting
On 12" x 18" (30 cm x 46 cm) lined newsprint, ask children to copy this sentence: "U is for umbrella (paste paper umbrella), uncle, and unhappy umpire."

Cooking

Umbrella Creation

Ingredients
- cheese squares
- cheese slices
- toothpicks
- plates

Directions
1. Put a toothpick into a cheese square.
2. Lay half of a cheese slice on top of toothpick to look like an umbrella.
3. Draw your recipe.
4. Clean up.

Interdisciplinary Topics

unkind	uncle	understand	uphill
underwater life	umbrella	underground	upset
umpire	unconscious	up	upstream
unhappy	under		

Short "U" The Ugly Duckling

Extension Activities (cont.)

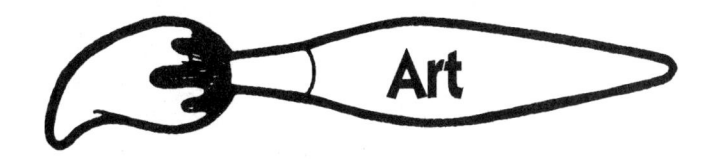

Art

Unhappy Flower
Materials
- paper plates
- construction paper
- magazine pages
- brad fastener
- glue
- marker
- scissors

Process
1. Cut trim off paper plate.
2. Cut and glue petals around plate.
3. Draw a frown face on the flower.
4. Roll a magazine page from one corner to form a stem and glue paper leaves to stem.
5. Attach flower to stem with brad fastener.

Unusual Undershirt
Materials
- T-shirts
- iron
- fabric crayons
- puffy paint (optional)

Process
1. Ask parents to provide their children with a plain T-shirt.
2. Follow directions on fabric crayon box for children to transfer a picture to the T-shirt.
3. If desired, the child's name and school may be written on the shirt with puffy paint.

"Us"
Materials
- "Us" pattern (page 353)
- 12" x 18" (30 cm x 46 cm) construction paper
- crayons or markers
- scissors

Process
1. Fold paper in half and then in half again to make four sections.
2. While still folded, trace pattern so hands and feet just reach folded edges.
3. Cut out and open to form a chain of "us" people.
4. Children decorate a person as themselves and three other friends.

The Ugly Duckling　　　　　　　　　　　　　　　　　　　　　　　　　　Short "U"

"U" Word List

umbrella	useful
uncle	upstairs
unicorn	universe
up	union
utensil	underground
umpire	uphill
United States	Utopia
unique	underwater
understand	unknown
unhappy	under

Short "U"   *The Ugly Duckling*

Shape Book

This Way Up!

by: _____

The Ugly Duckling   Short "U"

Flip Book

Flip Book Directions

1. Decorate the cover page of the book entitled "My Book of Short U Words."

2. Following the cover page, add some blank pages. (Use the pattern below.)

3. Stack inside pages on top of each other. Place cover on top and staple pages together.

4. Add short "u" words and illustrations to blank pages.

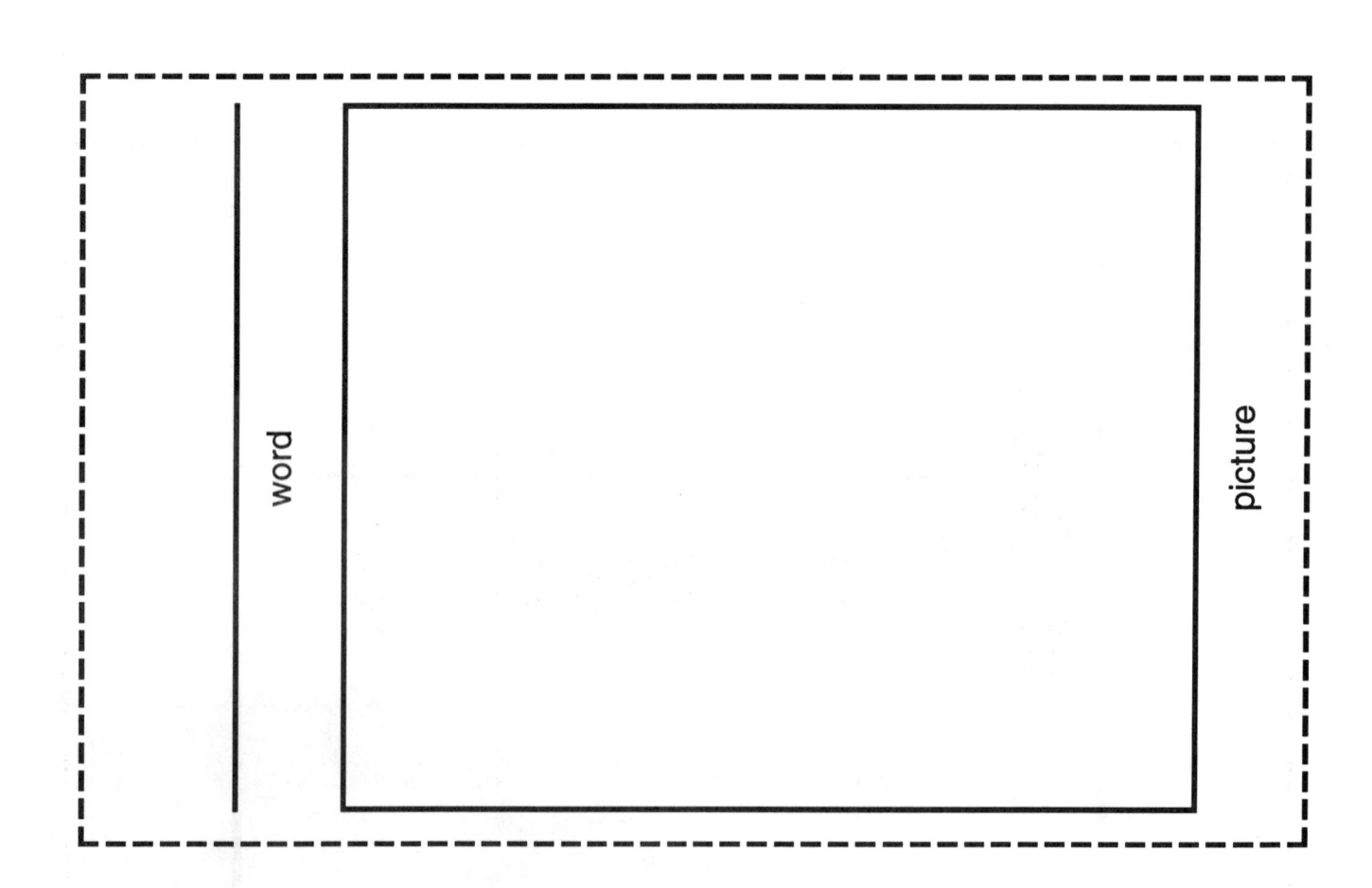

word | picture

Short "U" *The Ugly Duckling*

Flip Book Cover

Note to Teacher: Reproduce one cover page for every two students.

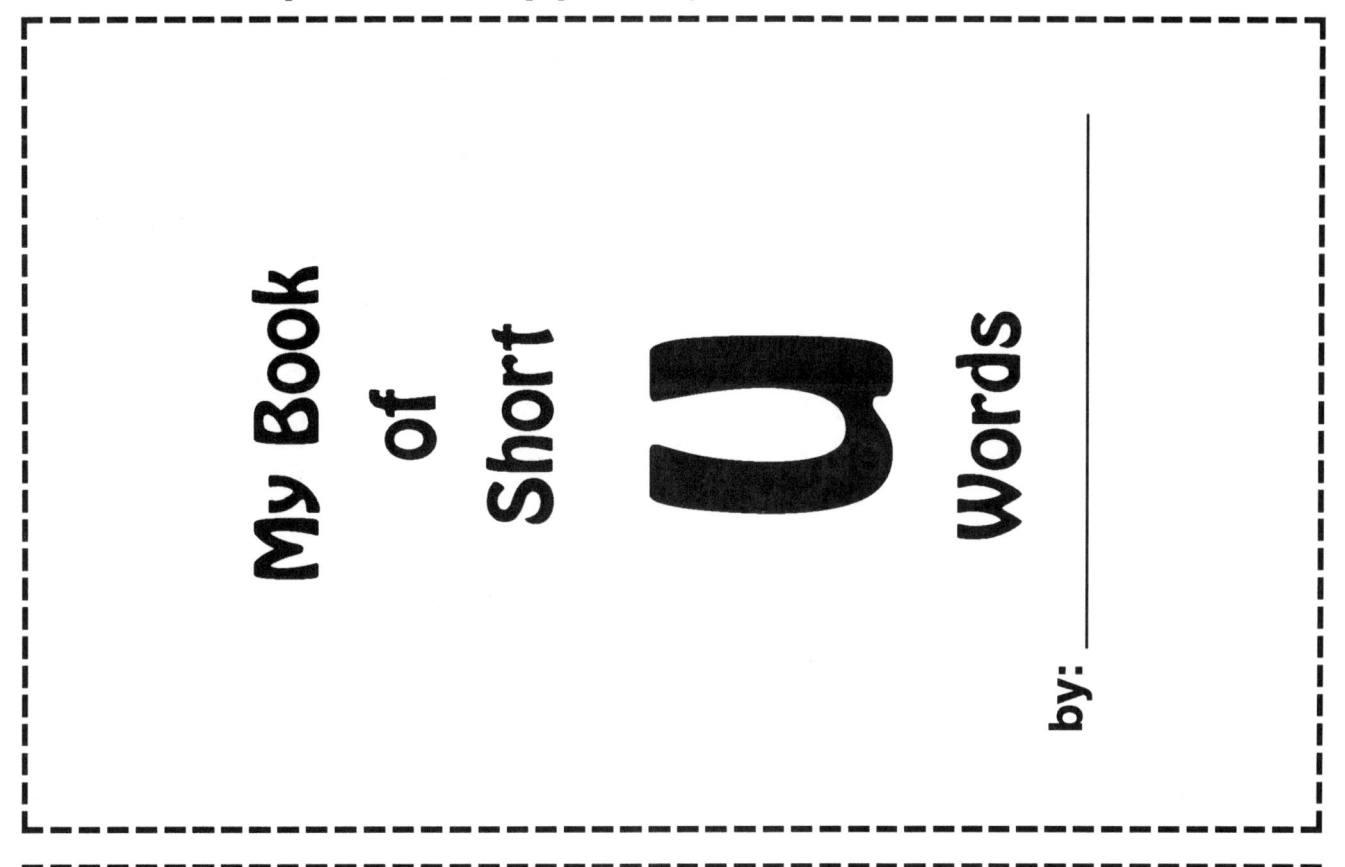

My Book of Short **U** Words

by: _____

My Book of Short **U** Words

by: _____

The Ugly Duckling   Short "U"

"U" Pattern

Short "U" *The Ugly Duckling*

"u" Pattern

©1995 Teacher Created Materials, Inc. 351 #791 Teaching Basic Skills through Literature: Phonics

The Ugly Duckling   *Short "U"*

Dog Pattern

_____
_____
(title)
by: _____

_____
_____
_____
_____
_____
_____
_____

#791 Teaching Basic Skills through Literature: Phonics   352   ©1995 Teacher Created Materials, Inc.

Short "U" | The Ugly Duckling

"Us" Pattern

Phonics Skills in Context: Long "U"

Book: *Stellaluna*
Author: Janell Cannon
Publisher: Scholastic, New York, 1993
Summary: After she falls headfirst into a bird's nest, a baby bat is raised as a bird until she is reunited with her mother.
Recommended Grade Level: K–2
Related Poetry: "The Unicorn" by Rainer Maria Rilke, *Eric Carle's Dragons, Dragons* (Scholastic, New York, 1992). For additional titles see page 389.

Skill Activity
Students take turns as they pantomime long "u" words.

Materials
- chart paper

Lesson
Introduce the Literature: Ask students what they know about bats.

Read the Literature: Read the literature selection. Allow time for discussion.

Introduce the Skill Lesson:
1. Brainstorm long "u" words with students and list on chart paper to use as a word bank.
2. Have students take turns selecting long "u" words from the chart paper.
3. Students must pantomime the word while other students guess their word.

Learning Center Activity: Allow students to make tube puppets, using empty paper tubes, construction paper, wiggle eyes, and yarn. Students can create stories using the tube puppets.

Cooperative Learning Activity: One student in the small group gives clues about an object in the classroom. Other members of the group try to guess the object.

Across the Curriculum: Health
Have students create a fruit fest. Ask them to brainstorm as many types of fruit as they can. Then, go back through the list and listen for the long "u" sound in the words.

Long "U" — Stellaluna

Extension Activities

Movement Activities
Stress the long "u" sound as students participate in the following movements: pretend to be a unicorn, play a ukulele, and make a unique face.

Multisensory Activity
On 6" x 8" (15 cm x 20 cm) tagboard, have children paste "u's" from magazines onto an upper and lowercase "u." Patterns are provided on pages 350 and 351.

Creative Writing
Have students work in partners. Each partner traces the other's body on butcher paper. On the paper students write what is unique about them.

Handwriting
On 12" x 18" (30 cm x 46 cm) lined newsprint, ask children to copy this sentence: "U is for unicorn (draw one), unicycle, United States, and unique utensil."

Cooking

Unicorn Salad

Ingredients
- ½ banana per child
- ¼ carrot per child
- raisins
- knife
- plates

Directions
1. Peel banana half.
2. Add ¼ carrot to the top of the banana for the unicorn's horn.
3. Add raisins for eyes, ears, and mouth.
4. Draw your recipe.
5. Clean up.

Interdisciplinary Topics

universe	ukulele	union	utensil
United States	unify	university	Utopia
unique	uniform		

©1995 Teacher Created Materials, Inc.

Stellaluna   Long "U"

Extension Activities *(cont.)*

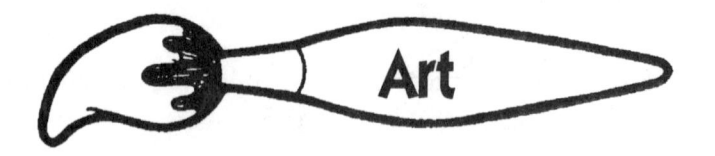

Art

Unique Unicorn

Materials
- cone-shaped cups
- yarn
- crayons or markers

Process
1. Decorate cups with crayons or markers.
2. Attach yarn to both sides of cup.
3. Tie to child's forehead.

Universe

Materials
- construction paper
- black paint
- silver glitter
- crayons or markers

Process
1. Paint a large black circle on a piece of construction paper.
2. Glue stars around the circle.
3. Sprinkle silver glitter on the stars.
4. Glue space objects onto the paper, such as planets and sun.

United States

Materials
- United States map (page 357)
- crayons
- pencils

Process
1. Give each child a United States map.
2. Have them color in the states.
3. Challenge them to write in the names of any states they know.

Long "U" *Stellaluna*

United States Map

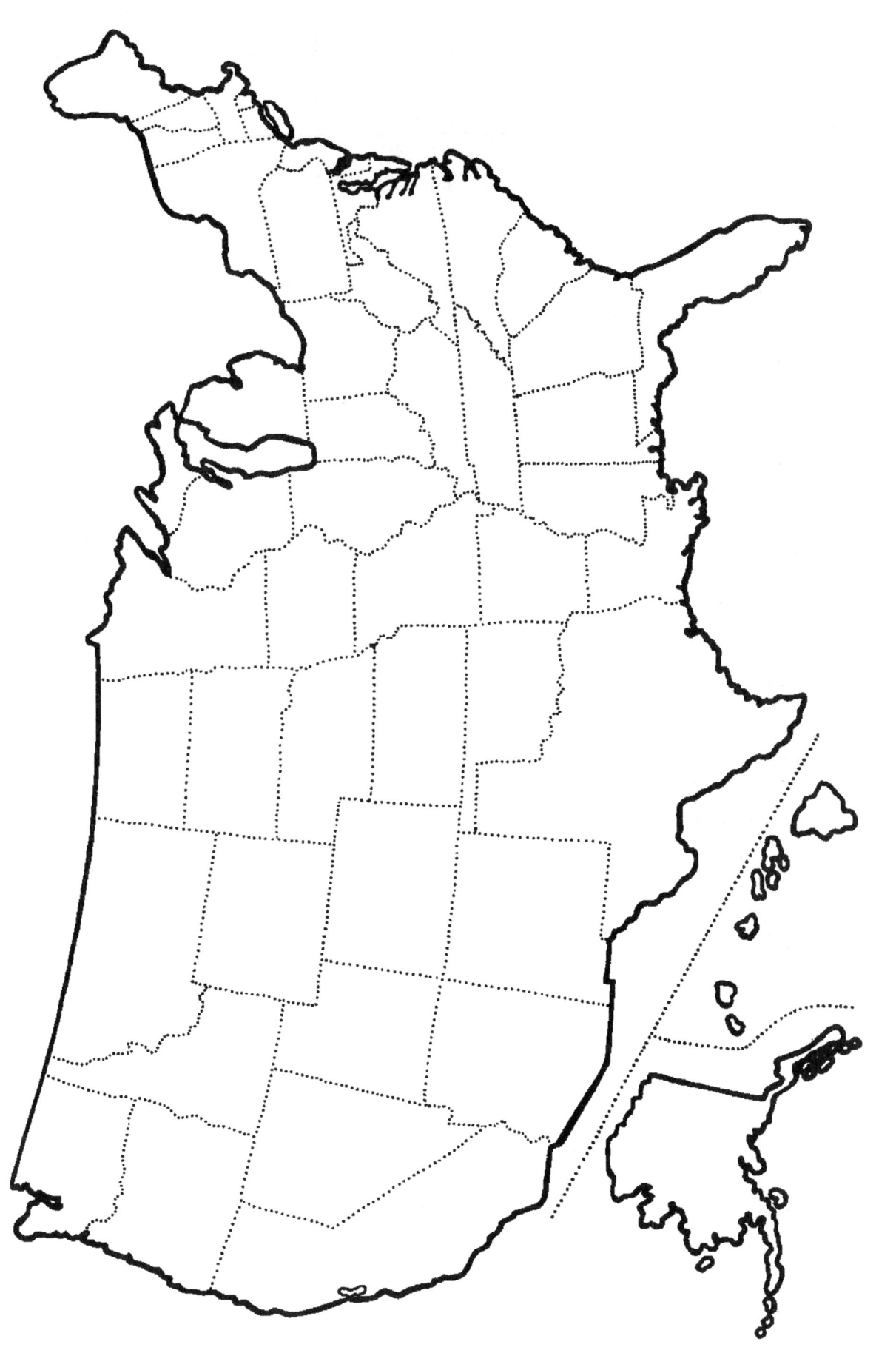

Phonics Skills in Context: "ch" Blend

Book: *Chatting*
Author: Shirley Hughes
Publisher: Candlewick Press, Boston, 1994
Summary: A child chats about all the places she likes to chat.
Recommended Grade Level: 1–2
Related Poetry: "Channels" by Shel Silverstein, *A Light in the Attic* (Harper & Row, 1974). For additional titles see page 389.

Skill Activity

Students will create their own chatting books.

Materials

- chart paper
- chatting book cover (page 361)
- crayons or markers
- scissors

Lesson

Introduce the Literature: Ask children if they know what it means to chat.

Read the Literature: Read the literature selection. Allow time for discussion.

Introduce the Skill Lesson:

1. Ask students to brainstorm any "ch" words they know. List them on chart paper to use as a word bank.
2. Give students the cover of the chatting book from page 361. Have them cut it out and decorate it with crayons or markers.
3. Students add pages to show who they like to chat with. They can use the prompt from page 362 to help with their writing.

Learning Center Activity: Allow students to make chalk drawings, using chalk and blue or black construction paper. Ask them to include as many things that begin with "ch" in their pictures as possible.

Cooperative Learning Activity: Allow students to chat for a while in small groups.

Across the Curriculum: Social Studies

Have students spend time in the library looking at books about China. Compile a class list of the things they learned about this country.

"ch" Blend   *Chatting*

Extension Activities

Movement Activities

Stress the "ch" sound as students participate in the following movements: run like a cheetah, chase a friend, jump up and down like a cheerleader, and churn butter.

Multisensory Activity

On 6" x 8" (15 cm x 20 cm) tagboard, have students paste colored chalk dust to the "ch" pattern on page 363.

Creative Writing

Have students write stories about a cheetah and a chimp who become friends and save the jungle. Cheetah and chimp patterns can be found on pages 364 and 365.

Handwriting

On 12" x 18" (30 cm x 46 cm) lined newsprint, ask children to copy this sentence: "Ch is for chair, checkers (glue on a checker), chocolate, and charming chief."

Cooking

Cheerios® Fun

Ingredients
- Cheerios®
- plates

Directions
1. Use Cheerios® to make a "ch" pattern on the plate.
2. Draw your recipe.
3. Clean up.

Interdisciplinary Topics

chainsaw	checkers	charity	chestnut
champ	cheetah	cheese	chick
chimp	channel	cherry	child
champion	chant	cherish	chow mein
chamber	chapter	chief	church
chance	chapel	chess	China
cheat	chariot		

©1995 Teacher Created Materials, Inc.   359   #791 Teaching Basic Skills through Literature: Phonics

Chatting   "ch" Blend

Extension Activities (cont.)

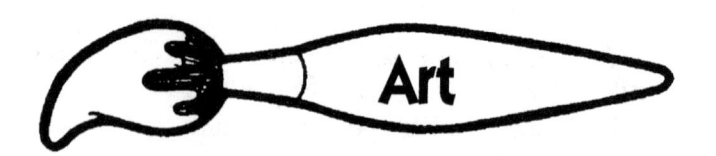

Art

Charcoal Drawing
Materials
- white paper
- charcoal
- hair spray

Process
1. Make a picture using charcoal.
2. Spray with hair spray to set picture.

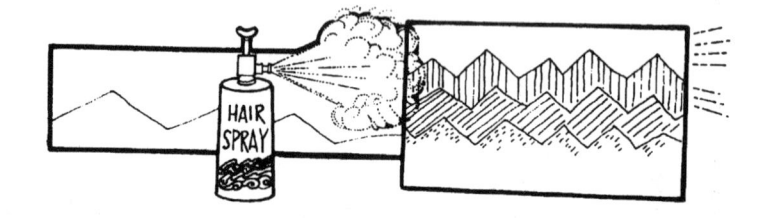

Checkers
Materials
- checkerboard pattern (page 366)
- pinto beans
- black crayons or markers

Process
1. Using a black crayon, color in the appropriate squares on the blank checkerboard.
2. Use pinto beans as markers and play checkers with a friend.

Chalk Flowers
Materials
- liquid starch
- colored chalk
- construction paper

Process
1. Paint a light coat of liquid starch on paper.
2. Draw in flowers with colored chalk.

Chalk Snowman
Materials
- blue construction paper
- white chalk
- cotton balls
- white paint

Process
1. Draw a snowman with the white chalk.
2. Add snow, using the cotton ball dipped in white paint.

"ch" Blend — Chatting

Chatting Book Cover

My
Chatting
Book

by:_____

Chatting   "ch" Blend

Chatting Book Page

I like to chat with _____

_____.

We chat about _____

_____

_____

_____.

picture

"ch" Blend   Chatting

"ch" Pattern

ch

©1995 Teacher Created Materials, Inc.   363   #791 Teaching Basic Skills through Literature: Phonics

Chatting

"ch" Blend

Cheetah Pattern

_____
_____ (title)
by: _____
_____
_____
_____
_____
_____
_____

"ch" Blend   *Chatting*

Chimp Pattern

_____ (title)

by: _____

Chatting   "ch" Blend

Checkerboard Pattern

Phonics Skills in Context: "th" Blend

Book: *The First Thanksgiving*
Author: Jean Craighead George
Publisher: Philomel, New York, 1993
Summary: This is a beautiful historical story of the first Thanksgiving.
Recommended Grade Level: 1–2
Related Poetry: "Thumb Face" by Shel Silverstein, *A Light in the Attic* (Harper & Row, 1974). For additional titles see page 389.

Skill Activity
Students will create a thank you letter for someone they care about and/or a community helper.

Materials
- thank you letter activity sheet (page 370)
- pencil
- crayons or markers
- chart paper

Lesson
Introduce the Literature: Ask students what they know about the history of Thanksgiving.

Read the Literature: Read the literature selection. Allow time for discussion.

Introduce the Skill Lesson:
1. Ask students to brainstorm words they know that begin with "th." Write these on chart paper to use as a word bank.
2. Discuss with students people they are thankful to have in their lives. Perhaps make a list of these people.
3. Have students write thank you letters to people personally important to them, using page 370.
4. If desired, have students write thank you letters to community helpers for their service.

Learning Center Activity: Challenge students to look up any words from the word listing in the thesaurus. Then, have students use the activity on page 371 to list other words that mean the same thing.

Cooperative Learning Activity: In small groups have students plan a Thanksgiving Day menu.

Across the Curriculum: Math
Bring in a thermometer for students to observe. Then, for the next week check on the temperature outside the classroom three times a day. Students can complete the data capture sheet on page 372 for this activity.

The First Thanksgiving   "th" Blend

Extension Activities

Movement Activities

Stress the "th" sound as students participate in the following movements: thrust a ball, thump their feet, thrash around the playground, and throw a baseball.

Multisensory Activity

On 6" x 8" (15 cm x 20 cm) tagboard, have students paste pieces of thread to the "th" pattern on page 373.

Creative Writing

Have students write a story about how they caught a thief trying to steal the Hope diamond.

Handwriting

On 12" x 18" (30 cm x 46 cm) lined newsprint, ask children to copy this sentence: "Th is for thank you, thimble (draw one), throne, and thunder."

Cooking

Thirsty Throat Specials

Ingredients
- fruit punch
- crushed ice
- cups

Directions
1. Pour fruit punch over crushed ice.
2. Draw your recipe.
3. Clean up.

Interdisciplinary Topics

theater	thoughtful	thigh	thistle
theme park	throne	thief	thorn
thermometer	thesaurus	think	thunder
thermos	thimble		

"th" Blend   The First Thanksgiving

Extension Activities (cont.)

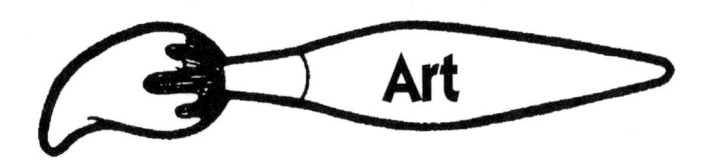

Art

Theater
Materials
- construction paper
- tape
- scissors

Process
1. Make characters from the story out of construction paper.
2. Tape a piece of construction paper in a "standing up" position onto a flat piece of construction paper. The paper standing up should be taped at the corners of the flat piece to form a half circle shape.
3. Add characters to the theater.

Thumbprints
Materials
- stamp pads
- construction paper
- thin black marker

Process
1. Make thumbprints on construction paper.
2. Add details onto the thumbs to create characters.

Thermometer
Materials
- construction paper
- thermometer pattern (page 374)
- crayons or markers
- scissors
- glue

Process
1. Cut out the thermometer pattern.
2. Using the red crayon or marker, color in the temperature of your choice.
3. Glue the thermometer to the construction paper.
4. Mark an appropriate temperature reading on the thermometer.
5. Have each child illustrate an activity, event, or season appropriate for the temperature chosen.

The First Thanksgiving   "th" Blend

Thank You Letter

"th" Blend *The First Thanksgiving*

Using a Thesaurus

Name _____

Use a thesaurus to look up words from the class word bank. Then, write down other words that mean the same thing. The first one is done for you.

1. _____thankful_____   _____grateful_____

2. _____   _____

3. _____   _____

4. _____   _____

5. _____   _____

6. _____   _____

7. _____   _____

8. _____   _____

©1995 Teacher Created Materials, Inc.   371   #791 Teaching Basic Skills through Literature: Phonics

The First Thanksgiving "th" Blend

Take the Temperature

Record the temperature outside your classroom three times a day for the next week.

Monday	Tuesday	Wednesday	Thursday	Friday

I recorded the temperature_____times during the week.

I noticed the following temperature pattern:

_____

_____

_____

_____

"th" Blend   The First Thanksgiving

"th" Pattern

©1995 Teacher Created Materials, Inc.   #791 Teaching Basic Skills through Literature: Phonics

The First Thanksgiving   "th" Blend

Thermometer Pattern

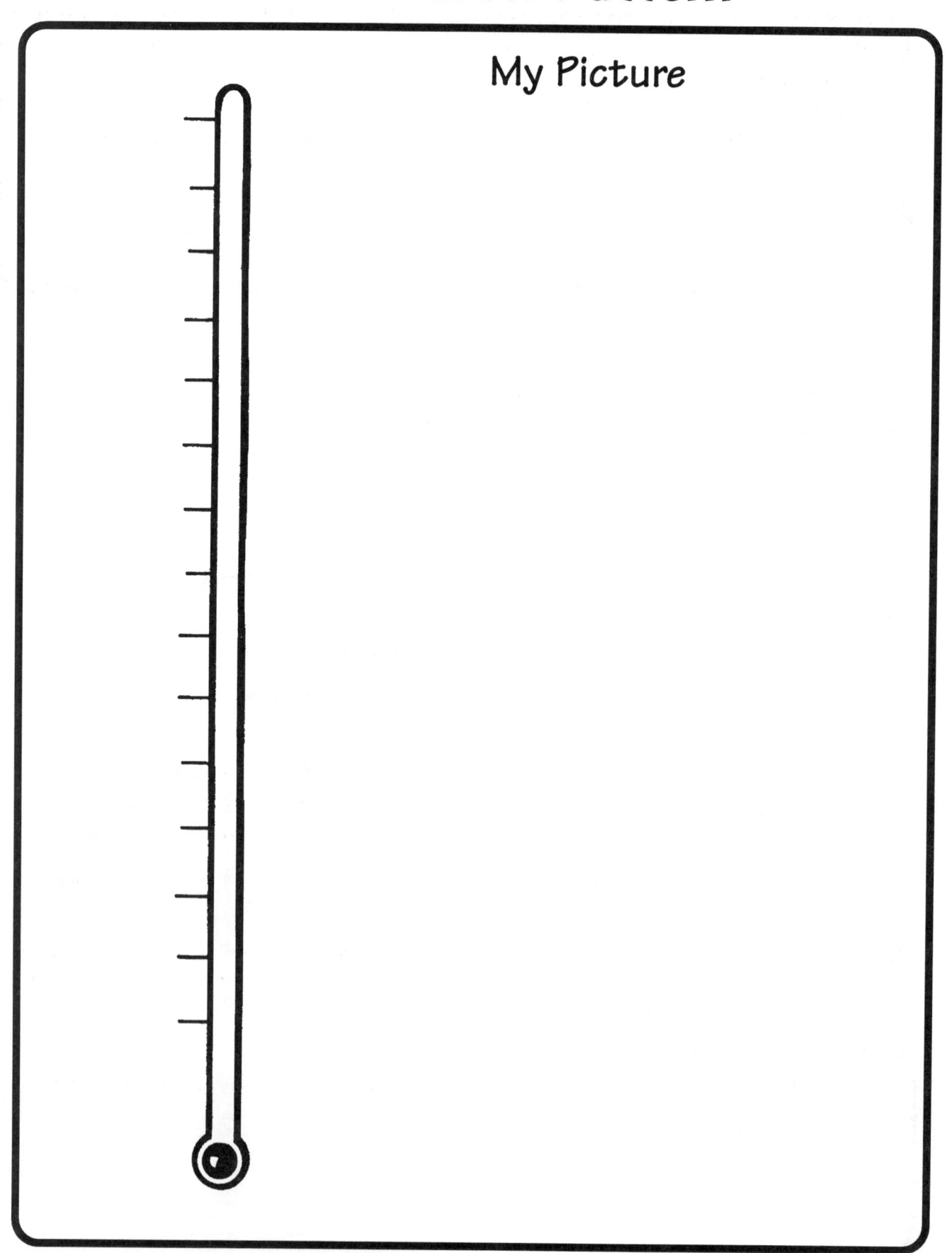

My Picture

Phonics Skills in Context: "wh" Blend

Book: *The Wheeling and Whirling Around Book*
Author: Judy Hindley
Publisher: Candlewick Press, Boston, 1994
Summary: This beautifully illustrated book shows all the things in the world that wheel and whirl.
Recommended Grade Level: 1–2
Related Poetry: "Whatif" by Shel Silverstein, *A Light in the Attic* (Harper & Row, 1974). For additional titles see page 389.

Skill Activity

Students will make a wheel shape book of "wh" words.

Materials

- wheel shape book cover (page 378)
- crayons or markers
- scissors
- chart paper

Lesson

Introduce the Literature: Have students brainstorm things that wheel and whirl.

Read the Literature: Read the literature selection. Allow time for discussion.

Introduce the Skill Lesson:

1. Brainstorm words that begin with "wh." List them on chart paper and display as a word bank.
2. Cut several blank wheel shapes to use as book pages. Use shape pattern (page 378).
3. Have students select words from the word bank to write and illustrate on the book pages.

Learning Center Activity: At the end of the book, students must find all the round, circular, and spinning things in the book. Challenge students to list as many as they can.

Cooperative Learning Activity: As a class brainstorm something important that recently happened at school. Then, ask the small groups to be reporters and find out who, what, where, when, and why it happened. They can use the data sheet on page 379 to record the information they receive.

Across the Curriculum: Physical Education

Allow students to wheel and whirl circular objects (balls, hula hoops, etc.) around the playground.

The Wheeling and Whirling Around Book   "wh" Blend

Extension Activities

Movement Activities
Stress the "wh" sound as students participate in the following movements: whimper, whirl around, whoop it up, whip around the playground, and whistle.

Multisensory Activity
On 6" x 8" (15 cm x 20 cm) tagboard, have students paste wheat germ on the "wh" pattern on page 380.

Creative Writing
Have students write stories about a whimsical whale. A cover pattern is located on page 381. Have students color the pattern and attach it to the front of the story.

Handwriting
On 12" x 18" (30 cm x 46 cm) lined newsprint, ask children to copy this sentence: "Wh is for whale (draw one), whimper, whistle, and White House."

Cooking

Wheat Treat

Ingredients
- wheat bread
- peanut butter
- plates

Directions
1. Spread peanut butter on a slice of wheat bread.
2. Draw your recipe.
3. Clean up.

Interdisciplinary Topics

whale	wheel	White House	whirlpool
wharf	whirlwind	whimsical	whisper
wheat	whisker	whey	whistle

"wh" Blend *The Wheeling and Whirling Around Book*

Extension Activities (cont.)

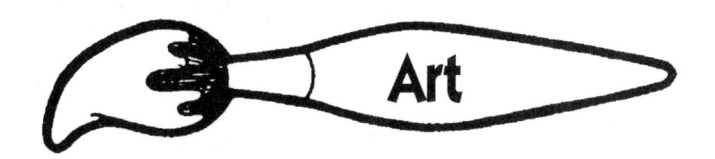

Art

Whimsical Clown
Materials
- clown pattern (page 382)
- bright crayons or markers
- scissors
- large piece of construction paper

Process
1. Cut out clown pattern.
2. Decorate him, using bright colors.
3. Glue clown on construction paper and add circus background.

My Whiskers
Materials
- cat pattern (page 63)
- black and blue construction paper
- scissors
- fishing line

Process
1. Trace the cat pattern on black construction paper and cut out.
2. Add features with blue construction paper.
3. Add fishing line as whiskers.

White House
Materials
- pictures of the White House
- construction paper
- crayons or markers
- pencils

Process
1. Draw the White House, using a pencil.
2. Draw in background.

The Wheeling and Whirling Around Book   "wh" Blend

Wheel Book Pattern

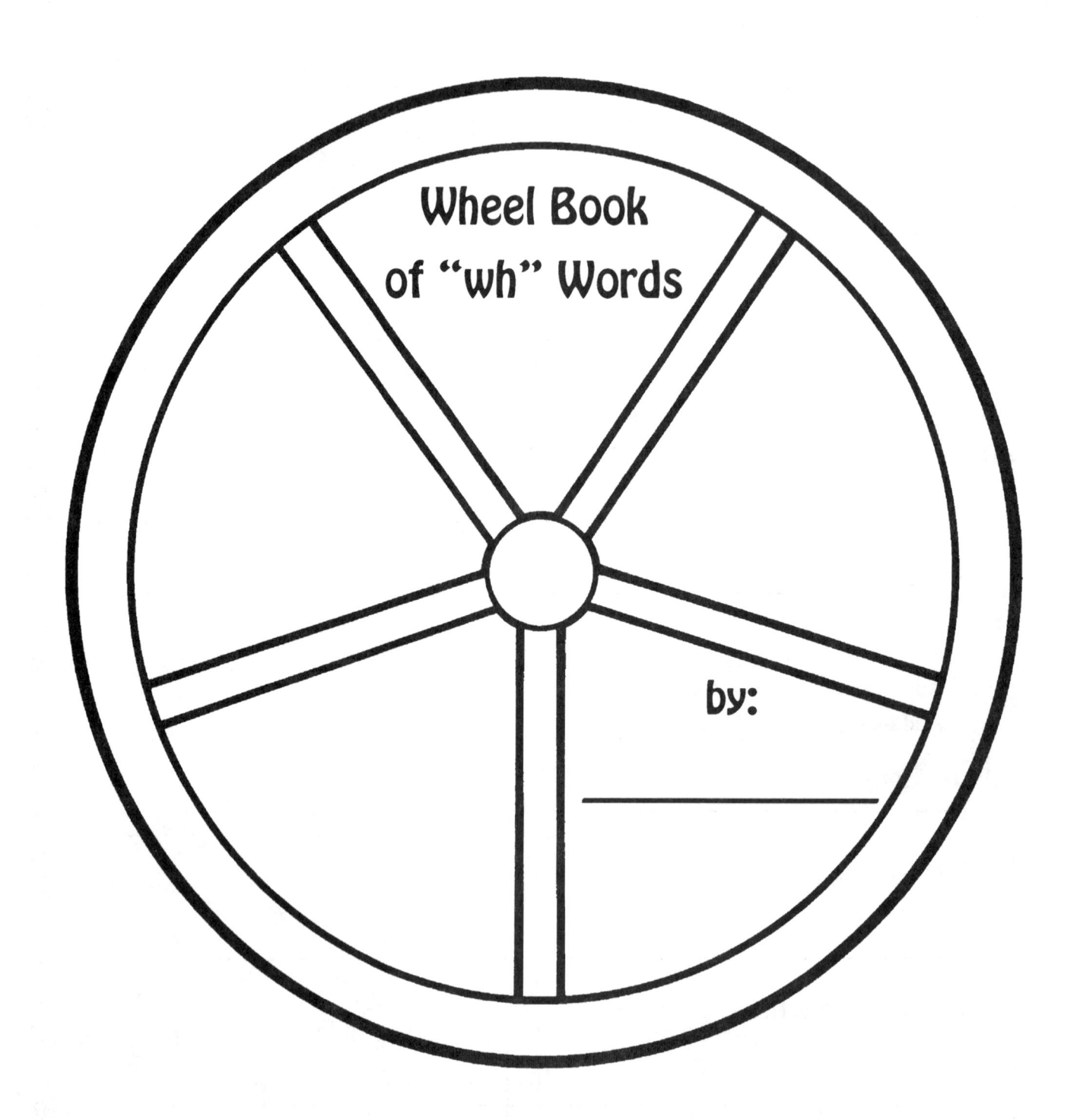

Wheel Book of "wh" Words

by: _____

"wh" Blend The Wheeling and Whirling Around Book

News Report

Name _____

Find out the details of a recent event at school.

```
┌─────────────────────────────────────┐
│                                     │
│                                     │
│                                     │
└─────────────────────────────────────┘
```
title

Who? _____

_____

What? _____

_____

Where? _____

_____

When? _____

_____

Why? _____

_____

©1995 Teacher Created Materials, Inc.   379   #791 Teaching Basic Skills through Literature: Phonics

The Wheeling and Whirling Around Book "wh" Blend

"wh" Pattern

"wh" Blend — The Wheeling and Whirling Around Book

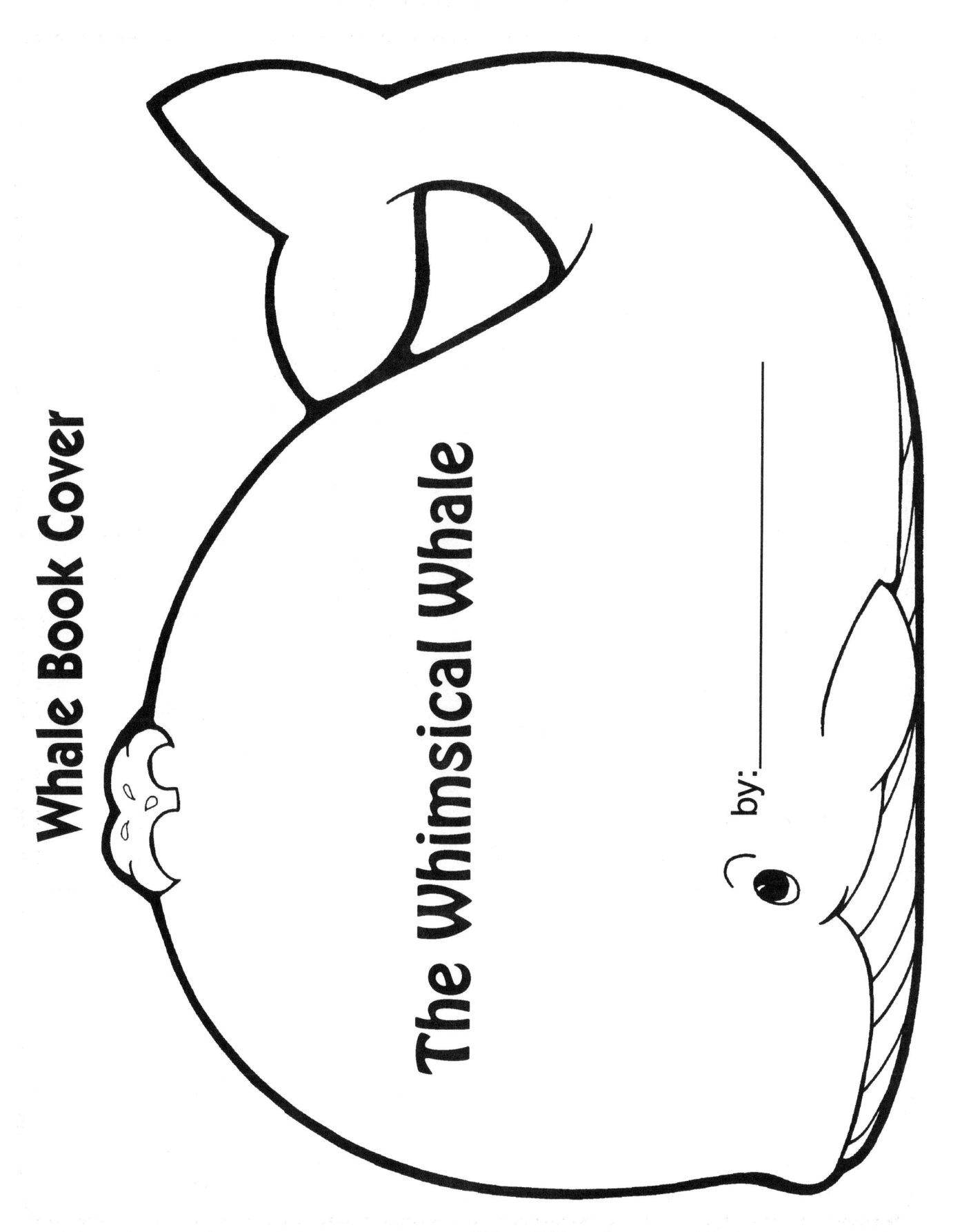

Whale Book Cover

The Whimsical Whale

by: _____

©1995 Teacher Created Materials, Inc. 381 #791 Teaching Basic Skills through Literature: Phonics

The Wheeling and Whirling Around Book   "wh" Blend

Clown Pattern

Reading Award

This award is presented to

_____

for

Outstanding Achievement

in

Reading

_____
Date

_____
Teacher

©1995 Teacher Created Materials, Inc. 383 #791 Teaching Basic Skills through Literature: Phonics

Related Poetry

Letter "B"

"Blame"
by Shel Silverstein
A Light in the Attic
(HarperCollins, 1981)

"Bubbles"
by Babs Bell Hajdusiewicz
Poetry Works
(Modern Curriculum Press, 1990)

"Furry Bear"
by A. A. Milne
Poems to Read to the Very Young
(Random House, 1982)

"Little Black Bug"
by Margaret Wise Brown
Poems to Read to the Very Young
(Random House, 1982)

Letter "C"

"Cubby Crunchies"
by Nancy White Carlstrom
It's About Time, Jesse Bear
(Scholastic, 1992)

"Animal Crackers"
by Christopher Morley
Poems to Read to the Very Young
(Random House, 1982)

Letter "D"

"Dickery, Dickery, Dare"
by Arnold Lobel
Random House Book of Mother Goose
(Random House, 1986)

Letter "F"

"Fish"
by Jack Prelutsky
Poems to Read to the Very Young
(Random House, 1982)

"A New Friend"
by Marjorie Allen Anderson
Poems to Read to the Very Young
(Random House, 1982)

"Fish?"
by Shel Silverstein
Where the Sidewalk Ends
(Harper & Row, 1974)

Letter "G"

"Hello and Goodbye"
by Mary Ann Hoberman
Yellow Butter, Purple Jelly, Red Jam, Black Bread
(Viking, 1981)

"Goops"
by Gelett Burgess
Poetry Works
(Modern Curriculum Press, 1990)

Letter "H"

"Hello and Goodbye"
by Mary Ann Hoberman
Yellow Butter, Purple Jelly, Red Jam, Black Bread
(Viking, 1981)

"Hippo's Hope"
by Shel Silverstein
A Light in the Attic
(HarperCollins, 1981)

"Hide and Seek"
by A. B. Shiffrin
Poems to Read to the Very Young
(Random House, 1982)

Related Poetry (cont.)

Letter "J"

"Jack Be Nimble"
by Arnold Lobel
Random House Book of Mother Goose
(Random House, 1986)

"Jack and Jill"
by Arnold Lobel
Random House Book of Mother Goose
(Random House, 1986)

Letter "K"

"A Kitten with Mitten"
by Polly Berrien,
Seesaw
(Charles Merrill Books, 1966)

"The Three Little Kittens"
by Arnold Lobel
Random House Book of Mother Goose
(Random House, 1986)

Letter "L"

"I'd Like To"
by Mary Ann Hoberman
Yellow Butter, Purple Jelly, Red Jam, Black Bread
(Viking, 1981)

"Llama"
by Gail Kredenser
The ABC of Bumptious Beasts
(Harlin Quist, Inc., 1966)

"London Bridges"
by Arnold Lobel
Random House Book of Mother Goose
(Random House, 1986)

Letter "M"

"Mice"
by Rose Fyleman
Poems to Read to the Very Young
(Random House, 1982)

"Merry Sunshine"
Anonymous
Poems to Read to the Very Young
(Random House, 1982)

"Good Morning"
by Muriel Sipe
Poems to Read to the Very Young
(Random House, 1982)

"In the Meadow"
by Christina Rossetti
A Child's Book of Poems
(Grosset and Dunlap, 1972)

Letter "N"

"I Had a Little Nut Tree"
Anonymous
Poems for Young Children
(Doubleday, 1986)

"The North Wind Doth Blow"
by Arnold Lobel
Random House Book of Mother Goose
(Random House, 1986)

Letter "P"

"There Once Was a Pig"
by Mary Ann Hoberman
Yellow Butter, Purple Jelly, Red Jam, Black Bread
(Viking, 1981)

"Parrot with a Pomegranate"
by Jack Prelutsky
Ride a Purple Pelican
(Greenwillow, 1986)

"Peter Piper"
by Brian Wildsmith
Brian Wildsmith's Mother Goose
(Scott Foresman, 1965)

Related Poetry (cont.)

Letter "Q"

"Almost Perfect"
by Shel Silverstein
A Light in the Attic
(HarperCollins, 1981)

"Questions at Night"
by Louis Untermeyer
Rainbow in the Sky
(Harcourt, 1963)

Letter "R"

"Rain"
by Robert Louis Stevenson
Poems to Read to the Very Young
(Random House, 1982)

Letter "S"

"A Sledding Song"
by Norman Schlichter
Poems to Read to the Very Young
(Random House, 1982)

"Sleeping Sardines"
by Shel Silverstein
Where the Sidewalk Ends
(Harper & Row, 1974)

"Sparrow"
by Kaye Starbied
Eric Carle's Animals, Animals
(Philomel, 1989)

Letter "T"

"A Little Turtle"
by Liz Cromwell
Finger Frolics
(Partner Press, 1976)

"Tired"
by Shel Silverstein
A Light in the Attic
(HarperCollins, 1981)

"Crowded Tub"
by Shel Silverstein
A Light in the Attic
(HarperCollins, 1981)

"Ticklish Mom"
by Shel Silverstein
A Light in the Attic
(HarperCollins, 1981)

"Twistable, Turnable Man"
by Shel Silverstein
A Light in the Attic
(HarperCollins, 1981)

"Squishy Touch"
by Shel Silverstein
A Light in the Attic
(HarperCollins, 1981)

Letter "V"

"Purple Violets"
by Louise Binder Scott & J. J. Thompson
Rhymes for Fingers and Flannelboards
(McGraw Hill, 1960)

"Five Little Valentines"
by Louise Binder Scott & J. J. Thompson
Rhymes for Fingers and Flannelboards
(McGraw Hill, 1960)

Letter "W"

"Who Has Seen the Wind?"
by Christina Rossetti
Poems to Read to the Very Young
(Random House, 1982)

"Pussy Willow"
by Kate L. Brown
First Poems of Childhood
(Platt & Munk, 1988)

"The Wallaby"
by Jack Prelutsky
Zoo Doings
(Greenwillow, 1983)

Related Poetry (cont.)

Letter "X"

"Extremes"
by James Whitcomb Riley
A Child's Book of Poems
(Grosset & Dunlap, 1972)

"The Three Foxes"
by A. A. Milne
When We Were Very Young
(Dutton, 1961)

Letter "Y"

"Yum! Yum!"
by Nancy White Carlstrom
It's About Time, Jesse Bear
(Scholastic, 1990)

"Yellow"
by David McCord
Poems to Read to the Very Young
(Random House, 1982)

"The Yipiyuk"
by Shel Silverstein
Where the Sidewalk Ends
(Harper & Row, 1974)

"The Yal"
by Jack Prelutsky
Zoo Doings
(Greenwillow, 1983)

Letter "Z"

"Zeppelin"
by Sylvia Cassedy
Zoomerimes, Poems About Things that Go
(HarperCollins, 1993)

"Zig-Zag Children"
by Liz Cromwell
Finger Frolics
(Partner Press, 1976)

"My Zipper Suit"
by Liz Cromwell
Finger Frolics
(Partner Press, 1976)

"Fuzzy Wuzzy"
Anonymous
Poems for Young Children
(Doubleday, 1986)

"Zero"
by Babs Bell Hajdusiewicz
Poetry Works
(Modern Curriculum Press, 1990)

"At the Zoo"
by A. A. Milne
Poems to Read to the Very Young
(Random House, 1982)

Short "A"

"Mix a Pancake"
by Christina Rossetti
Poems to Read to the Very Young
(Random House, 1982)

"The Acrobats"
by Shel Silverstein
Where the Sidewalk Ends
(Harper & Row, 1974)

"Cats"
by Mary Britton Miller
Poetry Works
(Modern Curriculum Press, 1990)

Long "A"

"Early One Morning"
by Jack Prelutsky
Ride a Purple Pelican
(Greenwillow, 1986)

"Rain"
by Robert Louis Stevenson
A Child's Book of Poems
(Grosset & Dunlap, 1972)

"April Fool's Day"
Old English Almanac
A Child's Book of Poems
(Grosset & Dunlap, 1972)

Related Poetry (cont.)

Short "E"

"As I Was Going to Sell My Eggs"
by Arnold Lobel
Random House Book of Mother Goose
(Random House, 1986)

"I Do Not Like the Doctor Fell"
by Arnold Lobel
Random House Book of Mother Goose
(Random House, 1986)

"E is the Escalator"
by Phyllis McGinley
Poems to Read to the Very Young
 (Random House, 1982)

Long "E"

"Little Bo Peep"
by Brian Wildsmith
Brian Wildsmith's Mother Goose
(Scott Foresman, 1964)

"The Happy Sheep"
by Wilfred Thorley
A Child's Book of Poems
 (Grosset & Dunlap, 1972)

"Three Little Trees"
by Gyo Fujikawa
A Child's Book of Poems
(Grosset & Dunlap, 1972)

Short "I"

"Silver Fish"
by Shel Silverstein
Where the Sidewalk Ends
(Harper & Row, 1969)

"This Little Pig"
by Liz Cromwell
Finger Frolics
(Partner Press, 1980)

Long "I"

"I Like Flies"
by Margaret Wise Brown
See Saw
(Charles Merrill Books, 1966)

Short "O"

"Poemsicle"
by Shel Silverstein
A Light in the Attic
(HarperCollins, 1981)

"Rock-a-Bye Baby"
by Arnold Lobel
Random House Book of Mother Goose
(Random House, 1986)

"The Ostrich is a Silly Bird"
by Mary E. Wilkins Freeman
A Child's Book of Poems
(Grosset & Dunlap, 1969)

Long "O"

"Here We Go"
by Mary Ann Hoberman
Yellow Butter, Purple Jelly, Red Jam, Black Bread
 (Viking, 1981)

"Jonathon Jo"
by A. A. Milne
When We Were Very Young
(Dutton, 1961)

"The Old House"
by Walter de la Mare
Peacock Pie
(Knopf, 1961)

"Snow"
by Mary Ann Hoberman
Yellow Butter, Purple Jelly, Red Jam, Black Bread
(Viking, 1981)

Related Poetry (cont.)

"Too Old for Naps"
by Jane Yolan
The Three Bears Rhyme Book (Harcourt, 1987)

"Oh Pennington Poe"
by Jack Prelutsky
Ride a Purple Pelican (Greenwillow, 1986)

"One Day in Oklahoma"
by Jack Prelutsky
Ride a Purple Pelican (Greenwillow. 1986)

Short "U"

"Rumpity Tumpity"
by Jack Prelutsky
Ride a Purple Pelican
(Greenwillow, 1986)

"Chubby Little Snowman"
by Liz Cormwell
Finger Frolics
(Partner Press, 1976)

"Hungry Mungry"
by Shel Silverstein
Where the Sidewalk Ends
(Harper & Row, 1974)

"Me a Mess?"
by Babs Bell Hajdusiewicz
Poetry Works
 (Modern Curriculum Press, 1990)

Long "U"

"The Unicorn"
by Shel Silverstein
Where the Sidewalk Ends
 (Harper & Row, 1974)

"Unicycle"
by Sylvia Cassedy
Zoomerimes, Poems About Things that Go
(HarperCollins, 1993)

"Ch" Blend

"Whole Duty of Children"
by Robert Louis Stevenson
A Child's Garden of Verses
(Scribner, 1933)

"Good and Bad Children"
by Robert Louis Stevenson
A Child's Garden of Verses
(Scribner, 1933)

"Green Cheese"
by Jane Yolan
What Rhymes with Moon?
(Philomel, 1993)

"Th" Blend

"This Bridge"
by Shel Silverstein
A Light in the Attic
(Harper & Row, 1974)

"A Thought"
by Robert Louis Stevenson
A Child's Garden of Verses
(Scribner, 1933)

"Wh" Blend

"Whole Duty of Children"
by Robert Louis Stevenson
A Child's Garden of Verses
(Scribner, 1933)

"Captain Blackbeard did What?
by Shel Silverstein
A Light in the Attic
 (Harper & Row, 1974)

"What Did"
by Shel Silverstein
A Light in the Attic
(Harper & Row, 1974)

"Who Ordered the Broiled Face?"
by Shel Silverstein
A Light in the Attic
(Harper & Row, 1974)

Children's Literature Bibliography

Letter "B"

Goldilocks and the Three Bears
by Jan Brett (Dodd, 1987)

Brown Bear, Brown Bear
by Bill Martin Jr. (Holt, 1967)

The Berenstain's B Book
by Stan & Jan Berenstain (Random House, 1971)

Bear Hunt
by Margaret Siewert & Kathleen Savage
(Prentice-Hall, 1976)

Letter "C"

A Pocket for Corduroy
by Don Freeman (Puffin, 1984)

Millions of Cats
by Wanda Gag (Scholastic, 1956)

The Very Hungery Caterpillar
by Eric Carle (Collins-World, 1969)

I Can, Can You?
by Ada Litchfield (Steck-Vaughn, 1971)

Letter "D"

Make Way for Ducklings
by Robert McCloskey (Viking, 1941)

Dinosaurs, Dragonflies, and Diamonds
by Gail Gibbons (Four Winds, 1988)

Dinosaurs, Dinosaurs
by Byron Barton (HarperCollins, 1989)

Harry the Dirty Dog
by Gene Zion (Harper & Row, 1936)

Walt Disney's 101 Dalmations
by Fran Manushlin (Disney Press, 1991)

Letter "F"

The Rainbow Fish
by Marcus Pfister (Scholastic, 1992)

A Fish out of Water
by Helen Palmer (Random House, 1961)

Fresh Fall Leaves
by Betsy Franco (Scholastic, 1994)

Blue Sea
by Robert Kalan (Greenwillow, 1979)

Frederick
by Leo Lionni (Pantheon, 1967)

Letter "G"

Goodnight Moon
by Margaret Wise Brown (Harper & Row, 1947)

Goggles
by Ezra Jack Keats (Macmillan, 1969)

Growing Vegetable Soup
by Lois Ehlert (Harcourt, 1987)

Letter "H"

Houses and Homes
by Ann Morris (Lothrop, Lee & Shepard, 1992)

Building a House
by Byron Barton (Trumpet Club, 1981)

Letter "J"

No Jumping on the Bed
by Tedd Arnold (Dial, 1987)

Hop Jump
by Ellen Stoll Walsh (Harcourt, 1993)

Anna Banana: 101 Jump Rope Rhymes
by Joanna Cole (Morrow, 1989)

Norma Jean, Jumping Bean
by Joanna Cole (Random House, 1987)

Children's Literature Bibliography (cont.)

Letter "K"
Momo's Kitten
by Mitsu & Taro Yashima (Penguin, 1977)

Katy No-Pocket
by Emmy Payne (Houghton Miffflin, 1944)

Mrs. Katz & Tush
by Patricia Polacco (Dell, 1992)

A Kiss For Little Bear
by Else Holmelund Minarik (Harper, 1968)

A Koala for Katie
by Jonathon Lindon (Whitman, 1993)

Letter "L"
Leo Paints it Red
by John McInnes (Garrard, 1974)

Lentil Soup
by Joe Lasker (Whitman, 1977)

Lyle, Lyle, Crocodile
by Bernard Waber (Houghton Mifflin, 1965)

Red Leaf, Yellow Leaf
by Lois Ehlert (Harcourt, 1991)

A Letter to Amy
by Ezra Jack Keats (Harper & Row, 1968)

Look
by Michael Grejniec (North-South Books, 1993)

I Like to be Little
by Charlotte Zolotow (Crowell, 1987)

I Know What I Like
by Norma Simon (Whitman, 1971)

Hop Like Me
by Jean & Gareth Adamson (Whitman, 1972)

Love You Forever
by Robert Munsch (Firefly Books, 1991)

Letter "M"
Papa, Please get the Moon for Me
by Eric Carle (Scholastic, 1986)

Goodnight, Moon
by Margaret Wise Brown (HarperCollins, 1947)

Wait Till the Moon is Full
by Margaret Wise Brown (HarperCollins, 1948)

More, More, More, Said the Baby
by Vera B. Williams (Scholastic, 1990)

If You Give a Moose a Muffin
by Laura Joffe Numeroff (Scholastic, 1991)

If You Give a Mouse a Cookie
by Laura Joffe Numeroff (Scholastic, 1985)

Mouse Paint
by Ellen Stoll Walsh (Trumper Club, 1989)

Mooncake
by Frank Asch (Prentice-Hall, 1982)

Letter "N"
There's Something in My Attic
by Mercer Mayer (Dial, 1988)

There's an Alligator Under My Bed
by Mercer Mayer (Dial, 1987)

No Jumping on the Bed
by Tedd Arnold (Dial, 1987)

Night in the Country
by Cynthia Rylant (Bradbury Press, 1986)

Never Talk to Strangers
by Irma Joyce (Golden Press, 1975)

Letter "P"
Little Penguin's Tale
by Audry Wood (Harcourt, 1989)

It's a Perfect Day
by Abigail Pizer (Lippincott, 1990)

Peter's Chair
by Ezra Jack Keats (Harper & Row, 1967)

Perfect the Pig
by Susan Jeschke (Holt, 1980)

Pentunia's Treasure
by Roger Duvoisin (Knopf, 1975)

Peter's Pocket
by Judi Barret (McClelland & Stewart, 1974)

Children's Literature Bibliography (cont.)

Letter "Q"

The Very Quiet Cricket
by Eric Carle (Philomel, 1990)

Quiet! There's a Canary in the Library
by Don Freeman (Golden Gate, 1969)

The Quiet Book
by Margaret Wise Brown (HarperCollins, 1993)

The Quilt Story
by Tony Johnston & Tomie de Paola (Scholastic, 1990)

The Keeping Quilt
by Patricia Polacco (Simon & Schuster, 1988)

The Patchwork Quilt
by Valerie Flournoy (Dial, 1985)

The Quiet Noisy Book
by Margaret Wise Brown (HarperCollins, 1993)

Letter "R"

The Rainbow Fish
by Marcus Pfister (Scholastic, 1992)

Planting a Rainbow
by Lois Ehlert (Harcourt, 1988)

The Runaway Bunny
by Margaret Wise Brown (Harper, 1977)

Little Red Riding Hood
by William Wegman (Hyperion, 1993)

Letter "S"

Swimmy
by Leo Lionni (Scholastic, 1989)

Small Pig
by Arnold Lobel (Harper & Row, 1969)

Sylvester and the Magic Pebble
by William Steig (Scholastic, 1969)

The Snowy Day
by Ezra Jack Keats (Scholastic, 1962)

Strega Nona
by Tomie de Paola (Scholastic, 1975)

Letter "T"

Tacky the Penguin
by Helen Lester (Houghton Mifflin, 1988)

Two Tiny Mice
by Alan Baker (Scholastic, 1990)

The Teeny Tiny Woman
by Barbara Seuling (Viking, 1976)

Tikki Tikki Tembo
by Arlene Mosel (Holt, 1968)

Letter "V"

The Very Busy Spider
by Eric Carle (Philomel, 1984)

Very Last First Time
by Jan Andrews (Atheneum, 1986)

The Very Little Boy
by Phyllis Krasilovsky (Doubleday, 1962)

The Very Little Girl
by Phyllis Krasilovsky (Doubleday, 1953)

A Very Special House
by Ruth Krauss (Harper, 1953)

A Very Tall Little Girl
by Phyllis Krasilovsky (Doubleday, 1969)

A Very, Very Special Day
by Frances Ullmann (Parents Magazine Press, 1963)

The Velveteen Rabbit
Margery Williams (Holt, 1983)

Growing Vegetable Soup
by Lois Ehlert (Harcourt, 1987)

The Village of Round and Square Houses
by Ann Grifalcooni (Little, Brown, 1986)

Children's Literature Bibliography (cont.)

Letter "W"
What Will the Weather be Like Today?
by Paul Rogers (Scholastic, 1989)

The Wind Blew
by Pat Hutchins (Scholastic, 1993)

Where the Wild Things Are
by Maurice Sendak (Scholastic, 1963)

Whistle for Willie
by Ezra Jack Keats (Puffin, 1989)

Baby Wolf
by Beth Spanjian (Longmeadow Press, 1988)

When I Was Young in the Mountains
by Cynthia Rylant (Dutton, 1982)

Letter "X"
Ox-Cart Man
by Donald Hall (Scholastic, 1979)

Hattie and the Fox
by Mem Fox (Trumpet Club, 1986)

Flossie and the Fox
by Patricia McKissack (Dial, 1986)

My Cat Likes to Hide in Boxes
by Eve Sutton (Parent's Magazine Press, 1974)

Box and Cox
by Grace Chetwin (Bradbury Press, 1990)

What's Inside the Box?
by Ethel & Leonard Kessler (Dodd, Mead, 1976)

Letter "Y"
Yummy, Yummy
by Judith Grey (Troll, 1981)

Little Blue and Little Yellow
by Leo Lionni (Scholastic, 1993)

Purple, Green, and Yellow
by Robert Munsch (Annick Press, 1992)

Hello Yellow!
by Robert Jay Wolff (Scribner, 1968)

Letter "Z"
Zomo the Rabbit
by Gerald McDermott (Harcourt, 1992)

Zella, Zack, and Zodiac
by Bill Peet (Houghton Mifflin, 1986)

Put Me in the Zoo
by Robert Lopshire (Random House, 1960)

Greedy Zebra
by Mwenye Hadithi & Adriene Kennaway
(Little, Brown, 1984)

Zoom Away
by Tim Wynne-Jones (HarperCollins, 1993)

Zoom at Sea
by Tim Wynne-Jones (HarperCollins, 1993)

Short "A"
Millions of Cats
by Wanda Gag (Scholastic, 1956)

There's an Alligator Under My Bed
by Mercer Mayer (Dial, 1987)

The Cat in the Hat Comes Back
by Dr. Seuss (Random House, 1967)

Long "A"
The Train
by David McPhail (Little, Brown, 1977)

The Train to Lulu's
by Elizabeth Fitzgerald Howard
(Bradbury Press, 1988)

Weather or Not: Riddles for Rain and Shine
by Rick Walton (Lerner Publications, 1990)

Short "E"
The Little Red Hen
by Paul Galdone (Scholastic, 1973)

The Empty Pot
by Demi (Holt, 1990)

The Right Number of Elephants
by Jeff Sheppard (Scholastic, 1990)

Children's Literature Bibliography *(cont.)*

Long "E"

The Sheep Follow
by Monica Wellington (Dutton, 1992)

Counting Sheep
by John Archambault (Holt, 1989)

Ten Sleepy Sheep
by Holly Keller (Greenwillow, 1983)

Sheep Out to Eat
by Nancy Shaw (Houghton Mifflin, 1992)

The Ear Book
by Al Perkins (Random House, 1968)

Matthew's Dream
by Leo Lionni (Knopf, 1991)

A Tree is Nice
by Janice May Udry (Harper & Row, 1956)

A Book of Seasons
by Alice & Martin Provensen
(Random House, 1976)

Greedy Zebra
by Mwenye Hadithi & Adrienne Kennaway
(Little, Brown, 1984)

How Many Feet in the Bed?
by Diane Johnston Hamm
(Simon & Schuster, 1991)

Asleep, Asleep
by Mirra Ginsburg (Greenwillow, 1992)

Short "I"

Small Pig
by Arnold Lobel (Harper & Row, 1969)

Swimmy
by Leo Lionni (Scholastic, 1989)

Itchy, Itchy, Chicken Pox
by Grace Maccarone (Scholastic, 1992)

Inch by Inch
by Leo Lionni (Scholastic, 1994)

Long "I"

Mirette on the High Wire
by Emily Arnold McCully (Scholastic, 1993)

Things I Like
by Anthony Browne (Random House, 1989)

All I Am
by Eileen Roe (Scholastic, 1990)

Ira Sleeps Over
by Bernard Waber (Houghton Mifflin, 1972)

Short "O"

Exactly the Opposite
by Tana Hoban (Greenwillow, 1990)

Hop on Pop
by Dr. Seuss (Random House, 1963)

Ten Black Dots
by Donald Crews (Scribner, 1968)

The Empty Pot
by Demi (Holt, 1990)

Long "O"

Over, Under, and Through and Other Spatial Concepts
by Tana Hoban (Macmillan, 1973)

N-O Spells No!
by Teddy Slater (Scholastic, 1993)

Oh, A Hunting We Will Go
by John Langstaff (Macmillan, 1974)

Roll Over
by Merle Peek (Houghton Mifflin, 1981)

The Polar Express
by Chris Van Allsburg (Houghton Mifflin, 1985)

The Snowy Day
by Erza Jack Keats (Viking, 1962)

A Color of His Own
by Leo Lionni (Pantheon, 1975)

Children's Literature Bibliography (cont.)

Short "U"
Six Little Ducks
by Chris Conover (Crowell, 1976)

Umbrella Parade
by Kathy Feczko (Troll, 1985)

Umbrella
by Taro Yashima (Viking, 1958)

The Runaway Bunny
by Margaret Wise Brown (Harper & Row, 1977)

Mud
by Wendy Cheyette Lewison
(Random House, 1990)

Make Way for Ducklings
by Robert McCloskey (Puffin, 1941)

Long "U"
Sarah's Unicorn
by Bruce & Katherine Correlle
(HarperCollins, 1979)

I Want to be a Musician
by Carla Greene (Children's Press, 1962)

Uncle Wissmo's New Used Car
by Rodney A. Greenblat (HarperCollins, 1991)

Uhu
by Annette MacArthur Onslow (Knopf, 1969)

Pelle's New Suit
by Elsa Beskow (HarperCollins, 1929)

"ch" Blend
A Chair for My Mother
by Vera Williams (Greenwillow, 1982)

The Chalkbox Story
by Don Freeman (Lippincott, 1976)

Peter's Chair
by Ezra Jack Keats (Harper, 1967)

Chicka Chicka Boom Boom
by Bill Martin, Jr., and John Archambault
(Simon & Schuster, 1989)

"th" Blend
Three Cool Kids
by Rebecca Emberley (Little, Brown, 1995)

Juba This and Juba That
by Virginia Tashjian (Little, Brown, 1995)

Yang the Third and Her Impossible Family
by Lensey Manioka (Little, Brown, 1995)

"wh" Blend
Why the Sky is Far Away
by Mary-Joan Gerson (Little, Brown, 1995)

What About Ladybugs?
by Celia Godkin (Sierra Club, 1995)

The 300 Most Frequently Used English Words

The following list is a rank-order representation of the 300 most frequently used words in the English language.

1-50

the	he	at	but	there
of	was	be	not	use
and	for	this	what	an
a	on	have	all	each
to	are	from	were	which
in	as	or	we	she
is	with	one	when	do
you	his	had	your	how
that	they	by	can	their
it	I	word	said	if

51-100

will	some	two	my	find
up	her	more	than	long
other	would	write	first	down
about	make	go	water	day
out	like	see	been	did
many	him	number	call	get
then	into	no	who	come
them	time	way	oil	made
these	has	could	its	may
so	look	people	now	part

101-150

over	live	name	old	too
new	me	good	boy	any
sound	back	sentence	follow	same
take	give	man	also	tell
only	most	think	around	came
little	very	say	where	want
work	after	great	help	show
know	thing	much	through	form
place	our	before	line	three
year	just	mean	right	small

#791 Teaching Basic Skills through Literature: Phonics ©1995 Teacher Created Materials, Inc.

The 300 Most Frequently Used English Words (cont.)

151-200

set	such	land	change	letter
put	because	different	off	mother
end	turn	home	play	answer
does	here	us	spell	found
another	why	move	air	study
well	ask	try	away	still
large	went	kind	animal	learn
must	men	hand	house	should
big	read	picture	point	American
even	need	again	page	world

201-250

high	last	light	along	life
every	school	thought	might	always
near	father	head	close	those
add	deep	under	something	both
food	tree	story	seem	paper
between	never	saw	next	together
own	start	left	hard	got
below	city	don't	open	group
country	earth	few	example	often
plant	eye	while	begin	run

251-300

important	sea	hear	watch	cut
until	began	stop	far	young
children	grow	without	Indian	talk
side	took	second	real	soon
feet	river	later	almost	list
car	four	miss	let	song
mile	carry	idea	above	being
night	state	enough	girl	leave
walk	once	eat	sometimes	family
white	book	face	mountain	it's

©1995 Teacher Created Materials, Inc.

Caldecott Award Winners

Awarded annually by the Children's Services Division of the American Library Association to the artist of the most distinguished American picture book for children, the medal is named for Randolph J. Caldecott (1846-1886), a British artist noted for the joyousness of his picture books.

1994 *Grandfather's Journey*
    by Allen Say

1993 *Mirette on the High Wire*
    by Emily Arnold McCully

1992 *Tuesday*
    by David Wiesner (Clarion)

1991 *Black and White*
    by David Macaulay (Houghton Mifflin)

1990 *Lon Po Po: A Red-Riding Hood Story From China*
    translated and illustrated by Ed Young (Philomel)

1989 *Song and Dance Man*
    by Karen Ackerman, illustrated by Stephen Gammell (Knopf)

1988 *Owl Moon*
    by Jane Yolen, illustrated by John Schoenherr (Philomel)

1987 *Hey, Al*
    by Arthur Yorinks, illustrated by Richard Egielski (Farrar)

1986 *The Polar Express*
    written and illustrated by Chris Van Allsburg (Houghton)

1985 *Saint George and the Dragon*
    retold by Margaret Hodges, illustrated by Trina Schart Hyman (Little, Brown)

1984 *The Glorious Flight: Across the Channel With Louis Bleriot*
    written and illustrated by Alice and Martin Provensen (Viking)

1983 *Shadow*
    by Blaise Cendrars, translated and illustrated by Marcia Brown (Scribner)

1982 *Jumanji*
    written and illustrated by Chris Van Allsburg (Houghton)

1981 *Fables*
    written and illustrated by Arnold Lobel (Harper)

1980 *Ox-Cart Man*
    by Donald Hall, illustrated by Barbara Cooney (Viking)

1979 *The Girl Who Loved Wild Horses*
    written and illustrated by Paul Goble (Bradbury)

1978 *Noah's Ark*
    written and illustrated by Peter Spier (Doubleday)

1977 *Ashanti to Zulu*
    by Margaret Musgrove, illustrated by Leo and Diane Dillon (Dial)

1976 *Why Mosquitoes Buzz in People's Ears*
    retold by Verna Aardema, illustrated by Leo and Diane Dillon (Dial)

1975 *Arrow to the Sun*
    written and illustrated by Gerald McDermott (Viking)

1974 *Duffy and the Devil*
    retold and illustrated by Margot Zemach (Farrar)

1973 *The Funny Little Woman*
    by Lafcadio Hearn, retold by Arlene Mosel, illustrated by Blair Lent (Dutton)

1972 *One Fine Day*
    written and illustrated by Nonny Hogrogian (Macmillan)

1971 *A Story, A Story*
    written and illustrated by Gail E. Haley (Atheneum)

1970 *Sylvester and the Magic Pebble*
    written and illustrated by William Steig (Windmill Books)

1969 *The Fool of the World and the Flying Ship*
    retold by Arthur Ransome, illustrated by Uri Shulevitz (Farrar)

1968 *Drummer Hoff*
    adapted by Barbara Emberly, illustrated by Ed Emberly (Prentice-Hall)

1967 *Sam, Bangs, and Moonshine*
    written and illustrated by Evaline Ness (Holt)

1966 *Always Room for One More*
    by Sorche Nic Leodhas, illustrated by Nonny Hogrogian (Holt)

1965 *May I Bring a Friend?*
    by Beatrice Schenk de Regniers, illustrated by Beni Montresor (Atheneum)

1964 *Where the Wild Things Are*
    written and illustrated by Maurice Sendak (Harper)

1963 *The Snowy Day*
    written and illustrated by Ezra Jack Keats (Viking)

1962 *Once a Mouse*
    written and illustrated by Marcia Brown (Scribner)

1961 *Baboushka and the Three Kings*
    by Ruth Robbins, illustrated by Nicolas Sidjakov (Parnassus)

1960 *Nine Days to Christmas*
    by Marie Hall Ets and Aurora Labastida, illustrated by Marie Hall Ets (Viking)

1959 *Chanticleer and the Fox*
    written and illustrated by Barbara Cooney (Crowell)

1958 *Time of Wonder*
    written and illustrated by Robert McCloskey (Viking)

1957 *A Tree Is Nice*
    by Janice Udry, illustrated by Marc Simont (Harper)

1956 *Frog Went A-Courtin'*
    retold by John Langstaff, illustrated by Feodor Rojankovsky (Harcourt)

1955 *Cinderella*
    illustrated and retold from Perrault by Marcia Brown (Scribner)

1954 *Madeline's Rescue*
    written and illustrated by Ludwig Bemelmans (Viking)

1953 *The Biggest Bear*
    written and illustrated by Lynd K. Ward (Houghton)

1952 *Finders Keepers*
    by Will Lipkind, illustrated by Nicolas Mordvinoff (Harcourt)

1951 *The Egg Tree*
    written and illustrated by Katherine Milhous (Scribner)

1950 *Song of the Swallows*
    written and illustrated by Leo Politi (Scribner)

1949 *The Big Snow*
    written and illustrated by Berta and Elmer Hader (Macmillan)

1948 *White Snow, Bright Snow*
    by Alvin Tresseault, illustrated by Roger Duvoisin (Lothrop)

1947 *The Little Island*
    by Golden MacDonald, illustrated by Leonard Weisgard (Doubleday)

1946 *The Rooster Crows*
    written and illustrated Maude and Miska Petersham (Macmillan)

1945 *Prayer for a Child*
    by Rachel Field, illustrated by Elizabeth Orton Jones (Macmillan)

1944 *Mary Moons*
    by James Thurber, illustrated by Louis Slobodkin (Harcourt)

1943 *The Little House*
    written and illustrated by Virginia Lee Burton (Houghton)

1942 *Make Way for Ducklings*
    written and illustrated by Robert McCloskey (Viking)

1941 *They Were Strong and Good*
    written and illustrated by Robert Lawson (Viking)

1940 *Abraham Lincoln*
    written and illustrated by Ingri and Edgar Parin d'Aulaire (Doubleday)

Newbery Award Winners

Awarded annually by the Children's Services Division of the American Library Association to the most distinguished book for children published during the preceding year, the medal is named in honor of John Newbery, noted British publisher and the first person to print and sell books for children.

1994 *The Giver* by Lois Lowry (Houghton Mifflin)

1993 *Missing May* by Cynthia Rylant (Orchard Books)

1992 *Shiloh* by Phyllis Reynolds Naylor (Atheneum)

1991 *Maniac Magee* by Jerry Spinelli (Little, Brown)

1990 *Number the Stars* by Lois Lowry (Houghton Mifflin)

1989 *Joyful Noises: Poems for Two Voices* by Paul Fleischman (Harper)

1988 *Lincoln: A Photobiography* by Russell Freedman (Houghton Mifflin)

1987 *The Whipping Boy* by Sid Fleischman (Greenwillow)

1986 *Sarah, Plain and Tall* by Patricia MacLachlan (Harper)

1985 *The Hero and the Crown* by Robin McKinley (Greenwillow)

1984 *Dear Mr. Henshaw* by Beverly Cleary (Morrow)

1983 *Dicey's Song* by Cynthia Voigt (Atheneum)

1982 *A Visit to William Blake's Inn: Poems for Innocent and Experienced Travelers* by Nancy Willard (Harcourt)

1981 *Jacob Have I Loved* by Katherine Paterson (Cromwell)

1980 *A Gathering of Days* by Joan W. Blos (Scribner)

1979 *The Westing Game* by Ellen Raskin (Dutton)

1978 *Bridge to Terabithi* by Katherine Paterson (Cromwell)

1977 *Roll of Thunder, Hear My Cry* by Mildred D. Taylor (Dial)

1976 *The Grey King* by Susan Cooper (Atheneum)

1975 *M.C. Higgins, the Great* by Virginia Hamilton (Macmillan)

1974 *The Slave Dancer* by Paula Fox (Bradbury)

1973 *Julie of the Wolves* by Jean Craighead George (Harper)

1972 *Mrs. Frisby and the Rats of NIMH* by Robert C. O'Brien (Atheneum)

1971 *Summer of the Swans* by Betsy Byars (Viking)

1970 *Sounder* by William H. Armstrong (Harper)

1969 *The High King* by Lloyd Alexander (Holt)

1968 *From the Mixed-Up Files of Mrs. Basil E. Frankweiler* by E.L. Konigsbury (Atheneum)

1967 *Up a Road Slowly* by Irene Hunt (Follett)

1966 *I, Juan de Pareja* by Elizabeth Borton de Trevino (Farrar)

1965 *Shadow of a Bull* by Maia Wojciechowska (Atheneum)

1964 *It's Like This, Cat* by Emily C. Neville (Harper)

1963 *A Wrinkle in Time* by Madeleine L'Engle (Farrar)

1962 *The Bronze Bow* by Elizabeth George Speare (Houghton)

1961 *Island of the Blue Dolphins* by Scott O'Dell (Houghton)

1960 *Onion John* by Joseph Krumgold (Crowell)

1959 *The Witch of Blackbird Pond* by Elizabeth George Speare (Houghton)

1958 *Rifles for Watie* by Harold Keith (Crowell)

1957 *Miracles on Maple Hill* by Virginia Sorensen (Harcourt)

1956 *Carry On, Mr. Bowditch* by Jean Lee Latham (Houghton)

1955 *The Wheel on the School* by Meindert DeJong (Harper)

1954 *...And Now Miguel* by Joseph Krumgold (Crowell)

1953 *Secret of the Andes* by Ann Nolan Clark (Viking)

1952 *Ginger Pye* by Eleanor Estes (Harcourt)

1951 *Amos Fortune, Free Man* by Elizabeth Yates (Dutton)

1950 *The Door in the Wall* by Margaret Henry (Rand McNally)

1949 *King of the Wind* by Marguerite Henry (Rand McNally)

1948 *The Twenty-One Balloons* by William Pene de Bois (Viking)

1947 *Miss Hickory* by Carolyn S. Bailey (Viking)

1946 *Strawberry Girl* by Lois Lenski (Lippincott)

1945 *Rabbit Hill* by Robert Lawson (Viking)

1944 *Johnny Tremain* by Esther Forbes (Houghton)

1943 *Adam of the Road* by Elizabeth Janet Gray (Viking)

1942 *The Matchlock Gun* by Walter D. Edmonds (Dodd)

1941 *Call It Courage* by Armstrong Sperry (Macmillan)

1940 *Daniel Boone* by James Daughtery (Viking)

1939 *Thimble Summer* by Elizabeth Enright (Rinehart)

1938 *The White Stag* by Kate Seredy (Viking)

1937 *Roller Skates* by Ruth Sawyer (Viking)

1936 *Caddie Woodlawn* by Carol Ryrie Brink (Macmillan)

1935 *Dobry* by Monica Shannon (Viking)

1934 *Invincible Louisa* by Cornelia Meigs (Little, Brown)

1933 *Young Fu of the Upper Yangtze* by Elizabeth Lewis (Winston)

1932 *Waterless Mountain* by Laura Armer (Longmans)

1931 *The Cat Who Went to Heaven* by Elizabeth Coatsworth (Macmillan)

1930 *Hitty, Her First Hundred Years* by Rachel Field (Macmillan)

1929 *The Trumpeter of Krakow* by Eric P. Kelly (Macmillan)

1928 *Gay-Neck: the Story of a Pigeon* by Dhan Mukerji (Dutton)

1927 *Smoky, the Cow Horse* by Will James (Scribner)

1926 *Shen of the Sea* by Arthur Chrisman (Dutton)

1925 *Tales From Silver Lands* by Charles Finger (Doubleday)

1924 *The Dark Frigate* by Charles Hawes (Atlantic/Little)

1923 *The Voyage of Doctor Dolittle* by Hugh Lofting (Lippincott)

1922 *The Story of Mankind* by Henrik Van Loon (Liveright)

Professional Book Bibliography

Braddon, Kathryn L., Nancy J. Hall and Dale Taylor. *Math Through Children's Literature* (Teacher Idea Press, 1993)

Gentry, J. Richard. *Spel is a Four Letter Word* (Scholastic, 1987)

Goodman, Ken. *Phonics Phacts* (Heinemann, 1994)

Goodman, Ken. *What's Whole in Whole Language* (Scholastic, 1986)

Griffiths, Rachel and Margaret Clyne. *Books You Can Count On* (Heinemann, 1988)

Hall, Nigel. *Writing with Reason* (Heinemann, 1989)

Jan, Lesley Wing. *Spelling and Grammar in a Whole Language Classroom* (Ashton Scholastic, 1991)

Johnson, Terry D. and Daphne R. Louis. *Bringing It All Together* (Heinemann, 1990)

Johnson, Terry D. and Daphne R. Louis. *Literacy Through Literature* (Heinemann, 1987)

Powell, Debbie and David Hornsby. *Learning Phonics and Spelling in a Whole Language Classroom* (Scholastic, 1993)

Rothlein, Liz and Anita Meyer Meinbach. *The Literature Connection* (Scott Foresman and Company, 1991)

Routman, Regie. *Invitations* (Heinemann, 1991)

Routman, Regie. *Transitions* (Heinemann, 1988)

Ryan, Concetta Doti. *Authentic Assessment* (Teacher Created Materials, 1994)

Wagstaff, Janiel. *Phonics that Works* (Scholastic, 1994)

Whitin, David, J. and Sandra Wilde. *Read Any Good Math Lately?* (Heinemann, 1992)

Yopp, Ruth Helen and Hallie Kay Yopp. *Literature-Based Reading Activities* (Allyn and Bacon, 1992)